Play Practice

Engaging and Developing Skilled Players From Beginner to Elite

SECOND EDITION

Alan G. Launder, MA

Wendy Piltz, MSc

Human Kinetics

Library of Congress Cataloging-in-Publication Data

Launder, Alan G., 1934-
  Play practice : engaging and developing skilled players from beginner to elite / Alan G. Launder, Wendy Piltz. -- 2nd ed.
      p. cm.
  Includes bibliographical references and index.
  1. Sports--Study and teaching. 2. Physical education and training--Study and teaching. I. Piltz, Wendy. II. Title.
  GV363.L39 2013
  796.07'7--dc21

                          2012020959

ISBN-10: 0-7360-9700-7 (print)
ISBN-13: 978-0-7360-9700-0 (print)

The web addresses cited in this text were current as of November 28, 2012, unless otherwise noted.

Acquisitions Editor: Scott Wikgren; **Developmental Editor:** Bethany J. Bentley; **Assistant Editors:** Tyler Wolpert and Derek Campbell; **Copyeditor:** Alisha Jeddeloh; **Indexer:** Bobbi Swanson; **Permissions Manager:** Dalene Reeder; **Graphic Designer:** Nancy Rasmus; **Cover Designer:** Keith Blomberg; **Photograph (cover):** Courtesy of David Mildren; **Photographs (interior):** © Human Kinetics, unless otherwise noted; photos on pp. 8 and 169 courtesy of Simon Munn; photo on p. 12 courtesy of Mark Orr; photos on pp. 19, 24, and 34 courtesy of Ray Titus; photo on p. 23 courtesy of Carolyn Pickering; photo on p. 42 courtesy of Nic Davel; photo on p. 46 © Photodisc; photo on p. 97 courtesy of Luke Greaves; photos on pp. 103, 159, 160, 183, 192, 193, 205, 215, and 221 courtesy of Wendy Piltz; photos on pp. 105, 116, 117, 121, 147, 172, and 187 courtesy of Bob Pearce; photos on pp. 132 and 136 courtesy of Alex Makeyeu; photos on p. 175 courtesy of David Eldridge; photo on p. 188 courtesy of Alan Launder; photo on p. 218 courtesy of David Mildren; **Photo Production Manager:** Jason Allen; **Art Manager:** Kelly Hendren; **Associate Art Manager:** Alan L. Wilborn; **Illustrations:** © Human Kinetics, unless otherwise noted; **Printer:** Sheridan Books

Printed in the United States of America   10 9 8 7 6 5 4 3 2 1

The paper in this book is certified under a sustainable forestry program.

Human Kinetics
Website: www.HumanKinetics.com

United States: Human Kinetics
P.O. Box 5076
Champaign, IL 61825-5076
800-747-4457
e-mail: humank@hkusa.com

Canada: Human Kinetics
475 Devonshire Road Unit 100
Windsor, ON N8Y 2L5
800-465-7301 (in Canada only)
e-mail: info@hkcanada.com

Europe: Human Kinetics
107 Bradford Road
Stanningley
Leeds LS28 6AT, United Kingdom
+44 (0) 113 255 5665
e-mail: hk@hkeurope.com

Australia: Human Kinetics
57A Price Avenue
Lower Mitcham, South Australia 5062
08 8372 0999
e-mail: info@hkaustralia.com

New Zealand: Human Kinetics
P.O. Box 80
Torrens Park, South Australia 5062
0800 222 062
e-mail: info@hknewzealand.com

                                                                        E5225

contents

foreword

Over the past quarter century, our understanding of how to best teach and encourage children and youths to become skilful players, to enjoy active participation in sport, and to commit to a physically active lifestyle has expanded enormously. Throughout this period, Alan Launder has played a pivotal role in creating successful approaches to teaching sports. Now in cooperation with Wendy Piltz, one of his former students and colleagues at the University of South Australia, he has produced a new edition of his successful book *Play Practice*.

This work extends the ideas presented in Launder's original work. It clarifies the Play Practice model and provides detailed information about how to use this innovative approach, helping learners understand sport through a series of experiences that gradually introduce them to the techniques and games sense needed for skilful play. Most important, it emphasises the satisfaction that can come from participating in a well-played game and explains the role that teachers can play in developing and sustaining good game habits that positively contribute to the sport culture of a school, a community, or a nation.

Alan Launder has combined a lifelong involvement in sport of all kinds with the roles of physical education teacher, teacher educator, coach educator, track and field coach, and world-class pole vault coach. His book *From Beginner to Bubka: An Australian Approach to Developing Pole Vaulters* has become the standard work in the field and has greatly influenced the teaching and coaching of this event around the world.

Wendy Piltz has also participated in a variety of sports, including representing Australia in women's lacrosse and cricket. Like Alan, she is an avid snow skier! Her professional expertise, developed through her roles as a physical education teacher and coach in a variety of sports and levels, along with her responsibilities in pre-service teacher education and coach education have continued to connect this approach to high-quality pedagogical practice.

Alan helped create an innovative formation program for physical education teachers at the University of South Australia, and Wendy has sustained it. There, Wendy has played a key role in embedding the principles and processes of Play Practice into the program, ensuring that the protocols for planning, observation, provision of feedback, reflection, and assessment are aligned with Play Practice. She has also carried out practice-based qualitative research with pre-service teachers around the efficacy of this approach for the consistent development of novice educators.

I have no doubt that *Play Practice, Second Edition,* will find a worldwide audience and will greatly enhance the capacity of teacher educators in physical education, physical education teachers, and school and youth sport coaches to not only help players develop skill and more advanced understandings of techniques and tactics but also communicate the positive role sport can and should play in their culture. This outcome will inevitably contribute to developing physical education and sport programs that positively affect players, coaches, parents, and the public.

Daryl Siedentop
Professor Emeritus
Ohio State University

preface

> The proper work of a writing is to arouse to thinking those who are fit for it.
>
> Leo Strauss

The aim of this book is to clarify key concepts of Play Practice and to extend and expand the practical advice presented in *Play Practice: A Games Approach to Teaching and Coaching Sports*, first published in 2001. This edition will ensure that the innovative ideas presented at that time continue to have a great influence on professional practice.

These ideas have become increasingly important because, especially in English-speaking countries, teacher-education programs have tended to move away from an emphasis on practical activities and sport and, associated with this shift, away from the vexed question of how best to teach them. Because physical activity and sport should be central in the focus of such programs, there is a need to show how the principles and processes of Play Practice could be embedded into professional preparation, both in teaching and coaching.

It was also important to outline both the theoretical (if retrospective) underpinnings of this innovative approach and to provide examples of similar ideas developed by other professionals in the field. These are included in the supplementary electronic chapters available with the book (visit www.HumanKinetics.com/PlayPractice). This was necessary because in the early stages of the evolution of Play Practice, there was no direct input from theory. Nor, apart from the work of Alan Wade, who introduced the use of small-sided games to teach the principles of tactical play in soccer, was there evidence of support for Play Practice in the work of other professionals at that time. Play Practice was initially

a purely pragmatic approach that was driven by the search by an inexperienced teacher to find worthwhile alternatives to traditional methods. In those early days, it was based solely on going with what appeared to work with youngsters, especially those reluctant and resistant learners who are found in every class in every school.

However, although the first edition of *Play Practice* was aimed at novice teachers, it rapidly became clear that teachers and coaches at all levels were attracted to the ideas presented in it. Given the many common elements in the roles of the physical education teacher and sport coach, this was not surprising.

With deep and diverse roots, Play Practice has taken shape through many years of reflective tinkering, where ideas have been developed, trialled, discarded, or improved and accepted. While this process did not meet the standards of rigor expected from formal research, it did partially meet the criteria for experimentation suggested by Richard Dawkins in his book *The Greatest Show on Earth*. There, he suggests that 'to experiment means that you do something, you manipulate, you change something in a systematic way and compare the change either with a control, or with a different change.' Since practice has preceded theory in many aspects of modern life, most notably in the evolution of the steam engines that powered the industrial revolution, it is clear that innovative ideas that have been generated through the same process of reflective tinkering could be useful in guiding future practice in our field. It is therefore interesting to discover the degree of support for Play Practice that has emerged since the first book was published. So it is now clear that Play Practice not only has sound theoretical underpinnings but also an expanding body of work from professionals in both teaching and coaching that supports it.

Here, it is especially worth noting the work of Paul Balsom, who in his booklet *Precision*

Football details an approach to improving critical elements of skilled play with elite soccer players that parallels Play Practice. Although Balsom arrived at his ideas independently, another highly successful coach, Mark Williams (a graduate of the University of South Australia), has built on the ideas presented in the original book to develop innovative methods for the teaching and coaching of Australian Rules football.

In the first book, it was suggested that juxtaposing the words *play* and *practice* might seem to create an oxymoron. For *play* implies free, open-ended activity, which is an end in itself, while *practice* suggests repetitive, closed behaviour that achieves future goals. However, the term was carefully chosen to describe an approach to sport education that harnesses the immense power of play to create challenging and enjoyable practice situations through which players, young and old alike, can be motivated to play their way to understanding, competence, and excellence.

The secret lies in the integration of play with practice through games and challenges that have been carefully structured to achieve specific outcomes. Of the latter, one of the most important for youngsters is the enjoyment gained from a growing sense of improvement and mastery. In fact, in his acclaimed television series, *The Ascent of Man*, Professor Jacob Bronowski captured this, the essence of both sport and of Play Practice, when he said 'The most important drive in the ascent of man is his pleasure in his own skill. He loves to do what he does well, and having done it well, he loves to do it better.' Clearly sport provides an ideal vehicle for young people to become involved in activities that they can do well, where they have the opportunity to strive to do better. However, with competition comes pressure to win, not merely to play for the sake of the game. This pressure can range from the need to meet the expectations of an entire nation when competing in the Olympic Games to dealing with the ill-informed comments of a single parent watching a junior competition. Whatever the source, pressure to win can lead to many of the problems that continue to bedevil competitive sport at all levels, from Little League baseball to the Olympic Games. Indeed, in an over-reaction to these problems, some members of the physical education community believe that competitive sport should be eliminated from the curriculum entirely and replaced with fitness, wellness, and co-operative activities.

However, while recognising these problems, we believe that it is impossible to ignore the immense power of sport to attract people into the world of physical activity. Whatever their limitations, professional sports provide a continual supply of role models, along with unending free advertising for the brand!

However, if it is to fulfil its potential as a humanising activity, we do need a radically different vision of sport that is far removed from a win-at-all-costs mentality, the sport entertainment industry, and the politically driven excesses of countries such as the former Eastern Bloc. It must always be rooted in the sport philosophy that has underpinned physical education for more than 100 years. It must be the sport of William Morgan, of Naismith, of De Coubertin, of Teddy Roosevelt, and of all those participants who have competed honourably and with respect for their opponents through the years. So if competitive sports are to be included in the physical education curriculum, they must always be structured to ensure that they remain both a humane and a humanising activity.

Here, the roles of the physical education teacher and the sport coach are critical, for who can better ensure that sport retains its value as a humanising experience? Many have had a lifetime of joyful involvement in sport; often, their whole lives have been changed by their participation. It has brought them many of their best friends, their most cherished memories, and their most significant achievements. They can, by their every word and deed, demonstrate a sound philosophy of sport in action.

We can begin by replacing all of the trite, hackneyed, misleading, and just plain wrong injunctions to win that are plastered around changing rooms with the Olympic motto, pure and simple. We must encourage youngsters to focus on the struggle and not the result, to treat their opponents in any sport as the surfer treats the big wave, as the skier approaches the mountain, as the kayaker views the turbulent river: as challenges, not as adversaries. As participants focus on the challenge, not on the opponent, they may experience not only greater enjoyment but also improved performance.

Above all, in schools and in communities everywhere, sport must be for all, not only for the elite. The essential premise of this text is that every child should have the opportunity to participate in enjoyable and challenging sporting activities. They may then learn fundamental truths about themselves and about life, and they may also become more tolerant supporters of sport and those who play it, as spectators, parents, or coaches in the future. Equally important, many may learn that they have infinitely more talent than they or their teachers and coaches could possibly imagine. For it is becoming increasingly clear that sporting talent is not the rare gift that we have often thought it to be but is often simply a function of the opportunity to participate, along with intelligent encouragement.

Teachers and coaches should remember that first experiences, like first impressions, can be crucial. This is especially important if youngsters have already had unfortunate experiences in community sport. They need to understand that many youngsters are more frightened of the possibility of failure than they are thrilled by the possibility of success. So Play Practice is underpinned by the idea that if youngsters develop a deep love and understanding of sport through positive early experiences, they are more likely to make a lifelong commitment to physical activity and a healthy lifestyle. As a result, Play Practice may prove to be an important tool for sport educators because it replaces mindless games and mechanistic training methods with purposeful practices and pertinent challenges. In this way, Play Practice may counter the serious threat posed by the sedentary amusements of television and computer games as we strive to capture the hearts and minds of young people.

It is important to understand that while the original driving force in the evolution of Play Practice was a search for better ways to encourage reluctant and resistant beginners to even participate, the principles that have emerged can be employed at the elite level. As training volumes increase in the drive towards excellence, play becomes work, enjoyment diminishes, and the motivation inherent in joyful participation is lost, prompting even talented athletes to retire early. Play Practice counters this by providing a framework for developing a vast range of enjoyable and realistic practice scenarios that simulate the demands of high-level competition while retaining the crucial element of play.

While it has a coherent framework, it is not necessary to understand and apply Play Practice as a complete package. Teachers and coaches can start by making one small adjustment to a practice situation or one simple modification to a game, by using a working model of technique, or by trying an innovation such as an action fantasy game. In this way, it is possible for them to gradually move towards this innovative approach. This means that they can trial elements of this model and begin to develop some confidence in it before they make a total commitment. Ultimately, this may prove to be the greatest strength of Play Practice because the history of education is littered with good ideas that were not successful in the harsh realities of schools.

An additional advantage, and one not to be undervalued, is that Play Practice can make the learning environment more enjoyable and professionally satisfying for the teacher, as well as for students. A teacher who creates enjoyable learning situations and sees a positive student reaction will respond with greater enthusiasm, and may even smile more often! This then becomes a reciprocal process, where the positive attitudes and improved performance of both teacher and students spiral upwards to create ever more positive learning environments. This is not a pipe dream. It is exactly what happens a thousand times over in the real world when inspired teachers and coaches give their lives to lead young people towards a better future.

While Play Practice can be especially valuable for sport educators at the beginning of their careers, it has already proved to be a useful resource for experienced teachers and coaches, who have quickly identified similarities between this approach and the methods they have devised for themselves. For them, Play Practice simply provides a framework that helps them to clarify and expand their own ideas. For example, the terms *simplifying, shaping, focusing,* and *enhancing* are only new definitions for processes that have always been used by effective teachers and coaches. However, when they are precisely defined, as in this work, the concepts they represent are easier to understand, employ, and improve upon.

It is now widely accepted that sports and games have the potential to make an immense contribution to the lives of individuals, to communities, and to nations. This places a huge responsibility on the shoulders of those who, like the authors, offer advice to teachers and coaches on how best to introduce youngsters to sport and physical activity. So while this work may 'merely' be about teaching sport, even using cartoons to make specific points, it is not a simple 'how-to' book, nor is it a 'dumb bunny's guide to teaching games'. On the contrary, it may force some readers to undergo a paradigm shift in their thinking.

Part I presents a radical analysis of the nature of skilled performance in sport. It begins by defining the key terms *skill* and *games sense,* goes on to detail the other elements of skilled performance in sport, and finally proposes how an understanding of the process of being skilful is critical to effective teaching and coaching. This analysis of the nature of skilled performance in sport is then integrated with a statement of the conditions under which youngsters best learn. The result is an innovative pedagogy that enables teachers and coaches to help youngsters become confident and skilful players who understand sports and want to continue playing as part of an active lifestyle. This is necessary because, despite the immense potential of sport to contribute to the lives of young people and to communities around the world, many critical issues in teaching and coaching remain unaddressed.

Part II supports these ideas with practical examples of how to introduce a range of sports and shows how a sound understanding of the nature of games can help students transfer teaching and learning principles across sports with similar structures. The practical information provided is invaluable to both the students and professionals who read this book.

As readers work through this book, they will discover that key ideas and concepts are repeated. This is intentional, since revisiting and repetition are critical in any learning situation, and they are absolutely essential when innovative concepts are encountered for the first time. For example, readers will find specific Play Practice mantras, such as 'What is tactically desirable must be technically possible', repeated in different contexts.

Finally, it is worth pointing out that while we believe that this book will help teachers and coaches meet the challenge of helping young people grow to love sport and incorporate it into an active lifestyle, it is not intended to be the definitive statement of how to teach all sports. Rather, we hope that it will provide a springboard for new ideas, ideas that will make the tasks of teaching and coaching easier, more rewarding, and infinitely more enjoyable.

acknowledgements

John Dickinson for initiating the second edition of *Play Practice*.

Daryl Siedentop for his very generous foreword and his long-time support and encouragement.

John Gormley for producing illustrations for this book.

Ray Titus, Carolyn Pickering, Bob Pearce, and schools in South Australia for allowing the use of some of their superb photographs.

David Kirk for his insightful feedback.

Len Almond for his ongoing support of the ideas presented here.

Chris and John Halbert for providing the initial impetus to publish these ideas.

All of the students upon whom we have practised in order to learn our trade.

Scott Wikgren and the folks at Human Kinetics who have brought this project to fruition.

The pre-service teachers who have contributed their voices about how this approach has supported their professional learning.

The teachers and coaches in the field who have used and grown these ideas and have persistently encouraged the development of this second edition.

The Influence of Sport

To teach people how to play and to want to play is to enhance their potential for humanistic experience. To develop a society of players and a culture devoted to play is to contribute to a civilized humanistic future.

Daryl Siedentop

Over the past 100 years, sport has become a dominant factor in the culture of most countries, even those poverty-stricken nations still struggling to provide basic services for their people. The great invasion games of basketball, field and ice hockey, lacrosse, and the various football codes are played and watched around the world by billions of people. The attraction of these games lies paradoxically both in their simplicity and their complexity. They are simple in the sense that ball possession and position clearly indicate the state of play at any instant but complex in that games of this type present the players with problems that can be solved tactically and technically with a vast range of responses. In the same way, net games, such as volleyball, tennis, table tennis, and badminton; target games, like golf, archery, lawn bowls, and tenpin bowling; and striking and fielding games, like cricket, baseball, and softball, all present players with innumerable technical, tactical, and psychological challenges.

While ball games are especially popular, the disciplines of track and field, the challenges of the alpine sports, the precision of gymnastics,

and the unique appeal of the aquatic sports all attract millions of participants around the world. In all of these sports, the skill of the great performers is such that their body control and movement represent images of perfection that are an ephemeral art form. At the same time, the tactical and strategic aspects of many ball games are akin to the magnificent game of chess. Most importantly, when played in the true spirit of competition, sports bring millions of young people into activities where they can begin the process of extending and defining themselves, thus expanding their awareness of their own potential. Indeed, sport has an almost unique capacity to provide experiences that can help us to achieve this, a notion superbly captured by Michael Novak (1988) when he wrote the following:

> If I had to give one single reason for my love of sports it would be this: I love the tests of the human spirit. I love to see defeated teams refuse to die. I love to see impossible odds confronted. I love to see impossible dares accepted. I love to see the incredible grace lavished on simple plays—the simple flashing beauty of perfect form—but, even more, I love to see the heart which refuses to give in, refuses to panic, seizes opportunity, slips through defenses, exerts itself far beyond capacity and forges momentarily of its bodily habitat an instrument of almost perfect will.

Sport flourishes because in one way or another, it engenders emotions such as these in billions of participants throughout the world. Unfortunately, the influence of sponsorship and advertising, of television and of money, often seem to overpower the true reality of sport, which is simply the story of one person's struggle against another or against the natural environment. Indeed, what is rarely mentioned is that the real attraction of sport is the pleasure that players experience when a movement task is done well. The sweet feeling of clean contact when a ball is properly hit, of mastery when it is controlled or caught, of satisfaction when intelligent teamwork produces a goal or thoughtful defense snares an interception, of thrill when a wave or a slope is mastered, of pleasure when a personal best performance is achieved: These are the magical moments we remember long after the result is forgotten. More than any other factor, they are the reason we continue to play even when our bodies can no longer sustain our dreams.

Perhaps one of the most astonishing manifestations of the attraction of sport occurs in Japan. Here, thousands of people, many of whom could never afford to play a round of golf on a real course, spend hours hitting balls from tees in tiered driving ranges that can accommodate hundreds of players at a time. Perhaps, as Pulitzer Prize winning author John Updike once suggested, the simple, clean contact with the ball, followed by the tracking of its flight towards the target, really is enough for one to gain pleasure from golf.

However, although some philosophers may disagree, there has to be more to sport than this, these mere ephemeral moments of pleasure. And, of course, there is! Indeed, the benefits of physical activity and sport have been extolled by physical educators for more than 100 years. Above all, sports have the potential to play a special role in the lives of young people growing up in the complex societies of the modern world. For while sport can contribute to the lives of people of all ages, it takes on special significance during adolescence. Dr. Roger Bannister, ever famous as the first man to run the mile in under 4 minutes, observed:

> What significance does sport have for the individual? I think adolescence can often be a time of conflict and bewilderment. These years can be weathered most successfully if a boy develops some demanding activity that tests to the limit his body as well as his mind. Each adolescent has to find this demanding activity for himself. It may be mountain climbing, running, or sailing, or it may be something quite different. It may not even be sport at all. But in the absorption in this pursuit, he forgets himself, and it fills the void between the child and the man.

Although we agree with the over-riding philosophy here, it is clear that his views apply equally to girls. However, instead of simply allowing adolescents to discover this demanding activity by themselves, they should be introduced to a range of experiences that are broad enough to provide a choice while ensuring a solid foundation.

While these initial experiences should be enjoyable, there is a growing acceptance that challenging and stretching youngsters in their formative years can contribute to their total well-being. Indeed the prophets of positive psychology argue that when people are totally committed to a task, completely absorbed in it, they operate in a state of flow (Seligman & Csikszentmihalyi, 2000). Here, as they draw on everything they have to meet the challenges they face, young people are contributing to their own development. Sport in all its varied forms provides an ideal vehicle to expedite this process, for it examines the qualities that have been crucial to the survival of our species over hundreds of thousands of years. Physical and moral courage, self-reliance, skill, speed, power, endurance, self-sacrifice, determination, dedication, perseverance, fairness, loyalty, and the pursuit of excellence have been valued by all societies throughout history. All of these qualities are necessary in sport, and many can be developed through sport.

Sport can also bring hope to young people in places where merely staying alive is an achievement. This is exemplified by the aptly named Fountain of Hope School in Lusaka, the capital of the African state of Zambia. Here, football is used as a carrot to encourage children to attend school and to begin pulling themselves out of the swamp of a life apparently without hope. Since 1981, the Harlem RBI (Reviving Baseball in Inner Cities) camps in New York have combined literacy and baseball programs, involving up to 700 youngsters between the ages of 6 and 18 every summer. Their success is evidenced by the fact that 90 percent of the youngsters who become involved in this program go on to college, compared with a 50 percent drop-out rate from high schools in the same area.

This is a story captured almost incidentally in the brilliant television series *The Wire* where, almost in an aside to the main theme, a former boxer attempts to draw youngsters away from the dangerous streets of Baltimore. It is repeated throughout the world in backstreet gyms where the heavy bag, punch ball, and sparring all play their part in providing potentially life-changing experiences; on the sun-baked grounds of Pakistan and India, where a dozen overlapping and informal cricket games are played simultaneously on a single field; on thousands of dusty pitches in Africa and South America, where anything remotely resembling a soccer ball is treated with reverence; on the battered concrete basketball courts of cities worldwide; on the running tracks of Kenya; in tiny sheds containing only a single table-tennis table, but an enthusiastic coach; and on the fields of Papua New Guinea, where youngsters commit themselves to an annual round of games of every kind. It is a story involving the young people of the entire world and it is a story worthy of serious study, because it reminds us that sport has an immense power to change lives. It need not be merely a vehicle for the casual entertainment of the masses nor the promotion of beer and razor blades, as sometimes seems to be the case with the advertisements that dominate great sporting events such as the Super Bowl in the United States.

While sport can go some way to alleviating the grinding poverty and sense of hopelessness that persists in many developing countries, it can play another role entirely with the more fortunate youngsters on this planet. Taking up an issue that was of concern to some of the most significant philosophers of the 20th century, Peter Arnold argued that sport can become a vehicle through which the privileged youth of more affluent communities can be tested, both physically and morally. In this way, he believed that the virility and vitality of humankind could be kept alive. In his seminal work *Education, Physical Education and Personality Development*, Arnold observed, 'In the absence of a way of life that will in a natural manner look after the physical and moral needs of society, we must turn instead to the artificed work of the physical educationist. It is to them that we largely entrust Man's supreme inheritance' (1968).

What is interesting here is that while the relationship between regular exercise and a longer, healthier, and more vital life is already generally accepted, studies are confirming that simple changes in lifestyle can positively affect many diseases. Evidence is growing that active children benefit in terms of obesity, lower blood pressure, improved glucose tolerance, plasma lipoprotein profile, and even intelligence. Experts have long agreed that fitness lowers cardiorespiratory risk factors and levels of anxiety and stress, enhances physical capacity, as well as improving self-concept and self-esteem.

Unfortunately, as nations, communities, and schools attempt to deal with this issue, they may be tempted to turn physical education into rigid and rigorous exercise programs. While this may lead to temporary improvements in fitness, it may also lead to a lifelong aversion to physical activity. This is why we believe that the best way to induce youngsters to make a lifelong commitment to a healthy lifestyle is to exploit the tremendous power of sport. Here it is worth considering the ideals of the Olympic movement.

The Olympic creed states with absolute conviction, 'The most important thing in the Olympic Games is not to win but to take part, just as the most important thing in life is not the triumph, but the struggle. The essential thing is not to have conquered, but to have fought well.' While this philosophy may be far removed from the realities of the modern Olympic Games, it still contains a vital message. This message must override the crass commercialism, rabid nationalism, myriad forms of cheating, and the use of performance-enhancing drugs. It must also be used to counter the more insidious problems that arise from a media-driven over-emphasis on national medal tallies. These range from distortions in funding that often leave little money available for development at the grassroots level to a push for the early specialisation deemed necessary to produce Olympic champions.

Above all, teachers and coaches must do everything in their power to combat the notion that winning is all that matters. Instead, they must apply the Olympic creed in everything they do. With this as a fundamental belief, it is then possible to add other Olympic principles, such as the importance of fair play, courage, self-control, and respect for officials, team-mates, and opponents. If we can convince youngsters of the truth of these ideas, we will have already achieved a great deal.

However, we need to go far beyond this if we are to ensure that all children have the kind of enjoyable and satisfying initial experiences that will leave them determined to continue their participation in the future. This is vital, because it appears that 70 percent of children who begin playing sport in the United States end up quitting by the age of 13. This statistic is a terrible indictment of a broken system. Unfortunately, it may well be replicated in other developed nations. So the challenge is to provide opportunities for determined children to pursue their dreams as far as they wish to go, without allowing this to distort the overall sport-development program. To achieve both of these objectives, it may be necessary to make fundamental changes to the physical education curricula and radically alter the philosophy of school and community competitive sport. This will not be easy.

Above all, we must try to improve the methods we use to introduce young people to sport. Traditional approaches have survived, even though they do not meet the needs of ordinary children and do little to help even talented and enthusiastic youngsters learn to play more effectively and enjoyably. Most importantly, these methods do not cater for reluctant or resistant learners who are not prepared to undertake the repetitive practice often associated with becoming proficient at sport and who drop out of any activity when it ceases to be fun for them. As David Kirk states in his insightful book *Physical Education Futures,* 'The dominant idea of physical education . . . is the pride of place given to the techniques of games and sports over the performance of the games and sports themselves' (2010).

Daryl Siedentop (1994) elaborates on this theme when he writes:

> Skills are taught in isolation rather than as part of the natural context of executing strategy in game-like situations. The rituals, values and traditions of a sport that give it meaning are seldom even mentioned, let alone taught in ways that students can experience them. The affiliation with a team or group that provides the context for personal growth and responsibility in sport is noticeably absent in physical education. The ebb and flow of a sport season is seldom captured in a short-term sport instruction unit. Physical education teaches only isolated sport skills and less-than-meaningful games.

Although this describes the scene in the United States, the methods he is referring to are still common throughout much of the developed world, including sport-crazy countries like Britain and Australia. Unfortunately, the skills and drills approach they describe is often replaced by the lazy 'let's have a game'. Inevitably, such games are dominated by the more aggressive and experienced players, while the remainder try to stay out of the way. Such a games lesson was captured superbly by Ken Loach in *Kes,* a film that should be required viewing for any aspiring physical education teacher. Produced by one of the most significant British film makers of the 20th century, *Kes* raises serious questions about the nature of English society and the place of both education and physical education in that society.

Play Practice can provide teachers and coaches with practical solutions to the challenges they face on a daily basis. This is possible because this innovative approach evolved through the most challenging of research environments—that is, teachers working with real students in real schools. As a result any dedicated sport educator who understands the philosophy of Play Practice and employs the methods we suggest can help young people play their way to understanding and competence. From competence comes confidence and positive self-esteem, qualities that may help young people develop the body image and feelings of self-worth they need if they are to cope with the 'slings and arrows of outrageous fortune' (as Hamlet would say) that are so much a part of life in our increasingly complex world.

We therefore hope that more teachers and coaches will take up the ideas presented in this book to induce even more youngsters to make a lifelong commitment to sport and physical activity. If so, it may indeed be possible to develop a society of players and a culture devoted to play, thus contributing to a more civilised humanistic future.

part I

Fundamentals of Play Practice

Despite the immense popularity of sports and their potential to enhance individual lives and revitalise communities, they are not always well taught. Given the incredible efforts to improve every aspect of performance at the elite level over the past 50 years, this is extremely disappointing. So although there are isolated pockets of excellence, sport education in schools and clubs often appears to be trapped in a time warp, where old ideas and methods are continually recycled.

Chapter 1 begins by examining the limitations of traditional methods of teaching games. It next outlines the origins of Play Practice and then details the advantages, key concepts, and conceptual framework of this innovative approach to teaching and coaching sport. The chapter closes with a brief consideration of the Teaching Games for Understanding approach.

Feedback from coaches and teachers has confirmed that the analysis of skilled play outlined in the first edition was of critical importance in improving their ability to analyse a sport, to assess the ability of both individual players and teams, and to plan practice sessions and lessons. Since very few, if any, other works in this field had even considered this issue, it seems that Play Practice was regarded as an almost revolutionary

contribution. As a result, chapter 2 greatly expands on the original ideas on the nature of skilled performance in sport by further clarifying terms and providing a range of examples to illustrate key concepts. Chapter 3 then considers the process of skilled performance and explores the implications of this process for teaching and coaching practice.

Chapter 4 introduces the processes of simplifying, shaping, focusing, and enhancing practices, and shows how the concepts involved can provide a framework to guide professional practice in both teaching and coaching. This chapter also shows how these processes can be used to plan pertinent learning experiences, ensure plenty of purposeful practice, and maintain engagement. This leads into chapter 5, which outlines how these processes are applied to develop specific elements of skilled play, namely technical ability, games sense, fair play, and resilience. Finally, chapter 6 outlines the *Ps* model of instruction, a working model that simplifies the complex process and so enables novices to begin the long work of becoming effective teachers and coaches. This chapter provides valuable insights relating to teaching and learning that can be easily understood and systematically applied to improve professional practice.

one

Approaches to Teaching and Coaching Sport

Doubt is the origin of wisdom.

Rene Descartes

This chapter examines the limitations of traditional methods of teaching sports, briefly considers the Teaching Games for Understanding approach, and presents the advantages of Play Practice.

Traditional Approaches to Teaching Games and Sport

As the introduction to this book suggests, with few exceptions, sports teaching appears to be trapped in a time warp. As a result, much of games teaching in schools and coaching at the junior level is still dominated by three outdated approaches: 'Let's have a game,' minor games and relays, and skills and drills.

'Let's Have a Game'

In the 'Let's have a game' approach, a group is divided into two teams. The children are thrown into a full game straightaway, even when there are more players than would be the case in a real game. Often, teams are picked by captains. This process wastes time and is demeaning and demoralising for the less-able youngsters, as evidenced by Janis Ian's poignant line, 'To those whose names were never called when choosing sides for basketball,' in her hit song 'At 17.'

Such games are inevitably dominated by the more aggressive or experienced players, while children with limited ability hover on the fringes, trying to make sense of the apparently chaotic whirl of play going on around them. They rarely touch the ball and quickly learn how to position themselves to stay out of the way. Softball, baseball, or cricket sessions can follow a similar pattern, where some children never touch the ball as fielders, while the batting side sit lined up, patiently waiting their turn. When it is finally time to bat, the youngster is on show and is often exposed to failure in front of the whole class.

Minor Games and Relays

Minor games are often used by well-meaning but untrained helpers or by teachers with a limited background in games. They select a minor game because of its title, such as soccer softball or circle soccer, and because a soccer ball is used. However, they have little understanding of the game's limited value for soccer development, for these games do nothing to help youngsters become better soccer players because they are too different from the real game.

However, if minor games are structured to have many similarities with the real game, they can be classified as lead-up games. End-zone games that are virtually identical to each other, such as line ball, skittle ball, bench ball, and goal ball, can be used to introduce children to the initial concepts of passing in games such as netball, basketball, korfball, and team handball.

Relays in various forms are very popular with children and are easy to organise. They are often used in teaching and coaching settings to keep large numbers of children active and involved, particularly in situations where it is necessary to manage large class numbers with little time for planning and organising the session. Unfortunately, teachers and coaches often use relays in an attempt to teach children the skills of major games. While it could be claimed that relays can be used to teach ball control, the fact is that children would get far more practice if they each had a ball!

Skills and Drills

The skills and drills approach appears to be the most professional and structured of the three methods. It is favoured by many teachers and coaches. With an emphasis on organisation, structure, and control, this approach can efficiently develop some aspects of skilled performance. However, careful analysis shows that while it may seem to save time, it is not always effective, and the vision of professionalism is often an illusion. The major problem is the over-emphasis on the development of the so-called fundamentals, or basic skills of the game, at the expense of other aspects of skilled play. This technique-oriented approach, with its pattern of skills first and game at the end, is still popular in schools and junior coaching. It also causes inexperienced teachers considerable grief as they face the unending calls of 'When are we going to play a game?'

Teaching Games and Sports Effectively

All of the approaches mentioned previously share fundamental problems:

1. They are based on a facile analysis of games and what is required to play them effectively.
2. They focus almost entirely on the development of technical ability—that is, the ability to control and direct the ball. They ignore other important elements of skilled play.
3. They often fail to meet basic requirements for safety, inclusion, engagement, collaboration, and successful participation for all children.
4. They ignore two of the most crucial factors in an effective learning situation, namely the amount of practice and the quality of that practice.

While these problems have been obvious to perceptive observers for many years, research that began in the late 1970s has provided objective evidence to support their opinions. It is now clear that what is termed *time on task* is fundamental to effective instruction. Time is precious, and it must not be frittered away through thoughtless planning, bad organisation, poor management, too much teacher talk, or poorly structured questioning. Studies have confirmed a direct relationship between the amount of time learners are on task (that is, practising) and the amount they learn. At the very least, this information suggests that it is better to give every child a ball for a series of basketball dribbling or shooting practices than to use relays, where five or more youngsters often share one ball.

While time on task can indicate the amount of activity, it cannot measure the quality of that activity. So, what we have termed *alignment* is also a critical factor in effective instruction. The fundamental principles of alignment, or what has been called *transfer of training,* emerged as perceptive coaches determined that there should always be a close relationship between practice and the real game. The closer the alignment— that is, the greater the similarities between a practice and a game—the more likely that the players can successfully apply what they learn in practice to the game. This is summed up by a coaching aphorism: 'Train as you play and play as you train.'

Unfortunately, assessing the degree of alignment between a practice and the game is not easy, since it becomes a subjective exercise that depends on the observer's deep understanding of the game. Figures 1.1 and 1.2 help clarify this important issue.

While learners may automatically transfer skills developed in practices that are closely aligned with the real game, this process will be enhanced if coaches and teachers point out the

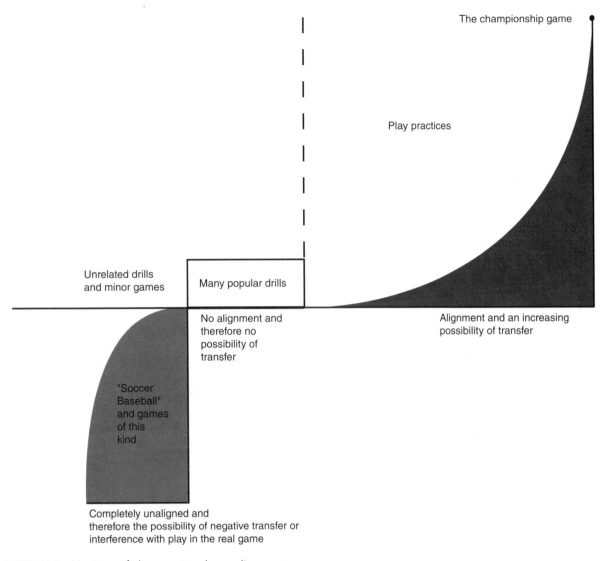

The championship game

Play practices

Unrelated drills
and minor games

Many popular drills

No alignment and
therefore no
possibility of
transfer

Alignment and an increasing
possibility of transfer

"Soccer
Baseball"
and games
of this
kind

Completely unaligned and
therefore the possibility of negative transfer or
interference with play in the real game

FIGURE 1.1 Versions of alignment and non-alignment.

similarities between the practice situation and the game, as well as any significant differences. Youngsters are also more likely to apply new learning in a game situation if it closely follows the practice.

Conversely, if there is little alignment between a practice and the game, there is unlikely to be any useful transfer between them. So, players are unlikely to improve! This is the case with many of the drills and unrelated minor games that have traditionally been used in sport education. See the shaded area of figure 1.1 for examples. In extreme cases, they may actually interfere with learning. Practices or games of this kind fall into the dark zone below the line.

Origin and Evolution of Play Practice

The limitations of the traditional methods outlined previously became abundantly clear to Alan Launder, who was an inexperienced, ill-prepared, and lonely young teacher in the winter of 1957, as he faced the problems posed by reluctant, even resistant learners in a rural secondary school in Norfolk, England. These methods simply were not effective with adolescent boys, especially those who had already been labelled as intellectually limited by an archaic educational system and who were simply

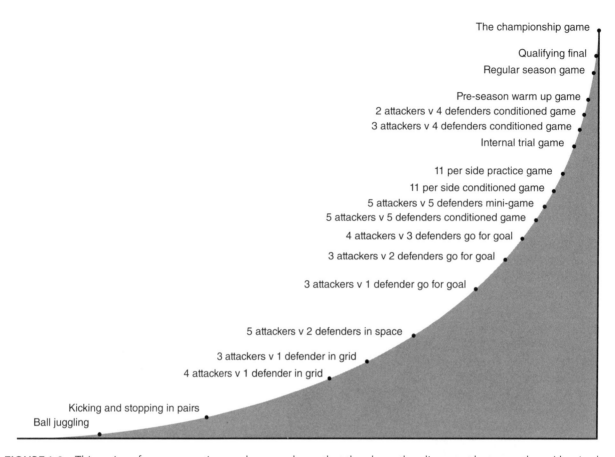

The championship game

Qualifying final

Regular season game

Pre-season warm up game

2 attackers v 4 defenders conditioned game

3 attackers v 4 defenders conditioned game

Internal trial game

11 per side practice game

11 per side conditioned game

5 attackers v 5 defenders mini-game

5 attackers v 5 defenders conditioned game

4 attackers v 3 defenders go for goal

3 attackers v 2 defenders go for goal

3 attackers v 1 defender go for goal

5 attackers v 2 defenders in space

3 attackers v 1 defender in grid

4 attackers v 1 defender in grid

Kicking and stopping in pairs

Ball juggling

FIGURE 1.2 This series of soccer practices and games shows that the closer the alignment between them (that is, the greater the similarities between the practice situation and the real game), the more likely it is that players will transfer new learning from the practice to the game.

serving their time before leaving school to find work at the minimum age of 15.

Alan faced the problems of very large classes, including a special population of students who were then termed 'maladjusted youths from a nearby hostel,' poor facilities, limited equipment, no mentors to consult, and a school that had not had a specialist physical education teacher for three years. Therefore, both his program and teaching methods were powerfully influenced by the responses of the students. Their ready acceptance of new ideas based on engaging every student and incorporating play-like elements into the program contrasted sharply with their negative reaction to traditional methods.

During these early days, the whole process was driven by an intuitive process of self-analysis and reflective tinkering, where ideas were developed, trialled, discarded, accepted, and improved. His key discovery was that students like to be challenged, but most of all, they

like to succeed and to have their successes noted. They do not like to fail or to be beaten, and they certainly do not want to be last at anything. Thus, the importance of ensuring early and continuing success for each youngster became a critical aspect of Play Practice.

It is important to remember that at this time, and for a considerable period afterwards, there were no books on pedagogy apart from the outdated *1933 Syllabus.* Only Barbara Knapp's *Skill in Sport,* first published in 1963, provided some theoretical insights into the problems of teaching sports. Even Mike Metzler's study of *Academic Learning Time,* one of the early pieces of modern research with clear implications for physical education, was not completed until 1979.

As a result, coaches associated with national sporting bodies served as the most significant external influences on what was to become Play Practice. Of these, the most important were as follows:

- 1958: Jack Carrington, the coaching director for the English Table Tennis Association, who stressed the importance of high levels of technical ability in racquet sports
- 1959: Alan Wade, the director of coaching for the English Football Association, who introduced the concept of principles of tactical play in teaching football
- 1961: Harry Crabtree of the Marylebone Cricket Club (MCC), who developed methods to help large groups of children master the techniques of cricket
- 1962: Tom McNab, who was the Southern Counties coaching coordinator for track and field in Britain

In fact, Alan's meeting with Wade in the summer of 1959 led to an epiphany that occurred at the perfect time to help him resolve some of the very real problems outlined previously. Wade's notion of using small-sided games to teach the tactical principles of soccer met the students' need to play, while simultaneously ensuring that they developed other aspects of skilled play—in other words, practising—without being aware of it!

When Alan took these ideas to Dr. Challoner's grammar school in Buckinghamshire, England, in 1960, they had an immediate effect. These changes rapidly brought the school recognition as a national leader in the fields of physical education and sport. Tom McNab's contribution during this period was recognising that the school's approach to teaching athletics was a major innovation. One result of this was the development of the five-star-award approach to teaching track and field, which was subsequently taken up by 27 countries.

While these early experiences laid the foundations for what was to become Play Practice, it only emerged in its present form after years of pragmatic experimentation. This included teaching physical education at both elementary and secondary levels, coaching a wide variety of sports, including track and field athletics at the Olympic level, deeply immersing himself in teacher education, helping young teachers solve problems similar to those that led to the initial stirrings of Play Practice, and making a major commitment to coach education. Subsequently, Wendy, a former student of Alan's at the University of South Australia, brought her considerable experience as a physical education teacher, teacher educator, and international games player to the developmental process.

In fact, it was only in 1994 when Alan and Wendy were developing the coach-education curriculum for lacrosse in Australia that the need to identify, clarify, and define the elements of skilled play in games became apparent. Until that time, sport educators appeared to rely on an intuitive, virtually unstated understanding of what was necessary to play the games they were teaching or coaching.

As the result of an ongoing process of reflection, it gradually became clear that Play Practice was effective because it harnessed the powerful forces released by play to motivate learners, first to participate and then to pursue excellence. Since it exploits the power of play, Play Practice recognises the fundamental truth captured by Bugelski's (1956) perceptive statement 'Learning can only be done by the learner, not by some kind of transmission process from the teacher.'

Put simply, unless learners make a commitment to mastery, the amount of time they spend practising and the degree of alignment of that practice with the real activity are both largely irrelevant.

Precepts of Play Practice

As Play Practice evolved, it became even clearer that it was very important to consider children's attitudes towards sport. While this awareness may be taken for granted in the 21st century, it was not a common notion 50 years ago! As a result, this complex issue was boiled down to the following characteristics that most, although not all, youngsters share:

- They desire to be good at sport.
- They prefer to play a game than to practise.
- They like playing real games or trying the real activity.
- They like to play in teams or groups.
- They prefer to play with their friends.
- They prefer central roles.
- They like to be successful.
- They prefer competition that is evenly balanced.

- They do not want to lose or be embarrassed.
- They would like to be seen as skilful by significant others.
- They see practice as a means to an end and not an end in itself.

While it is especially important to heed these precepts with beginners, experience suggests that they may apply equally to hardened professional players.

The key factors in inducing commitment to physical activity are the feelings of success, achievement, fun, and enjoyment that players can experience in sport. For most children, having fun is the dominant drive for their involvement; when an activity ceases to be fun, youngsters tend to drop out. However, *fun* is rarely defined, so there is a tendency to see it as synonymous with enjoyment. But while fun may be ephemeral, enjoyment is satisfying and lasts much longer. This is because it is derived from the feelings of success and achievement that can come from positive, even challenging participation. While completing a cross country run over muddy fields is rarely seen as fun, it can be immensely enjoyable. It is at least enjoyable

enough for many to want to repeat the experience the following week!

Therefore, Play Practice attempts to create situations that capture the enjoyment of the pick-up games and the challenges so common in children's play. However, while exploiting the power of play, these learning situations are carefully structured to create challenging and enjoyable practices that can motivate players, young and old alike, to play their way to understanding, competence, and excellence.

Because early success is critical, games and challenges are initially simplified to ensure that youngsters quickly begin to feel that they can do this! The process begins as the teacher

- introduces the activity safely and in a way that emphasises the sheer joy of playing or of meeting a challenge,
- simplifies activities so that children can cope with them, and
- builds a supportive climate in which youngsters can begin to develop the mental strength and resilience necessary to handle anything sport can throw at them.

This young player shows determination and a can-do approach, with commitment expressed in her eyes.

Lacrosse is introduced through the game of mitt-crosse, or grip-ball lacrosse, where the regulation stick is replaced with a softball glove or grip-ball pad. This enables absolute beginners to play a game that is like lacrosse in every other respect. In this way, they experience the joy of playing a game early on. From the very beginning, all learning is contextual, so youngsters gain an understanding of the fundamental nature of the game, of its rules, its tactics, and its mores almost incidentally as they play. They are then much more likely to make the commitment that will enable them to progress to the next level.

However, the Play Practice position is that once students have gained some understanding and liking for the game, they should be expected to commit themselves to mastering the techniques of scooping, carrying, catching, and throwing that are necessary if they are to play the real, more challenging game of lacrosse. Of course, during this time, the teacher may continually return to the joys of mitt-crosse, at least until this game is no longer a challenge for the group. A similar approach can be used in teaching hockey.

On the other hand, any analysis of skilled play in a game like table tennis confirms that sound technique, not an understanding of tactics, is the critical factor in early success and enjoyment for novices. The Play Practice solution is to introduce target games that encourage beginners to focus on developing effective technique, while still allowing them to enjoy the challenge of playing a game.

When it is not possible to develop technical ability effectively through games of this kind, coaches can use challenges to motivate youngsters. Examples from basketball could include 'How many shots will it take you to score 5 (or 10) baskets from 3-point range?' and 'How many consecutive layups can you make?' This approach can be used with any technique where accuracy is important. If coaches and teachers record performances and note improvements, the effect on the quality of practice may be profound.

Challenges should always be based on indirect competition, where players compete against their previous best performances, not on direct competition that pits one against another. The Play Practice approaches to introducing both cross country running and track and field are good examples of this. Youngsters take part in time trials instead of races, and everyone wins by improving their performance.

Although these approaches illustrate the driving forces of Play Practice, they represent only the first of many advantages that this innovative approach brings to sport education.

Benefits of Play Practice

1. *Play Practice gives teachers ongoing opportunities to interact positively with their students.* Once teachers accept the notion that learning can only be done by the students, it is clear that their primary function is to create practice environments that accelerate learning and make it enjoyable. If they are successful, their students may become so deeply immersed in learning that the teacher will be freed from the unending managerial tasks so common in physical education. Studies into the use of Play Practice at the University of South Australia (Piltz, 2008b) indicated that preservice teachers faced fewer management issues and saw higher levels of engagement, participation, and enjoyment. In this situation, teachers can devote more of their time and energy to the kind of positive interaction that builds valuable personal relationships.

This opportunity for one-on-one interaction can be especially important when children go through a rapid growth spurt or face difficult movement challenges. Sport educators who help young people to successfully pass through these experiences with confidence and optimism have contributed to learner transformation.

For example, a child who has just completed her first ever swim across the width of a pool is not the same individual who set out on that churning, gasping, scary challenge! And the relationship between that child and the teacher waiting to meet her at the side of the pool may never be the same!

In these most basic achievements, as students master a new challenge, improve on their previous best performance, feel the ball come sweetly off a racquet or a bat, co-operate in team play, see an arrow fly into the distance, or watch the ball drop cleanly through the hoop, lives can be changed. Educators have an opportunity to interact with youngsters on a personal level, possibly influencing their perception of the activity, of themselves, and of the learning process. These are the moments that can transform people and determine whether or not they make sport and physical activity a major part of their lives. In some cases, the influence may have even greater significance. It is for this reason that teachers and coaches must appreciate the vital importance of their role, even when some colleagues, administrators, and even parents do not!

2. *Play Practice can make the learning environment more enjoyable for teachers and coaches.* The teaching–learning process is like a mirror, where the attitude of the teacher is reflected back to them. Studies have confirmed that students can have a major effect on a teacher's performance by the way they react, whether positively or negatively. If children enjoy the experience of playing a game or meeting a challenge, they will show their pleasure. This affects the teacher, who in turn may become more positive and enthusiastic, causing the relationship to spiral upwards. No matter how experienced they may be, this is when teachers can rediscover the joys of their profession; for novices, these moments can be a revelation.

3. *Play Practice focuses on the learners and develops critically reflective practitioners.* The ongoing interaction between teacher and student tends to develop critically reflective practitioners who learn from every experience and every student. This is important because any instructional process should be based on a revolving, expanding analysis of student needs, which in turn depends on continuous, perceptive observation.

4. *Play Practice gives youngsters opportunities to co-operate with each other.* In many Play Practices, they can take on roles as supporters, commentators, feedback givers, and even assistant teachers or coaches. An emphasis on a helping attitude in sport is long overdue. If it can be nurtured from the beginning, it may be possible for young people to appreciate that sport is as much about co-operation and personal growth as it is about competition. It may also lead to thoughts of a future career in teaching, coaching, sport administration, or officiating. At the very least, it may introduce young people to skills they can put to good use when their own children begin to play!

5. *Play Practice provides a detailed analysis of skilled performance in sport.* This is one of the approach's major advantages because it

- shows that all elements of skilled performance are inter-related;

- suggests that in games, tactics often depend on the technical ability of the players;

- enables teachers and coaches to determine which elements of skilled play to emphasise as they plan learning experiences for a specific group of students or players;

- makes it easier for sport educators to understand the relationships among different sports and to appreciate the way in which good ideas and methods can be transferred from one to another;

- exposes the limitations of outdated methods that focus almost exclusively on the development of technical ability—commonly termed *ball skills* or *the fundamentals*—and which leave young players completely unprepared for the complexities of games; and

- raises serious questions about the value of approaches that emphasise tactics over technical ability when teaching games. The latter appear to be based on ideology rather than a reasoned analysis of what is actually required to play a specific sport well.

6. *Play Practice re-defines the term* games sense *and positions it as a critical element of skilled performance.* While the term *games sense* was originally used as a title for a series of workshops run by Rod Thorpe in Australia in the 1990s and has subsequently been used by some proponents of tactical approaches to teaching games, it was never precisely defined. Inevitably, this has led to confusion and to the notion that an understanding of tactics alone can drive the decision-making process in sport.

The Play Practice construct of games sense resolves this problem and makes it clear that to be effective, players need an understanding not only of tactics but also of the rules, of strategy, and of themselves (and of their team-mates, in many games) if they are to solve the problems posed by the game or by their opponents.

Defining games sense in this way opens up a broader understanding of the nature of skill in sport. With the constituent elements clearly identified, the concept of games sense is easier to understand and to teach.

7. *Play Practice introduces the strategies of simplifying, shaping, focusing, and enhancing.* The role of the teacher is to create situations where learning can take place efficiently and enjoyably. To that end, Play Practice recommends the use of practice situations that retain the essential feel of a sport but have the following characteristics:

- They are simplified to ensure early success.
- They are shaped to improve specific elements of performance.
- They are focused to ensure understanding and improvement.
- They are enhanced to maximise enjoyment and improvement.

8. *Play Practice emphasises the importance of time on task, maximum individual participation, and alignment.* These are captured in this Play Practice mantra: 'To become an effective performer, a learner needs plenty of perfect practice under conditions as similar as possible to the environment in which the new learning will subsequently be applied.'

9. *It is supported by a clearly defined action plan for the instructional process.* Play Practice provides a working model of instruction in the form of the *P*s of perfect pedagogy, detailed in chapter 6. This breaks the instructional task into components that can be more easily recalled, applied, and used as a template for critical reflection within the teaching process.

10. *Play Practice introduces the notion of working and advanced models of technique.* A working model is a technique stripped to the bare bones. While this concept is explored in chapter 5, working techniques in common use include the scissors high-jump technique in athletics and the dog paddle in swimming.

This notion of working models is important, because the techniques employed by elite performers are often complex. They usually require special physical qualities and may involve years of dedicated practice for mastery. On the other hand, youngsters can master working models of technique with minimal practice and can begin to play early on in the sport experience.

11. *It introduces the notion of working tactical models.* While experts can usually draw on a wide range of techniques and thus have a broad range of tactical options, beginners with limited technical ability must keep their tactics simple if they are to be effective. In soccer, young players should initially be encouraged to play direct football. They should continually look to make long forward passes instead of trying to employ the complex inter-passing methods of professionals. In table tennis, young players can be shown how to build a tactical game based on the forehand topspin drive and the backhand push, block, and drive.

12. *Play Practice can be used to introduce sports as varied as American football, skiing, track and field, swimming, surfing, and table tennis.* For example, while traditional approaches to teaching skiing have focused on the repetitive practice of specific techniques in one area of a slope, the Play Practice approach takes students on a trek across carefully chosen mountain terrain. The varied technical elements of skiing, including how to get up after a fall, are introduced and practised at appropriate points along the route.

This approach is effective because learning takes place in a real environment, which means that it is always contextual. Therefore, the motivation to improve is very high. Another advantage is that youngsters begin to learn how to read a slope and to choose a suitable route down or across it, which are important competencies at all levels of recreational skiing.

13. *It can be employed by elite coaches.* Here, as training volumes increase in the drive towards excellence, play becomes work, enjoyment diminishes, and the motivation inherent in joyful participation is lost. Many talented athletes may even stop playing.

Play Practice counters this by providing a framework for a vast range of enjoyable and realistic practice scenarios that can simulate the demands of high-level competition while retaining the crucial element of play. It is clear that even great players love the whole process of practising and competing in realistic scenarios.

14. *Play Practice lends itself to innovation of all kinds and is continually evolving.* As sport educators experiment with this approach, they will almost inevitably create something unique and exciting to add to the range of effective ideas. The process engages educators more deeply in the teaching–learning process and lays the foundation for a better understanding of professional practice. It encourages creativity and enjoyment

Play practice can be applied to a variety of activities such as surfing.

on the part of both teacher and student. In some cases, improvements occur through an ongoing, reflective process, as happened with the evolution of the five-star approach to teaching track and field. In contrast, some will arrive through moments of sheer inspiration, as was the case with action fantasy games, an innovation detailed in chapter 4.

15. *The potential of Play Practice has yet to be fully explored.* If sport educators or coaches connect with each other and share their ideas and experiences, the possibilities are unlimited. This is a completely open-ended process, since once the basic principles are understood, they can be applied to all levels of participation and to almost all sports.

16. *Play Practice can be taken up and applied piecemeal.* Teachers and coaches can choose to trial those ideas that are easiest to integrate into their usual methods and are most likely to be effective with their students or players. They can start by making one small adjustment

to a practice situation or one simple modification to a game, by using a working model of technique, or by trying a fantasy game. It is possible for novice instructors to begin with games little removed from pick-up games and then progressively modify them. In this way, they can gradually move towards the Play Practice approach to teaching and coaching sport. Ultimately, this adaptability may prove to be the greatest strength of Play Practice, because the history of physical education is littered with good ideas that did not survive the realities of schools.

17. *It has sound, if retrospective, theoretical underpinnings.* While Play Practice was originally driven by a process of reflective tinkering with limited input from theory, it is now clear that it is supported both by a large body of theory and by the work of other professionals in the field. (Please visit www.HumanKinetics.com/PlayPractice for supplemental material on the theoretical underpinnings.)

Differences Between Play Practice and TGfU

In 1982, the limitations of the traditional 'skills first, game last' approach were obvious to perceptive professionals, so Len Almond, Dave Bunker, and Rod Thorpe at Loughborough University proposed an alternative. Their innovative approach, Teaching Games for Understanding (TGfU), has been a seminal influence for many. It was initially outlined in a series of articles under the heading 'Games teaching revisited' in the 1983 edition of the *British Bulletin of Physical Education.*

The major contribution of this talented trio was their notion that the starting point should be a game, modified where necessary, that would engage youngsters in enjoyable activity and allow them to begin to understand the fundamental nature, rules, and tactics of the game as they played. TGfU has had a significant effect on the volume of research in the field, but until the turn of the century, there had been a void in the articulation of usable strategies to guide professional practice (Chandler, 1996; Piltz, 2003). As Almond suggested in a personal communication, a major reason for this was that the initial conceptual effort was not subjected to the deeper process of reflection and place-based experimentation needed to further flesh out the model. A second issue was that as some researchers and authors picked up this innovative approach, they placed too much emphasis on the development of tactics while often neglecting the importance of technical ability and other aspects in skilled performance.

Indeed, a major problem is that many who have championed TGfU appear to have rejected the possibility that the starting point in some sports should be with the development of technical ability, not tactics. As a result, there have been few attempts to develop games or challenges that could be used to help youngsters improve their technical ability or to consider other ways of developing this important aspect of skilled play.

However, TGfU brought a fresh direction to sport pedagogy and excited considerable interest as a potential alternative to traditional methods. The work of research practitioners such as Tim Hopper and Dennis Slade is particularly interesting. They have utilised their practical experience in teaching and coaching to expand the structure of the approach and align it to the complexity of the learning process. Hopper (2009) uses the concept of the game as teacher to illustrate the importance of teaching in game-centred environments and highlights the way in which learning emerges in these settings through the process of player adaption. This is aligned with the notions of teaching through the game and teaching in the game advocated in Play Practice as teachers and coaches shape and focus learning settings. Slade (2003) also advocates a game-centered environment to facilitate learning to play field hockey, and he illustrates how variables can be manipulated in a variety of tactical game challenges to both engage and transform learners' capabilities (2010).

Inevitably, comparisons will be made between Play Practice and the TGfU approach. In both cases, the innovators were immersed in the English tradition of physical education, had strong links with coach-education programs, and combined an ongoing practical involvement in teaching with personal experience in a wide range of sports. Both saw the limitations of traditional approaches. However, Play Practice is not an offshoot of TGfU, because it began to evolve on its own in the late 1950s with early publications on teaching and learning athletics and soccer being featured in the book *Modern Schools' Athletics,* edited by Tom McNab (1970), and the article 'Soccer for schools: A modern approach' in the November/December 1973 issue of *JOHPER* (Launder, 1973). The first introduced a radical approach to teaching athletics and cross country running, while the second outlined the importance of teaching tactical principles in soccer.

The fundamental difference between the two approaches is that the protagonists of TGfU were mainly concerned about redressing the balance between tactics and technique and foregrounding the game as the context for learning. The primary objective of Play Practice has always been to find ways to engage and motivate youngsters. The model guiding the process for Play Practice is based on a series of considerations starting with a thorough analysis of the activity and then determining which aspects of skilled play are most important for the particular group of learners. The learning environment is either simplified or shaped to facilitate learning. The starting activity might be an individual challenge, a target game, a sector game, or a mini-game. The processes of focusing and enhancing the play are also outlined as a part of the guiding framework. The original TGfU model in comparison presented a linear sequence to guide professional practice. It is based on presenting a modified game, addressing tactics and decision making, and then presenting the skills when needed. Whilst this model suggests both the activity and the learner need consideration when framing learning, there is limited guidance for this process.

Summary

Why is Play Practice so important? Teaching real children in real schools can often be a difficult and problematic task. Young teachers are especially vulnerable, since they face daunting and unremitting challenges on a daily basis. They need a framework to guide their practice and ideas and methods that work, ones that have already been proven in difficult teaching contexts. Play Practice provides this because every activity suggested in this book is authentic.

two

Elements of Skilled Performance

> The beginning of wisdom is when things are given their proper names.
>
> Chinese proverb

The preceding chapter suggested that traditional approaches to teaching and coaching games are ineffective for the following reasons:

- They ignore the importance of practice time.
- They do not ensure close alignment between the practice and the real game.
- They underestimate the importance of engagement and the commitment of each learner to mastery.
- They rarely account for the diversity of players within the group.

However, a more fundamental problem is that coaches have had a tendency to underestimate the true complexity of skill in ball games. Therefore, this chapter aims to clarify and define the elements of skilled performance in sport.

The problem begins when the word *skill* is used to describe both the action of controlling and directing the ball, as in ball skills, and the overall effectiveness of a player, as in a skilful person. Unfortunately, this leads many teachers and coaches to believe that once they have taught their players the skills of the game, they have taught them to be skilful! As a result, other critical aspects of skilled play are ignored, and players are left to solve the real problems posed by a game on their own.

Play Practice begins by defining the actions of controlling and directing the ball in games as *techniques,* not as 'skills,' 'the basic skills,' or even 'the fundamentals'. Then it is clear that kicking the ball in Australian Rules football, dribbling and shooting the ball in basketball, serving and volleying in tennis, along with all of the other examples shown throughout this book, are techniques. While this may require a paradigm shift in thinking, once this notion is accepted, it becomes clear that while technical ability is an important element of skilled play in ball games, it is only one aspect of skilled performance. This is because in order to play most of the major games well, the player needs the following:

- *A willingness to play fairly.* This underlies all participation in sport, since it is the foundation on which enjoyment and a sense of achievement are built.
- *Resilience and mental strength.* These enable the player to focus on the task at hand and to respond positively to setbacks.
- *Agility.* Often termed *athleticism* or *quickness,* this enables players to get into the right position when they want to get there.
- *Endurance, or fitness.* This allows a player to continue getting into good positions for the entire game and to maintain high levels of concentration and technical ability throughout.

- *Courage and physical toughness.* These ensure that players can cope with the physical challenges in the sport.
- *Communication.* In some games, players must also be able to communicate effectively with their team-mates.

Games Sense

In order to play skilfully, players need to understand the following:

- The rules
- Tactics
- Strategy
- Their own strengths and weaknesses and those of their team-mates

Play Practice draws these last elements together into the concept of *games sense,* which is the ability to use an understanding of the rules, of tactics, of strategy, and of oneself (and of one's team-mates) to solve the problems posed by the sport or by one's opponents (figure 2.1). In this way, games sense bridges the gap between understanding and action and incorporates the process of decision making, a truly critical aspect of skilled play in games.

Here, it is important to appreciate that coaches have always taught elements of games sense. In soccer, we find the adage 'If in doubt, give it a clout.' This seemingly crude advice captures an essential truth: If the ball is bouncing around loose in the penalty area, do not try to be clever. Move it as far out of the danger area as you can as quickly as possible! In basketball, games sense is captured in a series of tight phrases like 'pressure on the ball,' 'help and recover,' 'one foot in the paint on the weak side,' 'one bounce, one step,' 'move as the ball leaves the passer's hands,' and 'overplay the passing lane'. All are used to give players a better understanding of how to adjust their positions and play good defence. However, the clear definition of games sense provided previously enables teachers and coaches in all sports to better interpret their own experience and wisdom and to draw them together into a coherent package. If nothing else, this should allow them to communicate more effectively with their players.

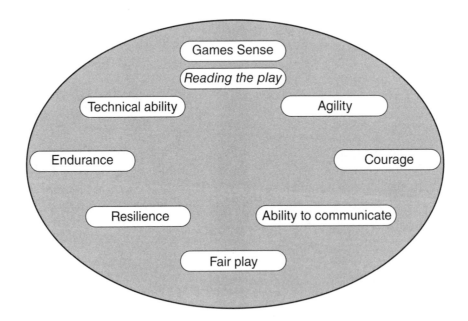

FIGURE 2.1 The elements of skilled play.

Complexity of Skill

Because even the idea that skill in games involves more than the ability to control and direct the ball may challenge long-held beliefs, consider the following scenario.

> In the deciding game of the WNBA finals, the crowd erupts as Lauren drives down the court against great defensive pressure to put up a perfect fade-away jumper for yet another three-pointer.

On the surface, the situation is simple: A great player has demonstrated her amazing talent yet again. Under the circumstances, it might seem ridiculous to ask if Lauren was being skilful when she took that shot. But what if her team was ahead by 1 point with 20 seconds left on the shot clock and 15 seconds left in the game? Would she have been skilful then?

The answer to this question provides a key to understanding the complex nature of skilled play in ball games.

Lauren was clearly good at shooting the ball. However, her coach and her more perceptive team-mates would question whether she was being skilful in taking a relatively low-percentage shot at that point in the game, even though she scored. Her team was ahead by 1 point with only 15 seconds left in the game, so with 20 seconds on the shot clock, she did not need to shoot! If she had missed, her opponents would have had a chance to rebound the ball and take it downcourt for a chance to score the winning basket. The skilful thing to do in that situation, and what the real Lauren would have done, would be to try to run the clock down until there was no time left for the other side to score. Even here, games sense is important! She would ensure that her team's best free-throw shooter had the ball in her hands, because in this situation, opponents are likely to foul in the hope of regaining possession to send the game into overtime.

Playing Skilfully With and Without the Ball

With games sense bridging the gap between understanding and action and incorporating decision making, it is possible to understand how, by relying on their games sense to make good decisions about when and where to move, players can play skilfully without the ball both in attack and defence. In soccer, individual players may be in possession of the ball for approximately 2 minutes in a game; for the remaining 88 minutes, they must employ games sense to play skilfully without the ball. In attack, they must continually adjust their position to support the ball player and to help their team keep possession while preparing for a strike at goal. In defence, they must continually move to ensure pressure on the ball, to support and cover the pressuring defender, and to track and mark attackers who may be breaking into dangerous positions.

Ferenc Puskás, a soccer player who scored three goals in the 6 to 3 demolition of England by Hungary in 1953, was actually on the ball for only 2 minutes and 3 seconds in that game. Similarly, Maradona, the best player in the World Cup final of 1986, was only on the ball for 1 minute and 38 seconds, while in the 1994 final between Italy and Brazil, the great Romário was in possession of the ball for only 53 seconds!

The book *Soccer Skills and Tactics* provides an extreme example of how it is possible to play skilfully without the ball. Jones and Welton (1978) analyse a brief passage of play in one of the greatest soccer matches ever played, the European Cup final between Real Madrid of Spain and Eintracht of Germany in 1973, in the following scenario:

Real's incomparable Di Stéfano breaks down-field, repeatedly inter-passing with several other players in a move that leads to a shot at goal by the great winger, Gento. Unnoticed, except by aficionados, his team-mate Del Sol has run almost the whole length of the pitch, continually moving into excellent support positions to be available for a pass from Di Stéfano. Although he never touched the ball in this move, Del Sol's determined running and good positioning continually distracted defenders, who expected the ball to go to him because of his great reputation.

This skilful play off the ball by Del Sol meant that Di Stéfano always had easier passing options to other players. A strike at goal by Gento was the result (see figure 2.2).

Extreme examples of the application of games sense can be found in both American football and Australian Rules football, games with a shared heritage extending back into the 19th century. Until recently, in both games, it was possible for a player to be skilful while scoring points for their opponents! In American football, this can still happen when a player concedes a safety and 2 points rather than turn the ball over to the opponents in the end zone. Similarly, until the rule was changed in 2007, in the Australian game, players under pressure could deliberately play the ball through their own goal to concede a single point if doing so robbed their opponents of a chance of gaining possession and scoring a goal, worth 6 points.

Integrating Games Sense and Technical Ability

While technical ability and games sense are both components of skilled play, the relative importance of each of these elements varies not only from one sport to another but also from one level of play to another. The key factors appear to be the ratio of the number of players to the ball and the tactical complexity of the game.

In golf, the challenge is to hit a tiny ball, often a considerable distance, to a specific spot using a relatively long lever. This must be done under the pressure of performing in front of anywhere from 2 to 200 hundred million critical eyes or more, and, of course, the pressure of the golfer's own expectations! The performance of one's opponents is, or at least should be, irrelevant. So, technical ability is a major factor in success in this great game, especially with beginners.

However, even when they are exceptional ball strikers, at the elite level golfers must employ games sense to solve the problems posed by the course and by the conditions on any given day. In fact, it is interesting to note the number of elite players who excel on the manicured courses of the United States but who fail on the links courses of Great Britain. There, the variable winds, frequent bouts of inclement weather, and the unforgiving rough can challenge a player's technical ability and dismantle the psyche of even the best.

While it is clear that technical ability is crucial to success in golf, it is possible that as many major tournaments have been lost by taking poor decisions at critical moments as have been won by making great shots. In his book *Ultimate Golf Techniques,* Malcolm Campbell states, 'There are many players with limited ability as pure ball strikers who have been highly successful on the course when it matters. Much of this is because they have had the ability to make the right decision at the right time; they have been able to assess correctly what is possible and stick with the decision' (1998).

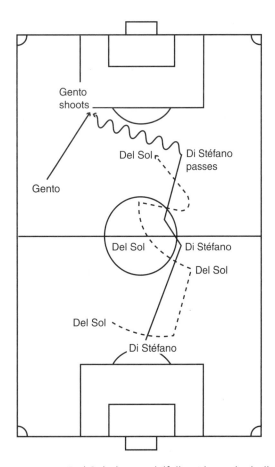

FIGURE 2.2 Del Sol playing skilfully without the ball.

This player demonstrates technical ability as he kicks the ball in Australian Rules football.

Now compare the individual sport of golf with rugby union football, with 15 players on each side. Here, the offside law that prevents forward passes, allied with draconian penalties for other rule infringements, leads to a tactically complex game where games sense is crucial for every player. Indeed, as in American football, some players may rarely, if ever, touch the ball in a game, despite playing superbly! It is also worth noting that in both games, the ability of players to withstand heavy body contact is often as important as their ability to control and direct the ball.

The previous examples appear to confirm that the relative importance of games sense compared with technical ability increases when there are more players in a game. However, games like cricket, baseball, and softball are exceptions to this general rule. This is because, although they are generally regarded as team games, their fundamental nature involves a contest between individual players within a team framework. In other words, it is a struggle between bowler and batter, pitcher and batter, with the fielders in support of the former in both cases. So

although decision making is still important, the technical ability of the key protagonists is the critical factor in skilled performance. In fact, hitting against a major-league baseball pitcher is among the most difficult challenges in sport.

In racquet sports, players have to be completely committed to controlling and directing the ball or the shuttle for half of the thousands of strokes played during a long match. Clearly, they need high levels of technical ability if they are to track and hit a small, fast-moving object, often to a precise point in their opponent's court. However, as they improve, games sense becomes increasingly important because the challenge is not just to hit the ball properly but to outwit an opponent in a kind of mobile chess game that may last several hours. They must make decisions about whether to go for it or just keep the ball in play. Which stroke? Where and how to hit the ball? All must be made instantly, in real time, with no opportunity to reflect. Then, as they execute a stroke, players must try to anticipate their opponent's reaction and move rapidly into the best possible position to deal with the return. Games sense drives all of these decisions!

Another important factor in determining the relative importance of games sense is the degree of unpredictability in a game. Where there are frequent turnovers, as in soccer, for example, the ability to recognise and react to the moment when the ball changes possession is critical. As players switch from attack to defence and vice versa, games sense determines when, where, and how they respond. In Australian Rules football, the unpredictable bounce of the oval-shaped ball makes this task even more complex. As in American football, the ability to gain possession of the loose ball becomes a critical component of skilled play.

So, technical ability and games sense are key components of skilled play. While technical ability is easy to comprehend, the concept of games sense may take some getting used to. However, if we consider each element in turn, the logic of this concept will become clearer. Technique is the dominant factor in performance only in sports such as gymnastics and diving. In ball games and many other sports, such as downhill skiing, surfing, and rock climbing, technique is a means to an end, not an end in itself. Although form follows function, there are no prizes for style in these sports!

Understanding the Rules

A major component of games sense is an understanding of the rules, for they both determine the fundamental nature of the game and influence the tactics, strategy, and techniques of the game.

Here, the concept of primary and secondary rules developed by Len Almond is valuable. Primary rules, such as the handball rule in soccer, determine the fundamental nature of a game; unlike secondary rules, they cannot be amended without changing the game completely. In basketball, while physical contact has always been controlled, the centre jump after every basket has been eliminated, the size and shape of the 3-second lane have been altered, and the time clock and the 3-point shot have been introduced. All these changes have occurred in an attempt to make the game fairer, faster, and perhaps more marketable.

Understanding Tactics

Understanding tactics is an important component of games sense. There is a tendency to think of tactics as a highly complicated aspect of ball games that is only important at the elite level. This is not the case; tactics are part and parcel of play at every level in all games, even when the players themselves do not know they are applying them! In team games, tactics are simply the ways in which attackers position themselves and combine with team-mates to keep possession of the ball and score, and the way in which defenders manoeuvre to regain the ball.

In most invasion games, the simplest offensive tactic is to get there 'firstest with the mostest.' In other words, the goal is to outnumber the other team at the critical point. Here, the moment of transition, that instant when the ball changes possession, is of critical importance. In an instant, defenders must switch roles and begin to counterattack. The fast break, counter attack, and rebound from defence are all names for this highly effective tactic that usually leaves defenders outnumbered. This is because only great teams fast break into defence as effectively as they rebound into attack.

Once the defence is organised, other simple tactics are needed. The give and go in basketball, the wall pass in soccer, and the one, two in

Good teams fast break into attack. Great teams fast break into defence.

Australian Rules are all different names for the same basic tactic: Pass the ball to a team-mate and then exploit any defensive error resulting from the ball movement. As figure 2.3 shows, this is usually done by cutting ball side or *blind side* into the space behind the defender to receive a return pass.

As defenders counter these moves and make it difficult to get open shots close to the goal, the tactical complexity of a game increases. In basketball, the terms *clear out*, *pick and roll*, *screen*, *penetrate and pitch out*, and *drive and dish* are simply shorthand for specific tactics devised to beat increasingly competent defenders, who pressure the ball, help out, and recover. In this game, as in many others, tactics evolve from a simple process of taking advantage of basic defensive mistakes into complex manoeuvres based on exploiting the predictability of defensive responses.

Tactics are continually evolving. As indicated previously, both the time clock and the 3-point shot have had a major influence on tactics in basketball. Another factor at the elite level in this game has been the increasing athleticism of the

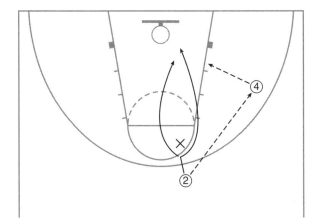

FIGURE 2.3 Example of tactics: cutting ball side, or blind side, into the space behind the defender to receive a return pass.

players and the games sense and technical ability they have developed in thousands of pick-up games, practice sessions, and competitive games. This enables them to play with great tactical freedom as they respond intuitively to the seemingly organised chaos of elite basketball. However, with young players, freedom can rapidly lead to real chaos, since every attacker tries to get open under the basket at the same time! It is therefore necessary to provide a framework through which they can begin to develop and to employ their games sense. Here, coaches often use a rules-based approach to teach games sense. So, when attacking zone defences, a player learns to overload, split the seams, reverse the ball, use the skip pass and the dribble draw, hit the open man, make inside cuts, use replacement cuts, and so on.

While a rules-based approach to tactics is well suited to a high-speed game like basketball, it is not as comprehensive and logical as that developed by English soccer coaches in the 1950s. At that time, they developed a set of principles of tactical play that can rapidly be understood and applied by youngsters. These principles are detailed in the soccer section (chapter 7), but they can readily be applied to other games such as field hockey and lacrosse.

In American football, coaches do their best to eliminate the need for players to employ games sense! Because of the limited time available once the ball is snapped, attackers use set plays and establish their tactics before the ball is put into play. This should make the decision making

process easier because the quarterback knows exactly what his team-mates should be trying to do after the snap. However, in practice, it is not that simple! As Jonah Lehrer observes in his book *The Decisive Moment*, 'The savage chaos of the game, the way every play is a mixture of careful planning and fierce improvisation, is what makes the job of any NFL quarterback so difficult. Even as he is immersed in the mad violence of the game—the defensive line is clawing at his body—the quarterback needs to look past the mayhem and make sense of all the moving bodies' (2009). So, despite the hours of planning before the game, games sense remains a critical element of skilled play in this role. Even in defence, as players read and react to this apparent chaos, games sense is important, especially in the key position of middle linebacker.

An understanding of tactics is the glue that holds a team together. When every player understands and applies key tactical principles, a team becomes more than the sum of its parts. When all players see the same problems and possibilities at the same time, an almost telepathic understanding can be generated. This builds trust, and it can lead to that powerful yet intangible motivational force, team spirit.

In racquet sports, tactics are based on intelligent positioning to cover the court in defence and the use of clever placement, speed, or spin in attack. In badminton, for example, the clear, smash, and drop shots are used in combination to force opponents into mistakes as they try to deal with the long and short tactics that the effective use of these techniques permits. In striking and fielding games, tactics are based on hitting the ball into the defenders' territory in such a way that attackers have enough time to seize a base or to score a run.

Understanding Strategy

As the standard of play increases, an understanding of strategy becomes important. While good tactics may lead to goals being scored, points won, or attacking moves blunted, a sound strategy is usually the key to winning a game. Although these terms are often used interchangeably, the difference between tactics and strategy is significant. This distinction must be appreciated by anyone who wants to fully understand the nature of skilled play in games.

In essence, players use their tactical knowledge to resolve the immediate problems they face in a game, but they use their understanding of strategy to decide which tactics to emphasise at particular points in a game. Most of the 1,000 incidents a soccer player may have to respond to require immediate decisions based on tactical understanding. However, the tactics a player chooses at any instant may depend on the game situation at that specific moment. The strategy of a team leading by one goal with 5 minutes may be to play a version of keep-away to retain possession of the ball. However, if it is trailing by one goal at the same point, it may adopt a completely different strategy and, with it, different tactics.

The more complex a game or the longer it lasts, the more important strategy becomes. While it is not a factor in tenpin bowling, strategy becomes critical in Test match cricket, a game played over five days on a pitch that may alter considerably during that time. The weather may also become a factor. Major golf tournaments, played over four rounds, often in variable weather and wind conditions, also require players to think strategically and to base their tactical and technical choices on a range of factors outside those required for a single stroke.

Sometimes apparently sound tactics may be poor strategy. Although a tennis player might win early games by pounding an opponent's weaker side, perhaps the backhand, this may gradually strengthen that stroke during a long match. Therefore, when critical points arise, the opponent can take the pressure and no longer yields easy points. A player with a strategic vision will only exploit a weakness of this kind on really critical points.

In the same way, table tennis players hold back their most devastating serves early in a match so that their opponents will be unprepared to deal with them when the crucial moment arrives. With strategy, it is important to plan for the whole game, or even a season, and not be concerned by early setbacks.

A sound strategy is also based on an analysis of individual and team strengths. For example, basketball coaches might base their strategy around full-court pressure defence. For a team that doesn't have players of great height or individual stars but instead has a group of athletic, quick, and determined players, such a strategy makes sense. Properly executed, it leads to a full-court, high-tempo game in which agility, fitness, hustle, and teamwork are as valuable as silky outside shooting and slick one-on-one moves. It can disrupt an opponent's controlled half-court game and cause many turnovers, while also exposing limitations in their fitness and mental toughness. Opposition stars who are made to work hard for every possession and who are not getting their normal quota of shots may even lose their cool as the pressure mounts. While such a strategy may seem to be essentially defensive in nature, it is a total package. This is because great defensive pressure leads to many easy baskets when the ball is turned over. In this strategy, the offence is not only built on good defence, it is driven by it.

While strategy might seem the sole province of coaches, it adds another level of interest for all participants. What is certain is that very few teams at the elite level will be successful without at least one player who has strategic vision. Schemers, quarterbacks, X-factor players, and play makers are all terms for this role that is essential in every team and, when well executed, can make a coach's task easy. This leads to another aspect of games sense—that is, the ability of players to factor in their own capacities as they try to solve the problems posed by the game and by their opponents. If there is a secret here, it is that good players exploit their strengths and cover any weaknesses.

In *The Melbourne Age* (2009), Martin Blake wrote about two of the greatest players in the history of cricket: 'Warne and McGrath have great physical gifts, no doubt, but it is nous and cunning that set them apart. It is working out what you can and can't do, and then applying the same logic to your opposition, that augments your great skills.'

Since every opponent brings unique strengths and weaknesses to the contest, this is a never-ending process. Players must learn to quickly assess their opponents and decide how best to exploit their relative strengths. In basketball, good coaches are always looking to exploit potential mismatches, where one of their players has an advantage of height, agility, or even sheer bulk over the direct opponent.

However, this process is virtually impossible for beginners, who have no idea what they are capable of. That said, teachers should be aware of the need to encourage youngsters to bring their own intelligence to bear on this aspect of skilled play.

At the elite level, this process also leads to the notion of developing a game plan, essentially a pre-packaged strategy, for every match. This game plan is based on an analysis of the relative strengths and weaknesses of the opposition gained from scouting reports. It is then prepared and practised ahead of time.

While it is convenient to separate games sense and technical ability in order to clarify the issues involved, in practice, there is a continual interaction among technique, tactics, and strategy in both individual and team sports. For example, in tennis, serve and volley tactics can only be used effectively by someone with technical ability in those areas, while in basketball, a player or a team with limited outside shooting ability will find defenders sagging off them to clog up the key and thus stop inside scoring. Conversely, good 3-point shooting pulls defenders out and creates space and scoring opportunities inside.

This notion is summed up by the phrase 'what is tactically desirable must be technically possible,' a simple idea that is repeated throughout this text. An example of this truism was captured when Philip Scolari (previously the coach of World Soccer Champions Brazil) was fired as coach of Chelsea football club in England in 2009. At that time, an associate remarked, 'You can't play Brazilian football without Brazilian feet!' While this may be true, it is also possible that the players he was expected to coach did not possess Brazilian games sense!

This is an important issue because games sense underpins the ability of players to

1. read the display,
2. interpret that display,
3. make good decisions, and
4. execute those decisions.

Because this complex process is central to skilled play, it is dealt with in great detail in chapter 3. However, some indication of the complexity of the task of reading the play in games such as basketball is superbly captured by John Wideman when he writes, 'Never forget what's coming up behind you: when you are dribbling the ball, leading a fast break attack on the opponent's basket, when it's a matter of peripheral vision, of the Janus look backward and forward so you're aware of who's in front of you and behind, also mapping 360 degrees all the other players on the court, the kaleidoscoping shifts, the evolving opportunities that your rush to the hoop engenders' (2005).

Important though it is, games sense must not be overvalued. Playing ball games is not a mere intellectual exercise. Skilled performance

An example of reading the play. With head up and eyes attentive to the surrounding action, this field hockey player is ready and able to make a quick and responsible play.

in games almost always involves the melding of games sense and technical ability with other elements of effective play. These elements provide a platform on which players can build skilled performance. For while the relative importance of the elements of skilled play varies with each sport and may even vary with a player's role in a team game, as we suggested previously, fair play, resilience, mental toughness, and the ability to focus are constants in sports at all levels. They create the essential platform for skilled play.

Fair Play

Some readers may find it difficult to accept the notion that fair play is an element of effective play. Even more may find it strange to see it listed as a key element underpinning skilled play. However, at a time when cheating in all its forms is common and bending the rules is generally accepted, the Play Practice position is that playing fairly is fundamental to sport at any level and is vitally important in any program of sport education.

We believe that playing fairly has major advantages, even at the elite level. This is because the ability to concentrate without being distracted by any external factors is a major influence in success in sport. Athletes at the highest level must take this notion much further and focus so intensely that no conscious thought, including the chimera of winning or distractions by an opponent, interferes with the uninhibited flow of action. As a samurai mantra states, 'If you have one eye on winning, you only have one eye to watch your opponent.' We would add that it also leaves you with only one eye to watch the ball!

Fair play should be emphasised from the very beginning of the sport experience and at every opportunity from that point on. It begins with imbuing youngsters with respect for their opponents. Once this simple notion is accepted, it will make the experience much more enjoyable, satisfying, and successful.

Resilience and Mental Toughness

To be effective, players need to be mentally and morally resilient and ready to play at all times. Young players often have a tendency to worry about the mistake they may have just made instead of focusing on the challenge they face in the next instant. Elite players, on the other hand, have the ability to put thoughts of past

The ability to focus is critical in this game.

three

The Process of Playing Skilfully

Live everyday as though it be your last; learn everyday as though you will live forever.

Mahatma Gandhi

Chapter 2 indicates that effective performance is a complex phenomenon where the relative importance of each element of skill varies from one sport to the next, as well as from one level of performance to another. However, our analysis suggests that the process of being skilful, of drawing together all of those elements to instantly solve a problem posed by the game or by one's opponents, may be even more complex.

The major aim of this chapter is to clarify this process and to highlight the importance of resilience as young people attempt to deal with these challenges.

Consider the excerpt from *Once an Eagle* by Anton Myrer (see sidebar). This astonishingly perceptive description of a single incident in a fictional game of baseball captures four of the key elements of skilled play in games: agility, games sense, technical ability, and intuition. Indeed, Myrer describes this scenario so well, one can only wonder where he gained his insights.

The commonly accepted information processing model of skilled performance in games suggests that

1. the player reads the (dis)play,
2. interprets it,
3. decides what to do, and
4. acts.

The problem is that this ordered linear sequence represents the reality of the skill process only in target games such as golf. Here, players stroll up to the ball, calculate the distance to the hole, note any hazards, consider where they are on the leader board, and factor in as objectively as possible what they are technically capable of achieving in this situation. Should they lay up or can they clear the water or bunker to reach the green? They then decide where to try to hit the ball as they consider the wind, the placement of the hole and the speed of the green, select a club, and finally execute the stroke. Apart from any last-second changes in the wind or weather, they are dealing with a fixed environment. The major elements in play are sound decision making, the technical ability needed to execute the stroke, and the mental toughness to commit totally to that stroke. What is important here is that the players are effectively under no time pressure as they carry out this process.

Of course, similar situations do occur in many other games. For example, when serving in court-divided games or shooting a free throw in basketball, the player is under no real time pressures. Soccer players are in a similar situation as they take a penalty kick, a free kick, or a corner kick, since although the display may change slightly, they have the time to consider their options and focus on the perfect execution of technique. On occasions, they may see the ball curling around and over the defence and into the goal from more than 40 metres (130 feet) out.

To use a film analogy, in these situations, the players (like the golfer) only need a single frame—a snapshot—to gain all the information they need in order to decide what they are going to do. However, the process of skilled play in

Playing Skilfully

1915. A unit of the United States Army at Camp Early, somewhere on the Mexican border. A baseball game. Company A is playing Company B in a grudge match, with no love lost between the teams! With two out and the winning run on first, the action begins with our hero Sam Damon in the outfield, thinking the game through.

The first pitch was in the dirt, Thomas making another fine stop and keeping Hassolt from breaking for second. The Company B crowd were all roaring and yelping now, riding Jumbo (the pitcher) for all they were worth. 'Now he'll groove this one, to try to stay even,' Sam thought, 'He'll put it right down the pipe and Davis will know it is going to be a fastball, a Fiji islander would know it's going to be a fastball, and he'll belt it.'

He crept back one step and came to the set position as Jumbo reared back and threw. Davis' bat licked around like a yellow wagon tongue, blue darter. It was coming toward him on a line, over Slattery's outstretched glove—then all at once, it began to curve, bending down and away from him toward left centre, coming very fast, bounced once flatly and kept on. He just had room to cut it off. Just barely.

He was vaguely aware of everyone roaring, a shrill cry from Devlin at third, the vaguely streaking figures—and then racing to his right, bending in the most luminous and evanescent of flashes of thought: 'Merrick will hold Hassolt at third, they're afraid of my arm, he won't gamble on tying it up now; he'll hold Hassolt at third and Hansen will come up and knock them both in. And here I am, running through this particularly heavy patch of scraggly old buffalo grass. . .'

Without any conscious thought, he dipped down, trapped the ball deftly, then spun round in the wilted yellow grass as though bewildered, took a step back. There was an outcry and he could hear Merrick distinctly now, shouting, 'GO ON, GO ON!' He wheeled and threw with all his might. The ball went in low, just to the right of the mound, skipped once, and everything took on a perfect clarity: Thomas, his mask off, standing like a bulldog, waiting, Hassolt racing down the line from third, the ball taking a nice hop into the big black mitt and Hassolt falling into his slide early, much too early, and Thomas reaching down to him, the cloud of ochre dust that hid everything for a second, and then Sergeant Major Jolliffe's arm shooting into the air. Out. Out by a mile. The game was over.

Captain Parrish: 'Damon, was that intentional?'

Sam Damon: 'Yes sir.'

Parrish: 'I played a good deal in my palmy days. Sometimes a fielder is unaware that he's trapped a ball in his glove.'

Damon: 'No sir. I knew I had it.'

Parrish: 'I see. That's interesting. You thought it out then, as you were playing the ball.'

Damon: 'No sir, it was more like a picture: Sergeant Merrick would hold Hassolt at third and Hansen would hit safely again. And then the grass around my feet.'

Parrish: 'I see. Remarkable.'

Damon (to himself): 'Was it remarkable?' He didn't know. It had happened: It had worked. That was all he could for the life of him say (Myrer, 1968).

many games ranges across a spectrum in which players usually need more than a snapshot. For example, in Australian Rules football, there are indeed calm, almost golf-like moments when a player takes a mark within scoring distance of the goal. He then has up to 30 seconds to focus on kicking the ball unimpeded by any opponent. However, for most of the time, this game involves continuous passages of fierce competitive action that rages almost non-stop from one end of the ground to the other. The ball player is nearly always under pressure.

In this game and in many others, players are faced with a complex and continually changing environment as team-mates, opponents, and the ball all move, often in a completely unpredictable manner. This is described by John McPhee in the book *Coach* when he suggests, 'Every time a basketball player takes a step, an entire new geometry of action is created around him. In 10 seconds, with or without the ball, a good player may see perhaps 100 alternatives, and from them, make half a dozen choices as he goes along' (2005).

In these situations, all players must be like a quarterback, capable of reading the play and making sound decisions even when they don't have the ball. They are like mobile chess pieces, relying on their games sense to counter the moves of their opponents while manoeuvring to keep or to regain possession. However, as they receive the ball under various degrees of pressure from defenders, they must meld games sense with technical ability. Now they must read and interpret the play, control the ball, decide what to do, and then deliver the ball accurately, all within tight time constraints because the ball always attracts defensive pressure. The problem is especially acute in games where the ball player can be tackled and perhaps lose the ball to a determined defender.

This issue is brought into focus by the way soccer is played in the English Premier League. Here, for historical and cultural reasons, the game is played in a highly combative manner and at an almost frenetic pace compared to that of the top leagues in other countries. As a result, mistakes abound and possession can change up to 1,000 times in a game. Because of this, many commentators tend to bemoan the low level of technical ability of the players in this league. While there may be some truth in this, the fact is that this apparent lack of skill simply reflects the reality that the ball players are rarely allowed space and time by the opposition, who close them down, pressure them, and even attempt to intimidate them with a strong physical presence. The evidence to support this perhaps contentious view is the number of players from other countries who arrive in England with world-class reputations but who cannot cope with the pressure, especially the lack of time they are allowed on the ball.

The problem in this game and many others is that even while new data are pouring in, players at this level are trying to execute decisions they have already made. This could involve a rapid acceleration into position to gain possession of the ball, perhaps to control it or to instantly redirect it at the goal or towards a team-mate, all the while dealing with a powerful physical challenge from an opponent. This overlap of accurate data retrieval and acquisition, rapid interpretation and prediction, clear decision making, and precise physical execution, all carried out in milliseconds, often while fatigued or emotionally stretched, is what makes the great ball games so challenging and interesting.

The huge number of continually interacting variables that players must access and interpret in many games means that it is impossible for them to deal with these problems through the rational and sequential process outlined previously. In fact, the complexity of the task that players face is now being linked with the term *combinatorial explosion*. This term, originally from mathematics and computing, describes the complexity of any situation in which a large number of variables begin to interact in such a manner that predicting the outcome of that interaction becomes difficult, if not impossible.

To imagine the demands of ball games, consider the fact that a field hockey ball can travel at 146 kilometres per hour (kmph), or 90 miles per hour (mph). Table tennis balls, baseballs, and cricket balls reach 160 kmph (100 mph), a tennis serve can attain more than 230 kmph (145 mph), while in the fascinating game of badminton, a smashed shuttlecock can begin its flight at 320 kmph (200 mph)! With speeds like these, it is clear that the time available to make decisions is measured in micro-seconds. When the challenge is to deal with a 155-gram (5.5 ounces) leather ball travelling towards one's head at anywhere from 100 to 160 kmph, time becomes a very important variable.

So, while the notion that the player reads the (dis)play, interprets it, decides what to do, and then acts may represent an acceptable theoretical model that is applicable to target sports, its simplistic nature has major limitations in helping us to understanding the nature of skilled performance in many other sports for the following reasons:

- It implies that the display is static. In reality, the sequence of action and complexity in many games is continually changing.
- It appears to be based on the assumption that players possess all of the other

elements of skilled play, especially technical ability, necessary to execute the decisions they have made.

- Above all, it does not indicate the time it takes a player to complete the sequence, which is often the critical factor in skilled performance.

Contemporary theory in motor learning has recognised the limitations of the linear model and now draws on nonlinear dynamical systems to represent learning in complex settings. Central to this theory is the interaction of variables associated with the performers, the environment, and the task that enables movement patterns to emerge through a dynamic, adaptive process of self-organisation (Chow et al., 2007; Davids, Button, & Bennett, 2007).

All of this has immense implications that will become clearer if we consider the differences between beginners and elite players as they attempt to solve the problems posed by their opponents.

Differences Between Beginners and Expert Players

Time is critical for beginners because they must work through each phase of the skill process cognitively, sequentially, and emotionally. As we have already suggested, this is not a problem in sports where the first three phases of the process can be completed at leisure, leaving the player to focus on the perfect execution of a technique. Gymnastics, diving, the field events of athletics, tenpin bowling, lawn bowls, archery, and golf are all examples of this.

However, when beginners play interactive games where they must continually compete with opponents for the ball, time becomes important. This is especially so in games where opponents can pressure them and even take the ball away. Players face the following challenges:

- They are faced with an unfamiliar, complex, and rapidly changing environment.
- They must interpret a mass of information with little or no idea of what is important in the picture they are seeing.

- They must decide what to do without a clear understanding of the rules or even of basic tactical principles.
- They have to move into position before they really know where or when to move, or even where they are in the first place!
- Often they are required to execute a technique they have not yet mastered.

If youngsters are introduced to the full version of such games, the result can only be chaos. In soccer, beginners simply do not have the time to be skilful! So, they bypass the first three phases. When they get the opportunity, they kick the ball in whatever direction they happen to be facing. Don't read the play, interpret the play, or make a decision, just bash the ball forward! Indeed, it is probable that soccer is the most popular game in the world because it can be played badly but enjoyably in this manner. What is interesting is that there are occasions when even highly skilled professionals do exactly the same thing! As the previous chapter shows, defenders faced with a ball bouncing around in their own penalty area who are surrounded by opponents will not waste a split second. They will simply belt it as fast and as far as they can. If in doubt, give it a clout!

However, many other games are not enjoyable when played badly. Unless youngsters grow up completely immersed in a sport (for example, basketball in many parts of the United States), most games must be greatly simplified for young players.

Ironically, it may be easier for readers to understand the problems that beginners face by examining the way experts resolve those same problems.

The fundamental difference is that while beginners must work through the process sequentially, great players can compress the skill process and thus minimise the time they take to complete it! It is only recently that some of the strategies they employ to do this have become clearer (Abernethy, Farrow, & Berry, 2003; Baker, Côté, & Abernethy, 2003; Phillips, Klein, & Sieck, 2004; Ross, Shaffer, & Klein, 2006).

The most obvious way that good players can compress the skill process (in milliseconds) is by rapidly executing the decisions they have made. Here, all of their behaviour, including the selection and performance of complex techniques, has been over-learned, so this is virtually an automatic and instantaneous response. Compare this with the problem facing beginners who may not know which technique to select in a given situation and who, even after they have decided, must consciously think about how to execute it.

Reading the Play and Executing the Desired Action

The non-conscious behaviour of experts as they move into position or execute a technique brings another major advantage; it enables them to multi-task! For example, elite soccer players can track and control the ball even while they are scanning the display. After an initial sighting of the ball, they can predict its flight and begin to move into position to receive it, even while transferring their attention to the overall display. Superstars can control the ball and play it without watching it. This ability to read the display while they are about to control the ball means that they can decide what they are going to do even before the ball arrives! This overlapping of all four phases compresses the time between reading the play and executing the desired action.

An example of this seemingly amazing talent is provided by Alan Smith, who said while writing about the great England and Chelsea midfielder Frank Lampard in the *London Telegraph* on January 31, 2009, 'No one is more skilled in the art of the quick fire pass under pressure, having expertly worked out distances and angles before the ball arrives at his feet. These calculations often result in a first time pass over the top to Drogba galloping away. If that is not on, he will choose something a little more conservative, if equally impressive in terms of peripheral vision and ability to spot the right pass in the blink of an eye.'

However, as they scan the display, elite players have another immense advantage. They intuitively know their own position on the field or the court to within centimetres, and also know where their team-mates should be! The virtually telepathic understanding that comes from hours of practising together means that they can deliver passes to team-mates they may not even see at the time they strike the ball. This was superbly captured by Sir Trevor Brooking, development director for the English Football Association, speaking about the Spanish player Ces Fabregas, 'He already has a picture in his mind of where all his team-mates are. His SATNAV is superior, so he rarely wastes the ball.'

Elite players not only know where their team-mates are, but they can also predict where their opponents are likely to be. Like chess masters, these great players seem to be able to draw on their past experiences and their intuitive understanding of the game to perceive and interpret the display from a single snapshot. They can then predict what is likely to happen next without being consciously aware of any of the cues that should be necessary to receive this information.

Eliminating the Time Lag

The ultimate compression of the skill process occurs when the time lag between the first and last phases is reduced or even eliminated, so that observation and action overlap. While this never becomes a reflex, it can be *intuitive*, as in the ability to instantly access the distilled essence of past experience to solve immediate problems. Here, the German concept of *fingerspitzengefuhl* (literally, fingertip feel), the players' deep intuitive sense of what is happening, where it is happening, and when it is happening, becomes important. For now, they can actually bypass two phases of the skill process—that is, interpreting the display and deciding what to do.

They can then use the time they have saved, no matter how small, in two different ways. They can ensure perfect execution of the obviously skilful thing to do or they may choose to deceive their opponents by doing something unexpected, leaving them bemused and baffled. Often, great players are unable to explain what they did or how they did it, even when their response is perfect!

Relying on Intuition

It is clear that expert players in any ball game can use their intuition, that distilled essence of past experience, to predict what is likely to happen. In striking and fielding games, expert batters can read the display before they prepare to strike the ball, or as they prepare to field it. In cricket, great batters appear to have the ability to process information that will tell them the line and length of the ball even before the bowler

This elite player reacts instantaneously, drawing on intuition.

lets it go. Yet it seems that they do not know what this information is or how they received it!

However, in racquet sports, players must be able to track and strike a rapidly moving target while simultaneously reading their opponent's movements, since this may determine how and where they will play the next stroke. Like batters and fielders in cricket, it seems that they can pick up cues that tell them where the ball is going even before their opponent hits it.

As Janet Starkes noted in *Bounce,*

> The exploitation of advance information results in the time paradox where skilled performers seem to have all the time in the world. Recognition of familiar scenarios and the chunking of perceptual information into meaningful wholes and patterns speeds up the process. As a result, Federer is able to see patterns in his opponent's movements in the same way that chess players are able to discern patterns in the arrangement of pieces on a chess board (Syed, 2010).

In fact, some have suggested that great tennis players use probability theory, based on prior knowledge of their opponent, to help them judge the likely speed and direction of the ball before it is played. It seems that spending time analysing opponents before a match gives players an advantage in predicting where, when, and how the ball will go when they meet these opponents in a game. In a sense, they use this pre-match analysis to refresh and focus their intuition. It also seems that in these games, great players can use their intuition to create tactical situations that allow them to be ahead of the game in the same way that a chess player sets up a checkmate many moves in advance.

Analysing Opponents

Other examples of skill compression come from the martial arts, where only an instant reaction will suffice. Here, the skill process is compressed to the point where the response appears to be instinctive. Expert performers perceive almost imperceptible clues in their opponent's movements that alert them to what is going to happen. These might range from slight changes in body position to minute movements of the shoulders, virtually unnoticeable except to the highly trained athlete, that occur before a punch starts. So while novices can only watch an opponent's hands, and so will usually respond too late, experts have picked up all the information they need not only to block the punch but also to take advantage of any errors their opponent may make as they deliver it.

Of course, experienced performers have other advantages over beginners. They are agile enough to get into good positions when they want to get there and have the endurance to keep on getting into good positions. They possess the physical courage needed to deal with the challenges they may face and can focus tightly on the task at hand. They understand their own limitations and can assess the strengths and weaknesses of opponents. They also have the psychological resilience to deal with setbacks. While beginners often waste time worrying about the mistake they have just made and so make even more errors, the experienced player simply prepares to face the next challenge. Beginners are always a work in progress; for them, the skill process is an experiment every time they attempt it. They have little idea what will work for them until they have tried it out, and even then, they may not be sure what actually produced the successful outcome!

Here, it is critical to understand that while a star player may need to glimpse only one frame of the action to predict what is going to happen and decide what to do, and experienced players need to see only a brief sequence to execute the process, beginners must wait to see the whole scene unfold before they can work out what is actually happening. It is virtually impossible for them to predict what is going to happen, and they often have little idea of what should happen.

The critical point is that it is possible to help players (in this case, soccer players) develop what may appear to be extremely complex elements of skilled play. In the *Saturday Telegraph* of November 22, 2009, Sir Trevor Brooking told how he 'had a picture in his mind' so that when the ball came in to him, he knew he had someone tight marking him or somewhere close: 'I didn't have to stop the ball, look up and think where do I go.'

How did he learn to do this? He describes how as a young player during training games, his coach Ron Greenwood would suddenly click his fingers and ask him to shut his eyes and describe where everyone else was on the pitch: Where had the opposition left space? Where were his best-placed team-mates? So whenever Brooking received the ball, he could make the right decisions.

While great soccer players like Frank Lampard can scan the play as they control and direct the ball, beginners must focus entirely on controlling and directing the ball. Only after they have done that can they take time to read the play and decide what to do. By that time, the situation will almost certainly have changed. This means that they may have to carry out the first two phases twice: the first time in order to decide where to move to gain possession of the ball and the second time to decide what to do with it!

Not only that, but differences exist between experts and beginners at an even more fundamental level. Professional soccer players can scan virtually the whole pitch and can also sense what is happening behind them. They even know where each of their team-mates is positioned and can predict where their opponents are likely to be. When they are on the ball, they can pass it through almost 180 degrees from a standing position using any part of their foot. They may also be able to drive it up to 50 metres (165 feet) from a single step and can even back heel the ball to a team-mate they know is behind them!

In contrast, beginners may only see what is happening directly in front of them. They may only be capable of playing the ball in the direction they are facing, often to a maximum of 20 metres (66 feet). This may be because they do not have the strength required in either the abductor or the adductor muscles to strike the ball sideways effectively with the inside or the outside of the foot. Even when striking the ball forwards, a lack of physical power often prevents them from directing the ball where they want it to go. This means that their passing options are always limited, while their intention to pass the ball in a given direction is automatically telegraphed to their opponents! What is tactically desirable must not only be technically possible, but also physically possible!

Complexity of the Total Skill Process

The complexity of the total skill process in games is well illustrated by the following basketball scenario (see sidebar), which in reality would only last for milliseconds.

If they choose to go to the basket, they face more decisions. As defenders move to help out against the drive, the ball player must decide whether to take the shot, dish off to open team-mates close to the basket, or pitch the ball out for a team-mate to take the three-pointer.

All of these decisions must be taken within an overall framework provided by the following:

- A game plan that reflects the coach's philosophy
- The tactical situation at that moment
- The score
- The time remaining in the game

Players' decisions may also be influenced by their shooting percentage from that spot and the way they match up with their direct opponent.

Do they have an advantage in quickness? Can they beat them on the first step? Do they believe they can? Is there a great shot blocker waiting in the lane? How many fouls do they (or their immediate opponent) have? Are they fatigued? Are there psychological considerations? All of this data will be instantly and non-consciously factored into the decision-making process. Players who are confident and on top of their game may choose one option, while ones down on confidence may choose a different one. Even the relationship between the player and coach may influence the decision taken! This complex process, in which games sense and technical ability are integrated with other elements of effective play, is repeated every time a player receives the ball during a game of basketball, and it is replicated in every similar game.

Ironically, the complexity of skilled play in games is perhaps best illustrated by the embarrassing mistakes that even professional players make. Captured in commercially produced DVDs, these humiliating errors should be compulsory viewing for all who teach children, and especially for those who think that attaining perfection in games is easy.

Complexity of Skill

On receiving the ball, players must decide what to do:

- Immediately shoot the three-pointer? Can they hit from there?
- Pass to any of the four possible receivers who may be in a better position than they are? Is anyone completely open? Is the alley-oop on? Do they need to get the ball in the hands of a team-mate who is being defended by a star opponent in foul trouble?
- Drive past the defender? Do they have the quickness to beat their opponent?
- Go down the middle towards defensive help, but get a key opponent to foul them?
- Drive the baseline away from defensive help for an open shot?
- Fake the drive and force the defender back to open up the jump shot?

Summary

The major objectives of this chapter were to outline the process of being skilful and to clarify the differences between the performance of experts and that of beginners. Only if teachers and coaches have a clear understanding of this process will they be able to appreciate the vast gap between the cognitive play of beginners and the non-conscious play of elite players. Equally important, they will be better prepared to help learners develop the psychological resilience necessary if they are to cope with the mistakes and failure that are inevitable when they are trying to master new challenges. It is now generally accepted that it takes years of committed practice to become an expert at anything, from playing the violin to hitting a golf ball. Most great games players begin honing their skill in pick-up games and through informal technical practice from a very early age, long before they are exposed to formal coaching programs (Berry, Abernethy, & Côté, 2008).

It is important to remember that when we watch great performers in sport, we are seeing merely the tip of the iceberg. We forget the thousands of hours of practice and the endless mistakes that have been an inevitable part of their journey towards excellence. As a result, it is easy to ascribe their seemingly effortless performance to a magical natural talent when, in fact, it is the result of dedicated effort over many years. Even then, they still make mistakes! This reality is captured in a Nike commercial, where Michael Jordan proclaims, 'I've missed more than 9,000 shots. I've lost almost 300 games. Twenty-six times I've been trusted to take the game-winning shot and missed!'

However, while elite sportsmen and -women have learned that mistakes and defeat are merely the price to be paid for participating in the glorious adventure that is sport, children do not like to fail, especially in front of their peers, whether it is in a physical education lesson, a club practice, or a competitive game. But some degree of failure is virtually inevitable for beginners. They must progress through the skill process sequentially and cognitively. Therefore, they often do not have enough time to complete the entire process before the situation has changed and the original information has become redundant.

Resolving these two factors—on the one hand, the complex nature of skilled performance, and on the other hand, the need to ensure that youngsters have positive early experiences—can be a severe test, even for coaches working with small groups of motivated youngsters. In physical education, where large classes are common and time, facilities, and equipment are often limited, the task becomes much more complex. If the class includes a sprinkling of reluctant or even resistant learners, it can become a daunting challenge.

Although we should aim to structure learning situations so that children will experience success, especially in the early stages, we cannot guarantee it. It is impossible to ensure success for everyone in a competition where all involved are striving to win. Youngsters must inevitably face the twin demons of failure and losing. This issue is of critical importance if we are to encourage children to develop and maintain an interest in sport and physical activity. We must help them to understand that mistakes, failure, and even losing in sport are not only normal but also often the foundation for future improvement. This is, in itself, very much a process. It will take time for children to accept the notion, especially those who suffer from low self-esteem or come from families or communities in which losing at sport is seen as worse than dying!

While it will not always be easy to convince children of this, teachers and coaches should continually return to the notion that losing can often provide a better foundation for later success than winning does. To help students accept this, we must first try to recognise their every success, even the smallest of achievements. In this way, we can help them understand that failure is often transitory and can be the springboard to success. This is not wishful thinking! The teacher can make recognising improvement and achievement part of the culture of the group by using comments and feedback effectively. Simply encouraging children to high five every positive event, especially examples of fair play, is a good starting point.

This is important because in the increasingly benign societies of the developed world, sport provides an opportunity for human beings to be pushed to extremes and so experience those elemental feelings of exhilaration that make us searingly aware of our own existence. If all sport educators were to promote the idea that mistakes, failure, and defeat are a small price to pay for such experiences, and that simply participating makes children winners, they could help young people develop the emotional resilience necessary to persist in the great adventure that is sport.

four

Strategies for Teaching Play Practice

. . . to find a method of instruction by which teachers may teach less but learners may learn more. . .

Comenius, Didacta Magna

One of the advantages of Play Practice is that it is easy to understand and relatively easy to employ. It involves the following processes:

1. Identify which elements of skilled play are important in a sport.

2. Determine which should be emphasised with a specific group of players, especially if they are beginners.

3. Simplify the activity to engage learners and ensure that they have early success.

4. Shape the practice by manipulating key variables to create a specific learning environment. This can be seen as teaching through the game.

5. Focus to re-emphasise key concepts, teaching cues, or behaviour relating to fair play and resilience. This involves teaching in the game.

6. Enhance practices by employing a wide range of motivational tools to engage the learner, maintain learner commitment, and maximise both enjoyment and improvement.

7. Provide a program of sport experiences so that every child has the opportunity to participate in the important roles of player, official, and administrator. Remember that practising is only a means to an end: that is, actually participating in sport activities confidently, competently, and joyfully.

In many ways, the first two processes are the most demanding. As chapter 1 shows, much of the teaching and coaching of games is based on a limited understanding of the complex nature of skill. And while chapters 2 and 3 help clarify this critical issue, teachers and coaches must still be able to assess the experience and ability of specific players, classes, or their teams. This takes knowledge, even wisdom, that can only come from experience. Once teachers and coaches have determined which elements of skilled play to emphasise, they must employ the following strategies.

Simplifying Activities

The first task is to capture youngsters' attention and then hold it long enough to help them build the self-confidence and resilience they need to cope with the challenges that even a well-structured sport experience presents. To do this, learning environments must be created to enable children to experience success or at least feel that they are experiencing success. The process begins with the teacher introducing the activity safely and in a way that emphasises the sheer joy of playing or of meeting a challenge. This approach is inclusive, maximises participation, minimises management issues, builds a positive psychological climate, and even makes the teacher smile more often.

Students learn best in a safe, challenging, and success-orientated environment.

To achieve this, do the following:

- Eliminate the need for physical courage and toughness by modifying the rules so as to minimise physical contact and reduce both fear and the risk of injury. Examples of games that do this are touch, flag football, non-contact lacrosse, and modified Australian Rules football.

- Minimise the agility demands. Poor agility is often the limiting factor in the performance of beginners.
  - Target tennis allows players to concentrate on successfully developing technique without continually moving into new positions to hit the ball.
  - Mini volleyball played in a smaller space enables players to get to the ball more easily.
  - Mini games of soccer, lacrosse, and field hockey are played on small pitches.

- Minimise the importance of endurance by controlling the dimensions of the playing area and the time allocated for a practice.

- Minimise the technical demands of a game to allow beginners to start playing as soon as possible. This can be done in the following ways:
  - Modify the rules. So, soccer is introduced on a field without sidelines or goal lines. This gives the players more space, and thus more time, to be skilful, allows play to continue almost without interruption, and eliminates the need for corner kicks and throw-ins, along with the rules involved.
  - Alter the equipment. Examples include replacing the stick with a grip-ball pad in lacrosse or using shorter racquets with larger hitting surfaces in some racquet sports.
  - Employ user-friendly balls. Use a black max ball for flag football, a soft touch ball in volleyball, slow-bounce tennis balls, or a volleyball or lighter soft-surface ball in the early stages of introducing soccer.
  - Introduce the notion of working technical models.

- Minimise the perceptual and timing demands. Tracking a ball or shuttle can present an enormous challenge for beginners, so it may be necessary to control the speed and direction of the target. Extreme examples are using a shuttle suspended on a string in badminton and hitting tees and very controlled feeds in baseball and cricket. While target games effectively make the delivery of the object more predictable, it may still be necessary to slow everything down, as in the use of low-compression slow-bounce balls in tennis or balloons in the initial stages of introducing badminton. Emphasis on early preparation for the technique can also reduce the timing demands, such as lifting the bat in cricket, keeping the racquet up in badminton, or taking the racquet back early in tennis.

- Minimise the tactical demands.
  - Play with small teams or in relatively large spaces. This makes decision making easier and gives players more time to be skilful.
  - Only emphasise the primary rules.
  - Use large goals to make scoring easy.

- Eliminate the tactical demands to create games that allow players to focus totally on developing a sound technique. Examples include target table tennis and sector games for cricket.

- Minimise both the technical and tactical demands of a game.

  ○ Give attackers a numerical advantage in 3v1 or 5v2 games in soccer, which are infinitely easier for youngsters to cope with.

  ○ Modify the rules in touch so that a dropped ball only costs novices two attempts instead of loss of possession.

- Allow both tactical understanding and technical ability to evolve concurrently by building games up from 1v1. This is the approach suggested for introducing the codes for rugby and touch and flag football.

Shaping Practices

Every major game is shaped by rules that define the size and shape of the playing area, how goals or points are scored, and the number of players. At the end of the 19th century, James Naismith manipulated just these variables to create basketball to meet a specific need for a game that could be played indoors during cold winters in Springfield, Massachusetts. William Morgan, also looking for an indoor game that minimised the importance of physical power, did the same thing when he invented minonette, the precursor of volleyball. Morgan's idea of separating the opposing teams by a net eliminated the physical contests that had led to deaths on the football field, while his use of a balloon instead of a ball made this game easy for ordinary students to play. Both are examples of games shaped to achieve specific objectives by manipulating critical variables.

Shaping play practices follows a similar pattern, except that it is possible to manipulate an even larger number of variables to develop an almost infinite range of learning situations that are suitable for every performance level. With beginners, the shaping process is used to simplify games and challenges, while at the elite level, it can replicate real game pressures in practice situations. The ideal is to employ play practices that retain the essential feel of a sport but are shaped to improve specific elements of skilled play with a specific group of players.

Here it is important to remember that in many games, the critical variable in skilled performance is time. While elite performers can short circuit the skill process and so minimise the time required to complete it, novices must work through the process cognitively and sequentially. Therefore, they do not always have time to complete the process before the situation has changed. So, teachers must continually monitor the variables that affect the time players have to be skilful as they play and practise. Consider the following equation:

Space = Time = Skilled play of value (good decisions and sound execution)

Interactive Team Games

While every effort must be made to create successful situations for beginners, once youngsters are committed, it is important to change the emphasis and to challenge them. At the elite level, practices should be structured to stretch players up to and beyond the edge of failure. This is the only way they will continue to improve. In interactive team games, this can be done by manipulating any or all of the following variables.

Number of Players

The fewer players involved in any game, the more opportunities there are for each to be involved. Games with a 3v3 setup ensure a good balance between improving technical ability and developing games sense in basketball, korfball, and netball, while 5v5 is an almost perfect learning laboratory for soccer, hockey, and lacrosse. While youngsters can cope with 2v2 in basketball and netball, it is still advisable to use 3v3. This format encourages decision making and helps players learn how to spread the defence by using width and depth.

In the rugby codes and American football, the game must initially be stripped back to 1v1 with beginners. This minimises both the technical and the tactical demands and allows students to play almost from the beginning. However, when introducing American football in a country where it is not part of the culture, it may be necessary to begin with some throwing and catching challenges.

Attacker-to-Defender Ratio

In a real game, the attackers may hold the numerical advantage, if only for an instant. The classic fast break in basketball pits 3 attackers against a single defender. With good passing, it usually results in an easy score. However, normal games are often chaotic because young players are pressured by defenders. So, they never have the space and time they need to execute the skill process.

To encourage beginners to pass the ball and help them to develop technical ability and games sense, attackers must always be given a numerical advantage. In basketball, where the ball is easily controlled, a single-player advantage is enough. However, in games such as soccer, hockey, and lacrosse, where controlling the ball is more difficult and where ball players must continually switch their focus from ball to opponent, it may be necessary to begin with 4 attackers against a single defender or possibly 5 against 2. But even here, it is important to understand that a second defender can present major problems for beginners in these games.

This is because beginners can watch both a single defender—or at least their feet—and the ball. However, a second defender completely changes the equation! Now ball players have to continually check where the second defender is before deciding where to pass the ball, all the while dealing with more pressure from the first defender who now knows that he has cover from behind! This is not a problem in basketball or netball, where the ball is more easily controlled and players can continue to read the play even as they prepare to pass to a team-mate, but it is a serious problem in games where the ball is more difficult to control.

Note that at the elite level, defenders may be given the advantage. For example, if a basketball team knows that their next opponents will probably employ aggressive full-court or half-court pressure defences, they can practise with 5 attackers facing 7 defenders. In this way, both the ball handler and the next logical receiver will be double teamed, with no one else completely open! Practice under those conditions should begin to prepare a team for any kind of pressure. It is interesting to note that in March 2000, as Michigan State prepared for their NCAA Final game with Florida State, a team whose strategy was based on intense pressure defences, they used exactly this approach. Another example of this was the strategy used by Coach Hayley, the volleyball coach at USC, as he prepared for a top-of-the-table battle with Washington State in September 2010. Recognising that the latter were a great blocking team, he used 4 front-line blockers in his practices instead of the usual 3.

Shaping play practices helps players to contend with the pressures of the game.

Primary and Secondary Rules

The fundamental structure of every game is determined by its primary rules, rules that cannot be altered without creating a different game. With beginners, start with as few rules as possible to allow play to flow, and introduce new rules only as they are needed. Modify any rule if it will make a play practice simpler and more enjoyable for novice players, but introduce the real rule as soon as it is feasible to do so.

Game Conditions

Play can be shaped in many ways, but especially by applying conditions that take on the power of rules for the duration of a specific practice. Very often, an apparently simple condition will have an immediate influence when first applied but will continue to shape the development of both tactical and technical ability over time. An example of this is the one-touch rule in soccer.

At the elite level in basketball, a game could be conditioned so that ball handlers can only go one on one to score, with no screens or give-and-go moves allowed. There will be a rapid improvement in their ability to operate from the triple threat position, combining outside shooting with fake and drive moves for the layup or the pull-up jumper. This condition can set the scene for a whole range of technical and tactical development when used by a knowledgeable coach. A precise sequence could focus on improving one-on-one defensive skill, then defensive help, in-and-out cuts to get open, offensive spread and balance, penetration and pitch-out moves, defensive recovery by the helping defender, drive-and-dish moves, and so on, until a whole range of skilled play in basketball has been explored and developed.

Goals

Since the goal defines the objective of the game, it can be used as a powerful tool in shaping the nature of a play practice. With this in mind, the goal can be whatever the teacher decides it is. The only rule is that with beginners, scoring should always be easy!

An easy goal encourages shooting, while a difficult goal tends to encourage more passing, so a game of basketball in which the goal is the backboard would immediately lead to far more shots. It would also quickly force defenders to put pressure on the ball and to stay much closer to opponents at all times. There would be no zone defences!

In the rugby codes, the goal is the whole width of the pitch, but it is possible to use such a goal in practices for many other games. When developing one-on-one dribbling skills in soccer, hockey, or basketball, the goal of the dribbler can be to get the ball over the goal line at any point. This forces defenders to be honest and to try hard to prevent the dribbler from going past them.

Very large goals in soccer encourage players to lift their vision and shoot from long distances, while very small goals encourage them to inter-pass or dribble for a good close shot. Four-goal soccer encourages attackers to switch play from one side of the field to the other to counter defenders, who use the principle of concentration to stop them. In lacrosse, attackers must learn how to play behind the goal, so turning the goal around encourages players to use this space.

Differential Scoring

Differential scoring systems can be a valuable tool in shaping play. In basketball, the 3-point shot was introduced to help resolve some of the problems the professional game faced when defenders jammed the scoring lanes.

With beginners, the problem is worse because of poor shooting ability. Allocating 10 points for an outside 5-metre (15 foot) shot that hits the rim and 20 points for a basket forces defenders to play honestly. This in turn opens up other attacking options, such as a layup for 5 points! One idea that has yet to be developed is the notion of allowing players to add points or goals to their score in a practice for specific aspects of skilled play—for example, exhibiting sporting behaviour or executing a specific tactic.

Playing Area Dimensions

The basic rule is that while beginners need plenty of space to play effectively, good players must learn to play in limited space. The first soccer game for beginners should have no boundaries, so space is almost unlimited. On the other hand, a game of 5-a-side soccer played on a 20-by-30-metre (70 by 90 feet) pitch encourages players to value space, apply the principles of play in attack and defence, support the ball player intelligently, and pass accurately. Five-a-side long soccer, played on a pitch 80 metres long by 30 metres wide (260 by 90 feet) and with 20-metre (70 feet) goals, develops long passing and long shots for goals, provides many opportunities for players to control high balls, and forces players to lift their vision.

Equipment

Balls used in invasion games should be appropriate to the age and experience of players. Even the simple modification of using a volleyball in the early stages of teaching soccer immediately encourages a more open game instead of the moving scrimmage that develops when a regulation ball is used. When teaching American football, the black max mini ball allows youngsters to throw farther with greater accuracy, thus opening up greater tactical possibilities.

Reining in Star Players

To ensure that every child has an opportunity for meaningful participation, it may be necessary to limit players from becoming stars. This can be done by restricting the dribble in basketball, allowing only two touches in soccer or hockey, or stating rules that players can never move in front of the ball in attack or should not shoot at the goal. This strategy promotes inclusive practice. Handled properly, it encourages leadership, brings less-able players into the game more, and actually helps the stars improve their own play. It can be extended to team conditions in a similar way.

Time

Limiting the time of games minimises the endurance demands, keeps the score closer, and maintains player commitment. The following sections deal with this concept in more detail.

Racquet Sports

With beginners, technical ability is the critical element of skilled play in racquet sports. To help players improve their technique, games are shaped to maximise their opportunities to hit the ball while minimising the importance of agility, endurance, and tactics. This is helpful because the techniques of these games do require practice, practice that is likely to be riddled with errors early on. In target tennis, points can never be lost; they can only be won. This helps youngsters build their confidence. It also immediately shapes and focuses consistent stroke play, thus helping improve technique. In

his excellent book *Bounce* (2010), Matthew Syed, an Olympian and four-time Commonwealth table tennis champion, describes how Marty Reissen, a great American player, took this notion to the extreme by using a single cigarette standing on end as his target.

As players improve, games can be shaped to demand increasing levels of tactical and technical ability, while simultaneously putting pressure on their agility and endurance. For example, in tennis, if points can only be won by shots played into the service area, players will be encouraged to exploit sharp angles, a strategy employed with great success by Andre Agassi. This variation forces players into rapid changes of direction, fast movement into position, and decisions about where to play the ball. It also encourages great racquet control.

The shaping process can improve both games sense and technical ability up to the highest level by specifying which strokes can be employed and how points can be won. For example, using an elevated net, even a rope, immediately slows the game down. In the case of table tennis, it encourages players to use high looping shots. Another approach with young players is to use low-compression slow-bounce tennis balls. However, teachers and coaches can improve any element of skilled play, including endurance, by manipulating these simple variables. They can also differentiate the learning challenge to include diversity within a class by simply adjusting the dimensions of playing space, the size of the target, the equipment, and the conditions of play for each participant. For example, in target table tennis, each player can select the size of the block target, while in a short–long badminton target game, players can personalise the size of their back target area based on their technical ability.

Syed (2010) provides an example of an innovative approach to shaping when he describes how his coach, Chen Xinhua, made him defend a table that was 50 percent larger than the regulation area. Inevitably, this forced him to improve his positional skills, footwork, and speed, which he could then transfer back into his competitive play on the real table!

Another stunning example of shaping that Syed mentions occurred purely through serendipity. He describes how when Desmond Douglas, arguably Britain's best ever table tennis player, first appeared, he brought an almost amazing approach to the game. He stayed right up by the table and relied almost entirely on the speed of his reaction and his apparent ability to determine where his opponent would play the ball before he hit it! It gradually emerged that he had developed his method, over thousands of hours, in a tiny shed. There, he was forced to stand with his back against the wall, right up against the table—there was no space to retreat. The size of the shed that was the home of his school's table tennis club shaped his method.

Striking and Fielding Games

Technical ability is of great importance in these games. A combination of sector and target games can develop the critical elements of technique involved in striking, fielding, and delivering the ball. In cricket, it is especially important to eliminate the need for the rapid decision making when batting. Sector games allow youngsters to concentrate totally on the execution of a specific technique. However, as indicated in the cricket section of this book, these games must usually be preceded by practising the specific movement patterns required to produce most of the batting strokes and the bowling action, since these movements are not natural.

In sector games, it is possible to allocate a negative score when a hit is caught. If the penalty is large, it will certainly encourage players to keep the ball on the ground! However, in baseball and softball, where a sacrifice fly is a tactical ploy, it may be necessary to work out a scoring system that rewards a long hit even when it is caught.

Target Sports

In most of these sports, shaping is achieved by altering the nature and size of the target or its distance from the aiming point. Markers can create corridors and zones that provide immediate knowledge of results and allow for differential scoring. Tenpin bowling, of course, is an exception to this general rule. Fortunately, it is possible to use raised side barriers to prevent gutter balls, so learners can at least convince themselves that they are bowling quite well! In archery, teachers and coaches can use a range of targets to help players improve technique. In

games like bowls or bocce, situational scenarios can be shaped to encourage technique, tactics, and games sense.

Play practices can shape performance in a range of sports. In swimming, a horizontal body position is essential. However, beginners who have yet to learn how to deal with water around their noses find this position impossible. Simple races where swimmers blow a table tennis ball across the surface of the water are a playful introduction to this important ability. In skiing or surfing, the selection of the practice environment can have a powerful effect on the speed of learning, while with an activity like dancing, in all its varied forms, careful selection of the music has a major influence on the ease with which beginners learn.

Focusing Practices

Focusing practices maximises understanding and improvement. Teachers cannot simply set up a play practice, even one that has been carefully shaped, and let it run without any intervention. They must be prepared to teach in the game by using the process of focusing to help players understand key concepts, to restate technical cues, or even to maintain complete commitment.

The freeze replay is critical here. Choosing the moment carefully, teachers use a specific signal to freeze play so that everyone must immediately stop moving. They then use the same technique to wind the action back to a specific point, and then use guided discovery to replay the scenario and draw out key points. However, students dislike having a game continually disrupted, so interventions must be carefully chosen.

Carefully handled, this strategy allows instructors to capture great teaching moments and use them to help players better understand the game. It is also a very effective way of controlling the chaotic scramble at the beginning of many games and of reducing the high error rate that is inevitable when beginners play. Sometimes a particular condition may lead to results teachers did not anticipate. They must therefore be prepared to take advantage of any situation and focus it in a positive direction. They can also use this process to point out the similarities and differences between a specific play practice and the real game.

However, it is also worthwhile to allow teams to call a limited number of short tactical time-outs (30 seconds) to discuss what they are doing, raise questions about the rules, or make necessary adjustments to their play. Used as a focusing strategy, the tactical time-out can help youngsters better understand the nature of the game and the specifics of skilled play.

Coaches can use the process of focusing to ensure continual progression throughout a practice session. At an advanced level, they can focus play in the simple game of two-touch soccer to help players develop very sophisticated skills. They might begin by stressing the importance of supporting ball players to give them many easy passing options. Next, they could show how intelligent calls of 'Player on,' 'Hold,' and 'Turn' can help alert ball players to how much space and time they have, thus enabling them to be more skilful in their distribution. Finally, they might begin to encourage players to read the play even as they prepare to control the ball, as well as to call out the name of the team-mate they intend to pass the ball to before they receive it!

A half-court basketball play practice in which players are only allowed to score from outside the 3-point line could shape play in several directions. First, it will lead to many off-balance shots as players try to walk the walk. This in itself could be a valuable learning experience! More important, it is likely to lead to many rebounds, which will give the perceptive teacher or coach the opportunity to focus on positioning and blocking out. Without intelligent intervention of this kind, many valuable learning opportunities will be lost.

Teachers and coaches can then focus this practice on the importance of teamwork to help players get open shots. They can emphasise tactics such as a reverse pass, the dribble draw, the pick and roll, and penetrate and pitch out. Finally, they can direct the focus to the defenders as they try to find a balance between putting pressure on the ball and helping out. Again, time is a useful aid for focusing play. Teachers may require players to focus on specific tactics or techniques for 2 minutes, then change the focus for the next 2 minutes.

Teachers and coaches can focus play practices to help players improve technique and commitment.

Enhancing Play Experiences

The notion of enhancing play to maximise enjoyment and improvement is vital because of the Play Practice mantra that 'learners improve most rapidly when they are absolutely committed to mastering the task.' This means that teachers and coaches can employ a variety of motivational strategies to induce learner interest and maintain an engaged learning state. Clearly, the personality and skill of the teacher are important factors here. Those who are liked, admired, or simply respected by their students will always draw greater commitment and improved performances. If, like great coaches, they have higher expectations of those students than the latter have for themselves and they insist that everyone strives to meet those expectations, then the scene is set for remarkable things to happen.

The commitment level of even the most reluctant learners can be enhanced, or lifted up, in the following circumstances:

- They know exactly what is expected of them.

- They see the task as worthwhile and achievable.
- They can see that the new learning will improve their performance and that of the team.
- They understand that what they are practising will quickly be put into a real game.
- Practices are varied and well paced.
- The time remaining in a play practice is counted down.
- Novel tasks or environments that stimulate curiosity are included.
- Players have some degree of choice within the learning environment: for example, with equipment, rules, size of their target zone, or playing partner.
- The number of repetitions to be completed is counted down, using the strategy employed by fitness instructors.
- Indirect competition is used.
- Performances in tests or challenges are recorded.
- Fantasy or simulation games are used.
- They know that they are preparing for exciting culminating activities.
- Competition is balanced and fair.

This last point is very important. While most children love to play games, they will only make a complete commitment for as long as the game seems fair and the result stays in doubt. This, of course, is not unusual in adult play, even with highly paid professional players! So, it is important to ensure a continual rotation of opponents and a rebalancing of teams.

Controlled Playing Time

Another way this can be done is to control the playing time for a game. Even a cursory glance at the contemporary sporting scene shows that critical periods occur, usually at the end of the game, when time seems to stand still. Seconds feel like hours and players commit everything as they strive for victory.

By limiting the playing time in a practice to between 2 and 3 minutes, the score stays close. The sense of urgency and purpose is captured and the quality of play is enhanced. Now every move counts and every score is important. In

this way, the quality of the games experience is heightened. With playing time limited in this way, fatigue is less likely to contribute to poor performance or to lower motivation. It is also fair to add that many youngsters have a limited attention span, even when they are playing a game.

The ultimate use of time as a motivating factor is with randomly timed play practices. These may last anywhere from 30 seconds to 5 minutes, or even longer, depending on the whim of the teacher or coach. Once players get used to the shock of the idea, random-time games will ensure complete commitment from the very first instance.

It is possible to enhance the performance of star players, rather than merely control them, by giving them leadership roles such as playmaker, schemer, or quarterback, with the suggestion that they must try to play like a local or national hero known for the great ability to provide assists and to lift their team. The better players can also be given a coaching role with the task of improving their team. This provides stars with the recognition they might otherwise seek by dominating the game, giving them a real chance to try on a leadership role and perhaps to expand their own technical and tactical abilities. Few youngsters can resist this opportunity, especially when they are acknowledged as being real team players. They may also become role models for the rest of the group.

This naturally leads to the idea of assigning students other roles such as scorer, referee, feedback giver, or commentator. This can, in turn, lead to the latter nominating the play of the day, the catch of the match, and the award of prizes such as the golden boot, bat, bowling pin, arrow, or racquet.

Fantasy Games

The culmination of the Play Practice approach is using action fantasy games to enhance practice in both individual sports and team games, thus giving all youngsters the chance to experience magical moments. The fantasy games concept has been used extensively across the whole range of sports played in Australia, which takes in most of the games played around the world! In these games, youngsters love to emulate their sporting idols and take on their identities when playing. Indeed, the struggle to be a particularly favoured hero is often as hard fought as the game itself.

The concept is simple. The instructor presents a scenario such as the following: 'It is two sets all in the Wimbledon final. Federer is down three games to four in the final set against Rafael "Rafa" Nadal. Nadal is serving at 30 to 15.' The youngsters choose who they wish to be, or toss a coin in the case of a dispute, and then play the match out. Here is another example: 'The United States, with the ball, trails Australia 90 to 86 in the women's Olympic basketball final with 4 minutes left to play.' Teams of 3 toss for the right to represent a country and then play the game out in a half-court format. In this way, it is possible to combine action fantasy games with mini games to create cameo situations in which young players commit themselves fully as they become immersed in the fantasy.

The sports chosen and the game situations highlighted can involve teams at any level, from local leagues through national leagues, World Series games, test matches, world championships, and the Olympic Games. You can set the scenario in the future or re-create critical situations or periods from famous games of the past. In many ways, these short fantasy games are very much like the simulations that elite coaches use to prepare their players for those same critical periods or situations that can occur in any game.

Fantasy games can stand alone as one-off situations or they can be part of a tournament. For example, they could be the initial round-robin tournament in a World Cup or Olympic Games, where teams compete in pools of 4 for the right to advance to the next stage. At the conclusion of the pool stage, teams move into the finals and begin to play off in groups for positions 1 to 4, 5 to 8, 9 to 12, and so on. This could all be part of a festival of sport at the culmination of the unit or the season.

Fantasy Game Cards

The information on the card sets the scene (see figure 4.1), and the students can either choose

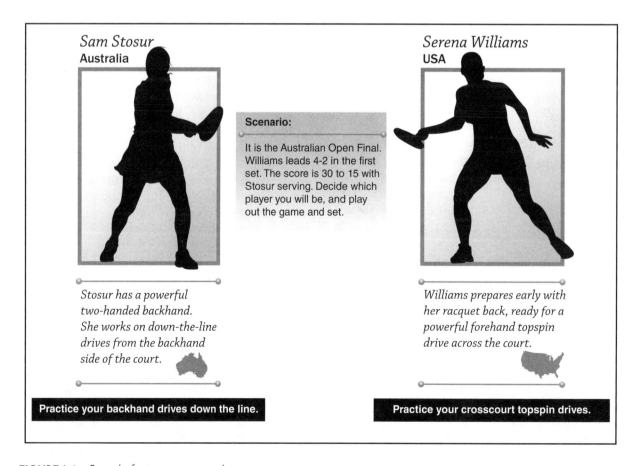

FIGURE 4.1 Sample fantasy game card.

which player they want to be or toss a coin to decide. In either case, they play out the match as if it were a real championship. An additional benefit of using the cards is that the teacher is now free to help students who might be experiencing difficulty and who can benefit from one-on-one tutoring.

Teachers can use action fantasy games to deal with some of the major problems encountered in teaching a game such as tennis, where youngsters with a wide range of abilities are often dispersed over a large area. Surprisingly, it is often the more experienced players who quickly lose interest and begin to practise or play very casually. Their careless attitude rubs off on classmates nearby so that the quality of work from the whole group deteriorates. One method of dealing with this is to give the better players coaching roles. However, this means that they're not always developing their own potential.

Our experience indicates that many youngsters actually begin to take on the persona of their star player. For example, students playing as Lleyton Hewitt most invariably begin by turning their caps around. As a result, they are able to accept a lost game more cheerfully because they are not personally involved; games are played in much better spirits than would otherwise be the case. On some occasions, however, teams become so involved in the competition that examples of bad sporting behaviour surface. In spite of this negative aspect, the fantasy game approach can also give teachers opportunities to deal with issues of critical importance.

The solution is to make up a series of fantasy game cards based on great athletes playing in major tournaments (see figure 4.2 for some examples). At the beginning of the session, children pair up and select a fantasy game card randomly from a box or from a computer tablet. After deciding who they will be, they play out the game.

Practice Tasks

The next step is to put a brief but specific practice task on the reverse side of each card, which must be completed before the match can begin. To maintain the fantasy element, these practice tasks should be set up as either the match warm-up or as practice just prior to a restart after a rain delay or an injury. In the most recent development of this concept, the practice cards require the players to hit forehand drives like Williams, or to keep the ball in play like Nadal. They also carry information about the way that player executes a particular stroke. With digital files, it is easier to create, code, update, and access these challenge cards.

FIGURE 4.2 Sample Fantasy Scenarios

LAKERS VERSUS BULLS

It is the opening game in the final series. Before starting the game, the Lakers warm up with a 2v1 fast-break. The Bulls warm up with 3 attackers outside of the key and 2 defenders.

It is the last 4 minutes of the game. The Lakers are up by 1 point, 50 to 49. The ball is passed to set up a player with a clear shot.

ITALY VERSUS ARGENTINA

It is the World Cup. Italy focuses on controlling the ball quickly and playing it off, using just two touches. They work in a 3v1 square. Argentina focuses on a 2v1 break to score a goal from 20 metres (66 feet).

It is 5 minutes from half time and the score is 0–0. Two attackers dribble and pass to get past the goalie to score.

WILLIAMS VERSUS STOSUR

It is the final at the U.S. Open. Both players work on their serve to improve consistency. Williams looks at placing the ball with depth in the serve. Stosur focuses on placing the ball wide in the serving area.

It is the final set. Scores are one set all and it is 4–4 in the third.

Using fantasy games at the beginning of a session encourages children to get ready quickly so they can start playing, although, as indicated previously, it is possible to build in a practice task that can be presented as an extended warm-up for the match. For example, when the children randomly select a card from the appropriate box, if the fantasy game is facing them, they can immediately begin the game. But if a practice task is facing them, they must complete it before they can start the game.

The element of chance involved makes this approach very acceptable to students, and they respond well to it. Another bonus is that when the majority of players begin practising quickly and purposefully, the instructor is free to deal with the inevitable personal problems and minor organisational matters that arise at the start of any session.

Teachers can also use the cards in a variety of ways during a session to keep the better players on task, as a reward for students who have worked particularly well at a practice task, or to free themselves to provide individual assistance. The fantasy game concept can be applied in many creative ways, and not only in the area of ball games, as this wonderful example confirms (see sidebar).

Culminating Events or Activities

Elite sport is characterised by a wide range of culminating activities that provide a focus for training and preparation. While the Olympic Games and world championships in a vast range of sports are the most significant examples, there are a host of other culminating activities, including national, regional, and state championships. In the United States, many teams view just making the playoffs as a major goal. With this in mind, consider organising sport festivals for children that represent these tournaments. If you announce that students are preparing for a significant culminating activity at the beginning of a unit of work, there is little doubt that they will commit themselves even more enthusiastically.

While culminating activities can have a major influence on a unit of work, the aim should be to provide a program of sport experiences that gives every student the opportunity to participate in the important roles of player, official, and administrator. Remember that practising is only a means to an end—that is, actually participating in sports. This is why school and community sports should be structured to support and extend the school physical education

Example of the Fantasy Game Approach

In 1984, Sam White, an Adelaide student teacher, was required to teach a unit of work dealing with the maintenance of cycles and safe road riding. To motivate a class of difficult boys and to encourage purposeful and careful riding habits as well as to ensure perfectly maintained cycles, he created the 'Tour de West Lakes,' which was the name of the area around his school. Sam modelled his race on the world-renowned Tour de France and brought as much information to school as he could find about this great sporting event.

Each lesson included a ride of several miles that made up a stage of the race. To eliminate racing and its attendant dangers, Sam used the beautifully simple device of determining the finishing position and time randomly. As the riders finished each stage, they picked a card from a box that allocated a position and riding time so that the student who finished first might well draw a card that placed them last! This arrangement made actual racing pointless. When combined with a system of time penalties for traffic offences or careless riding, it ensured that the students rode sensibly and safely. Naturally, Sam also had a time bonus system for all bicycles that were well maintained.

Sam published stage results and awarded prizes for the winners. The race leader, as in the Tour de France, wore the famed yellow jersey. There were special sections for sprints and hill climbs as in the real tour, even though no hill of any kind could be found within 24 kilometres (15 miles) of the school! A well-organised presentation of prizes took place at the end of the race. Though there is no research evidence to support this, we believe that few of the children involved will quickly forget this experience.

This is dedicated to Sam, who was tragically killed in Adelaide while preparing for a triathlon on his cycle.

program. At the very least, all youngsters should have access to appropriate facilities and the opportunity to practise as often and as long as they wish. Most importantly, they should have the opportunity to participate in both organised and informal pick-up games throughout the year.

Summary

Sport Education is a proven model for providing students with the opportunity to participate in an authentic sports experience during the physical education program (Siedentop, Hastie, & van der Mars, 2011). The Sport Education program framework engages participants in a variety of roles associated with sport participation, and its focus on small-sided game play for extended weeks of play time enables the development of sport literacy. A problem that some teachers may confront is that they do not have the content knowledge to sustain the motivation of students for the longer season of play. However, once they begin to appreciate that their students need extended periods of focused practice to develop and improve their technical ability, plus considerable time in the learning laboratory of the game to acquire games sense, they may discover that they really do not have enough time! Our experience suggests that it is possible for any committed teacher to become an expert in virtually any aspect of sport and physical activity, especially when they are prepared to grow with their students and be partners in learning.

five

Teaching Specific Elements of Skilled Performance

Perfection does not come from doing extraordinary things; it comes from doing simple things extraordinarily well.

Anonymous

It is possible to use Play Practices to facilitate the development of all of the elements of skilled play in games. However, instructors should initially aim to help young players appreciate the importance of fair play, develop their technical ability, improve their games sense, and build their resilience. This chapter shows how these goals can be achieved.

Developing Fair Play and Resilience

Fair play and resilience are fundamental to enjoyment and to its apogee, fun. They provide the platform on which all the other elements must rest if sport is to fulfil its potential in education. Sport educators must treat the development of these two elements of skilled play as seriously as they do technical ability and games sense.

Of the many lessons that players can learn, one of the most important is that sport must always be about risk, victory and defeat, success and failure, mastery and mistakes. This may lead not only to greater enjoyment for all involved but also to improved performance as players focus on the challenge, not the opponent. It is also important for students to be introduced to a philosophy that values opponents in the contest and where ultimate competition is true cooperation as players choose to come together to play. These ideas are expressed by Tim Gallwey (1976) in his 'Inner game' series of books and encapsulated in the wisdom of the late Robert Paddick, who in a personal communication said, 'It is obvious that to treat opponents as enemies in a situation valued for its own sake by all the players, all of whom are necessary for the continuation of the activity, is absurd, being a denial of the whole agreement for coming together: to play'.

In Play Practice, every game or challenge can be a learning laboratory for fair play and an opportunity to help players to build resilience. Resilience can be developed as players are encouraged to persist with effort to improve personal performance, to keep on trying even in difficult circumstances, and to value making mistakes as a part of the learning process. An example for developing fair play is when students play fantasy games, often with the furious intensity of a world championship. These games have the potential to generate the aggression often common at the senior level, so they provide hundreds of opportunities for youngsters to be involved in situations where they must make choices between one action and another. They also provide the perceptive sport educator with ongoing opportunities to initiate discussion about appropriate behaviour and the fundamental nature of the sport experience. Students will quickly begin to understand how rules structure a game to make it fair and enjoyable. This can be used to lead them to the understanding that any time a rule is broken, the game is broken.

In addition, Play Practice provides many opportunities for youngsters to take on officiating roles. This puts them on the other side of the fence, where they get a different perspective of the rules and of those individuals who deliberately infringe them. It also brings home the difficulty of the official's task and will help players understand and tolerate the mistakes that the former makes. The emphasis on small-sided games where team rosters are continually adjusted also ensures that players discover that yesterday's opponent is today's team-mate. Then when undertaking challenges, students often work in pairs or small groups, giving them opportunities to take on helping roles as commentators or 'coaches' providing feedback. This involvement with classmates makes it easier for them to appreciate each other and also helps them develop respect for a good performance, even on the part of an opponent.

However, while all of these experiences may help students understand the importance of playing fairly through a process of osmosis, educators must plan for these outcomes and seize every teachable moment. In the early stages, this can include using game situations to introduce or to clarify fair play: for example, by encouraging youngsters to shake hands before and after a game, by acknowledging a great piece of skilled play by an opponent, or by recognising player behaviours contributing to fair play.

Coaches, who may question the importance of fair play, should remember that the ability to concentrate on the critical elements of performance without being distracted by any external factors is one of the keys to success. Elite athletes must take this notion much further, focusing so intensely that no conscious thought, including the chimera of winning, interferes with the uninhibited flow of action. This notion is captured in two samurai maxims: 'If you have one eye on winning, you have only one eye to watch your opponent' (or the ball) and 'In battle, as in life, anger will defeat you.'

Improving Technical Ability

The importance of technical ability has been undervalued in much of the recent discussion on the teaching of games. With its mantra 'What is tactically desirable must be technically possible,' Play Practice attempts to redress the balance. This is essential because no matter the tactics employed, if players are to score a goal or win a point, they must be able to control the ball and direct it to where they want it to go!

However, there are other reasons to emphasise technical ability with young players. The first is that players can find great joy in executing a sport technique successfully, even outside the context of a game. Kretchmar (2005) describes this feeling as 'delight,' while Pulitzer-winning author John Updike alluded to the same feelings of joy when he watched a golf ball soar away into the air, then bounce and roll down the fairway. This is clearly the sensation that Japanese golfers feel as they swat ball after ball into the distance at a driving range. The joy of seeing a ball drop through the hoop, rocket between the posts, or knock down a stump in the cricket nets, even when no batsman is in place! The satisfaction of maintaining a rally while focusing on a specific element of technique when practising

Modify practices to ensure they meet the needs of individuals.

tennis! The joy when the ball comes sweetly off the boot, bat, racquet, or club! And who has never felt a buzz after getting a strike in tenpin bowling? The pins go down with a clatter and everyone knows you have been successful.

The results of good technique are obvious, while the most successful use of tactics may slide by unnoticed. Helping participants improve their technical ability gives teachers and coaches the opportunity to recognise a thousand small successes and improvements.

It is easy for teachers and coaches who have had long and successful involvement in sport to forget how important apparently simple achievements can be to children. For youngsters, scoring a goal or winning a point can be highly significant, remembered long after the result of the game is forgotten. In that single act, they feel that they have demonstrated their ability.

So while skilful play involves many elements, everything possible must be done to make scoring goals, winning points, registering improvement, or attaining personal bests as easy as possible for beginners. It is also important to encourage partners, team-mates, and opponents to support the teacher in recognising any achievement, for this contributes to the development of a positive and supportive climate and that critical belief, 'I can do this!'

Children growing up in a particular sporting culture master the techniques of a game, such as dribbling and shooting a basketball, almost through a process of osmosis. However, when this is not the case, mastering these techniques often requires commitment and considerable practice, much of which may need to be done informally in the player's own time. Here, it is important to remember that it is far more difficult to modify poor technique than it is to master the movement correctly at the start. So, it is crucial for young players to develop effective technique from the very beginning. This is where working models of technique are valuable because they enable youngsters to quickly master a stripped-down version of the advanced technique of the experts.

Models of Technique

Elite players often use advanced technical models. These exploit biomechanical principles and usually require special physical qualities such as strength, flexibility, excellent body control, or superb hand–eye coordination. In addition, the mastery of advanced techniques often requires years of high-quality practice and training and in some cases access to specialised and expensive equipment.

The concept of working models of technique evolved in parallel to the Play Practice approach when it was clear that few youngsters could master the advanced techniques involved in the field events of athletics. The major advantage of working models is that they enable young players to take part in the real activity much earlier than if they had to wait until they had mastered more advanced techniques. They also make it possible to delay the introduction of advanced techniques until novices are better able to cope with their complexity and thus less likely to develop bad habits.

A working model is technique stripped to the bare bones! This notion is further developed in the section on table tennis, but working techniques in common use include the sliding wedge in skiing, the pat-a-cake tennis serve, the scissors high-jump technique in athletics, and the dog paddle in swimming. However, a working model must always provide the framework for continued development towards the advanced model. In other words, it cannot be a dead-end technique, one that allows participants early success but then blocks them from further progress.

Understanding Why Techniques Are Effective

While tactical understanding has been a major focus of instruction for several years, the importance of understanding in the development of technical ability has been virtually neglected. Yet experienced teachers and coaches know that a clear understanding of why things are important in a specific technique is often a critical element in the learner's successful mastery of that technique. Two contrasting examples illustrate this point.

An understanding of how top spin is produced by the upward swing and contact patterns between bat and ball can help learners improve this important aspect of technique. At a slightly more advanced level, as learners strive to improve their performance in the apparently

Individual challenges provide a strategy to enhance the development of technical ability.

simple flop technique of high jumping, experience suggests that they may improve if they understand why accelerating around the curve is so important in setting up the correct body position at take-off.

The point is that a clear understanding of why a specific technique is effective often helps learners improve more rapidly. Indeed, there will come a point where their improvement may falter if they do not understand why they are executing a specific movement pattern. Of course, many intelligent learners of any age are curious about why things should be done in a particular way.

Shaping, Focusing, and Enhancing to Develop Technical Ability

Teachers will find the processes of shaping, focusing, and enhancing practices (detailed in the preceding chapter) invaluable as they attempt to motivate students to undertake high volumes of quality practice. The shaping process can be used to minimise or even eliminate the importance of other elements of skilled play so that the student can focus almost totally on developing a sound technique. However, sport educators can also improve the volume and quality of technical practice if the following conditions are met:

- Organisational and management strategies maximise individual practice opportunities.

- Sufficient equipment is available. This means a ball for each child in a basketball dribbling practice, a ball for each pair of students for kicking and stopping practices in soccer, and the smallest possible team size compatible with achieving the tactical or technical objectives of a play practice.

- Students understand why a specific technique is important and how it fits into the overall pattern of the game. If players understand the relevance of new learning to the game, they are more likely to practice purposefully.

- The practice becomes a challenge. With novices, this must be handled carefully. For example, asking children how many baskets they can score out of 10 attempts creates a situation where a few may fail to score even one. On the other hand, asking them to see how many shots it takes them to score five baskets gives everyone a chance to succeed. It is far easier to find extension tasks for the better players than to reassure children who feel that they have failed. Having completed the original task quickly, the more experienced players in a group might be asked to establish their shooting percentage with 10 shots taken from 3-point range.

- The importance of individual improvement is emphasized and there are no comparisons made between students.

- Learners can clearly see the results of their performance. In some activities, such as basketball shooting and kicking for goal, knowledge of results is automatically built in, which supports player engagement and fosters learning through the task itself.

- Record performances in challenges because this demonstrates the importance attached to the learner's efforts and provides data against which subsequent improvements can be assessed. Sometimes it provides evidence that certain players are not as good as they think they are!

- Learners know the amount of practice time for an activity, or the number of attempts they will make, from the beginning. Avoid letting practices drift along for an indefinite period of time.

- A build-up teaching method is employed, which is very valuable in any repetitive practice situation. For example, when practising digging a volleyball, instead of encouraging students to make as many consecutive attempts as possible from the beginning, teachers can ask them to try for two consecutive digs. After accomplishing this, learners can then build up to three or four. When the sequence breaks down, they go back to two, and then build up again. This ensures more stable progression and rewards consistency.

- The practice is enjoyable, with an element of novelty and fun where possible. An example is moving targets in archery.

- The practice involves a lot of variation around a specific technical theme. For example, lacrosse techniques of scoop, carry, and throw can be combined into partner target challenges.

- An obvious progression leads towards the application of the technique in the real game.

The section on teaching dribbling in basketball provides examples of how all three of these elements can be achieved at the same time. However, when it is still difficult to maintain high levels of motivation and commitment, educators must reassure learners that they will be playing a game and applying their new expertise within a clearly defined time frame. To do this, teachers and coaches can use a parallel approach. Instead of using long blocks of repetitive practice, they simply switch from practising key techniques to playing a game and then back again throughout a session. The combination of technical practice with grip-ball games when teaching lacrosse is a good example of this strategy. Clearly, teachers must use good pacing and focusing to ensure that the session does not become too bitty. They can also use their skills in positioning and providing positive reinforcement and feedback to ensure that learners stay involved throughout the practice task.

It is often worthwhile to give students time to review previously acquired techniques at the beginning of every session. This allows them to re-establish both their technique and their confidence, thus building that important 'I can do this' feeling before they move on to new challenges. While it is especially important with challenging activities such as skiing, this strategy can also be valuable with ball games.

Devoting Time to Practice

Finally, and most importantly, there is a growing acceptance that opportunity and time to practise, rather than talent, are the key factors that determine the final level of performance. Since time is often scarce in school physical education programs, teachers must emphasise helping youngsters gain a love of sport, develop at least a working model of technique, and get a clear understanding of how best to practise in their own time. This is another recurrent theme in this work.

Here, it is vital for sport educators to understand that while youngsters can master the movement patterns of many of the basic techniques of sport with relative ease, they must often undertake many hours of repetitive practice before they can consistently reproduce those techniques in the chaos of a real game.

Developing Games Sense

While the improvement of technical ability is relatively straightforward, teaching games sense may present a challenge for those coming to the concept for the first time. Games sense is not a mystical key to success in sport but is merely one element, albeit a very important one, in skilled performance. The only time understanding is the most critical factor is in games like chess. However, it is worth noting that games sense, or common sense applied to sports, is important in many other activities: as climbers study the route up a rock face, surfers consider the size of the waves rolling in, or skiers assess the possibilities and dangers of those narrow black diamond chutes.

Many great players appear to have been born with games sense. They seem to intuitively know what to do in any situation. However, in Play Practice, intuition is defined as the ability to instantly access the distilled essence of past experiences to solve immediate problems. So while there may be a genetic component, it seems highly likely that this intuitive ability comes from playing in endless pick-up games from an early age. It also seems likely that the opportunity to play and practise with more experienced players is a key factor in developing games sense.

Coaches have always known that games sense is an important element of skilled play—they just did not give it a label. However, the definition of games sense as the ability of players to use an understanding of the rules, tactics, strategy, and themselves to solve the problems posed by the game or by their opponents achieves two important goals. First, it clarifies what may sometimes appear to be complex, almost mystical elements of skilled play. For example, great players in soccer and basketball have an almost uncanny ability to lose their defenders at critical moments. However, while this may appear to be uncanny, it is possible to analyse exactly how they do it and to teach anyone else how to do it!

Second, this definition provides the key to helping players acquire games sense. For example, in many American cities, almost every youngster can dribble a basketball. Many can drive to the basket to shoot a layup or dribble behind their backs with either hand. But how many, if any, of them would know how to get an open shot for a team-mate by using a dribble draw (figure 5.1a) or how to use the dribble to create a better passing angle (figure 5.1b)? Yet a simple explanation or demonstration of these tactics could ensure that young players immediately grasp a simple idea that may make them more effective throughout their career. A teacher or coach who can present the concepts that underpin games sense and who can create learning situations that develop these important aspects of skilled play can have a powerful and lasting influence on young players.

The key to helping players acquire games sense lies with the fact that it is defined as the ability of a player to use an understanding of the following:

- Rules
- Tactics
- Strategy
- Their own ability to solve the problems posed by the activity or by their opponents

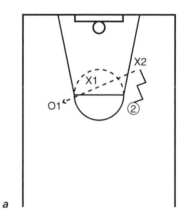

FIGURE 5.1 Using a dribble to create (a) space for a team-mate and (b) a better passing angle.

With games sense unpacked in this way, Play Practice provides an ideal vehicle to introduce these components of games sense, thus helping players translate understanding into action. By playing a game as early as possible and continuing to play in every session, youngsters can begin to understand the fundamental nature of an activity from the outset. So, it is easy for them to appreciate the relevance and importance of rules, tactics, strategy, and techniques when these are introduced. Indeed, the key to developing games sense lies in ensuring that youngsters have the chance to play in realistic scenarios that gradually increase in complexity.

The opportunity to play in carefully structured small-sided games gives them many more opportunities to recognise the cues that are the basis for decision making and to trial possible responses. In this way, teachers and coaches can fast forward the learning process so that students quickly master elements of games sense that might otherwise take years of informal play to acquire. While it may take months to improve agility or endurance, it is possible for youngsters to become better players almost instantaneously by learning how to exploit a rule or employ a new tactic, by grasping a key element of strategy, or by learning to play to their strengths.

Rules

Since an understanding of the rules is critical to both fair and skilful play, they must be emphasised early on. Some primary rules must be emphasised even before play begins. Secondary rules, like the offside law in soccer, can and should be altered or even omitted if this simplifies the game for beginners. Teachers can then introduce them as opportunities arise in the context of the game, letting play continue until an incident occurs that leads to a dispute. The held ball situation in basketball and netball are good examples of this. The teacher simply freezes play and guides a discussion about what has occurred in order to lead players towards an appropriate rule. When this is done, everyone involved is more likely to understand why the rule is necessary and how it is enforced. They are also more likely to abide by rules arrived at in this way.

Many games have unwritten rules that need to be observed if play is to be fair and rewarding for everyone. These rules are part of the tradition of a game. In some sporting cultures, they are often more powerful than those that are written down. Since they are usually ethically driven and may sometimes run counter to a win-at-all-costs philosophy, they often engender considerable discussion.

However, while the rules are important to make the game fair for all and to prevent rough or even dangerous play, they also influence the tactics, strategy, and techniques of a game. Volleyball is a great example of this. Here, the rules that allow a team a maximum of three clean touches influence all of the elements of skilled play. In rugby, the rules that prevent forward passes but allow forward kicks have created a game where physical toughness and courage are critical elements of skilled play. While they don't eliminate the need for technical ability, these qualities tend to overshadow that element of skilled play in this game. This, of course, is a major reason why youngsters should be introduced to the rugby codes through the less-complex 7-a-side game or through touch football, which does not require physical toughness.

Tactics

With its emphasis on the use of simplified or shaped games, which are potential learning laboratories, Play Practice provides an ideal vehicle to help players use an understanding of tactics to improve their play. However, the clear and precise definition of games sense provided earlier is critical for the following reasons:

1. The player's ability to use an understanding of tactics to solve problems is more important than mere understanding.

2. Tactics cannot be viewed in isolation from other elements of skilled play, especially technical ability.

3. A continual two-way interaction exists between tactics and other elements of skilled play. While 'what is tactically desirable must be technically possible' is a Play Practice mantra, the effective use of tactics enables players to reduce the technical demands of controlling and directing the ball.

Great soccer teams like Barcelona make the game look simple as they make one pass after another to open team-mates. But this is only possible because every player is using his understanding of tactics to continually move into good positions so that each new ball player has several easy passing options. In the same way, great tennis players like Federer appear to have all of the time in the world to play their shots. However, it is their tactical understanding that gives them the time because it enables them to anticipate their opponent's stroke and to move into position early.

Play Practice uses three practical strategies to speed up tactical understanding in players:

- The first, simplifying play by eliminating the technical demands, enables youngsters to solve the tactical problems of the game from the very beginning. This is best illustrated by the use of mitt-cross or grip ball to introduce lacrosse.
- The second, focusing play through the judicious use of freeze replays to capture great teaching moments, has long been used by teachers and coaches.
- The third strategy, shaping play, is of immense value in helping players learn to apply tactical principles in games. This is because the shaping process can reinforce the use of a tactical principle, not simply help players understand it.

The game of four-goal soccer, described in chapter 7, illustrates this perfectly. Here, with a goal in each corner of the field instead of in the middle, players can use the tactical principle of width to switch the attack from one goal to the other as they try to outflank defenders. This inevitably opens up more scoring opportunities, so players can immediately appreciate the advantages of this tactic.

As we have already seen, tactics evolve from a simple process of taking advantage of basic defensive mistakes into complex manoeuvres based on exploiting the predictability of defensive responses to force mistakes. This is an important concept, especially for coaches. There is no point in trying to get players to try to play like Brazil if they don't have Brazilian feet or Brazilian games sense!

The development of tactical understanding is facilitated as youngsters play in carefully shaped games that allow them many opportunities to be successful.

Strategy

While strategy might seem the sole province of coaches, it adds another layer of complexity to games, making them even more interesting for all participants. Unfortunately, this term is often used interchangeably with tactics, naturally leading to confusion. In essence, players use their tactical knowledge to resolve the immediate problems they face in a game, but they use their understanding of strategy to decide which tactics to emphasise at particular points in a game. While good tactics may lead to goals being scored, points won, or attacking moves blunted, a sound strategy is often the key to winning a game.

Although understanding strategy is not initially as important as the ability to understand and apply tactics, it will gradually become more significant, especially if youngsters begin to play in formal competitions. It brings an intellectual component to the games experience that makes sport more interesting and challenging. At the very least, it may help youngsters become more perceptive teachers, coaches, and even spectators in the future. In general, the higher the level of play, the more complex the game. The longer it lasts, the more an understanding of strategy becomes important.

Individual Ability

Players' ability to factor in what they are capable of doing is critical to games sense. It is also central to understanding the contribution that Play Practice can make to sport education. This is because once this idea is accepted, it is obvious that players need much more than a mere understanding of tactics to deal with the problems posed by the game or by their opponents. In many games, players must draw on their total knowledge of themselves—their agility, their endurance, their mental toughness, their courage, their technical ability, and even their use of their signature move—as they decide what to do in the game.

Individual challenges, variation in the task, and the use of novel targets such as balloons or a moving target ensure that motivation is enhanced when developing technical ability in archery.

In a sport like golf, where players compete against the course and nature, the challenge is to psychological toughness, resilience, and technical ability. It may come down to the simple question 'Am I good enough to hit over that water, bunker, or tree, or must I play safe and lay up?' However, in interactive games, where opponents can disrupt their plans, players must resolve the question 'How can I do what I do well and force my opponent to do what they do poorly?' In basketball it might be 'Can I beat him with my quickness on the first step to get in for a layup?' Or 'Should I take her in to the low post where I can use my height and strength advantage to get a shot and draw the foul?'

In these situations, games sense, technical ability, and the players' strengths are melded, hence the repeated Play Practice mantras 'What is tactically desirable must be technically possible' and 'What is technically desirable must be physically possible.' Never forget that while it is easy to present tactics in a book or on a white board, it is another thing entirely for players to execute those moves. What coaches term *game slippage* is a reality at every level of play because even professional players cannot always do what is expected of them. Indeed, even great players sometimes make amazing blunders.

So although unpacking games sense can help readers better understand what is involved, in many sports, players must be able to instantly draw together all of these elements as they try to solve the problems posed by the game or by their opponents.

The fact that games sense can be acquired through carefully structured experiences enables intelligent but less physically gifted youngsters to use their heads to compensate for a lack of agility or strength. They now have a template that enables them to read the game, anticipate what is likely to happen, and begin to move into position early. Gaining possession of a loose ball in soccer is not simply a footrace in which the fastest player gets to it first. The thinker also has a chance. In racquet sports, this means that players can be in position earlier, with more time to select and execute a stroke. Games sense gives a more diverse group of young people the chance to participate successfully.

Reading the Play

Before players can begin to use games sense, they must be able to read the play—that is, to see what is happening and interpret what they see. Students will improve their ability to see if they are encouraged to scan. This involves keeping their heads up and watching other players, even while undertaking the simplest of practices. When dribbling a basketball or running with the ball in soccer, they should be asked to watch a partner, shadowing or mirroring them even as they are controlling the ball themselves. For the same reason, in interactive games, at least one defender should force the ball player to continually scan the playing area and begin reading the play. This is especially important in soccer and field hockey, where the ball is usually at ground level and where the ability to control the ball easily becomes a factor in a player's ability to look up to read the play. The process can gradually be made more demanding by adding defenders, increasing team sizes, or decreasing the size of the playing area.

Naturally, players must improve their ability to respond to what they are seeing. The challenge is to progressively bridge the gap between the cognitive performance of beginners and the non-conscious play of experts. This can be done by putting learners into practice situations that progressively increase the amount of information they must process or that reduce the time they have to be skilful. This means bringing practices back closer to the real activity. At the elite level, it may involve tipping the balance against attackers. This is where the skill of the instructor can be severely tested. On the one hand, players need to be challenged, but on the other, they must not continually fail.

Developing Communication Skills

The ability to communicate effectively is an important aspect of skilled play in a number of team sports, since it builds cohesion while improving a team's performance. In games where the player with the ball can be pressured, a call of 'player on,' 'run,' or 'time' from team-mates can provide vital information to guide the decisions of the ball carrier. When using a helping player-to-player defence, calls of 'my ball,' 'help left,' 'help right,' or simply, 'help' are examples of how communication can assist a defensive unit to work effectively. Players must understand the significance of communication so that teachers and coaches can continually strive to help them improve their capabilities. This can be done by adding a communication element to any of the scanning activities suggested previously and by focusing on communication during periods of play in small-sided games.

This book emphasises the use of small-sided games wherever possible because they give more students the opportunity to be positively involved. However, it is important to use the actual game with real equipment on occasion. For example, it is difficult, if not impossible, to introduce some elements of the rules, such as the offside law in soccer or the tactics needed to defeat a zone defence in basketball, unless learners have an opportunity to play the full game.

Summary

Chapters 2 and 3 earlier confirmed the complexity of skilled performance in sport. It should now be clear that helping players to progress from the cognitive play of beginners to the intuitive, non-conscious behaviour of highly skilled performers is a challenging and much underrated task. This chapter has focused on the development of the three critical aspects of skilled play with beginners: playing fairly, games sense, and technical ability. However, it must be remembered that the development of technical ability alone to the level required to play games like basketball, tennis, and golf competitively requires considerable practice, and learning to ally technical ability with games sense takes even more time.

This reality has major implications for the structure of sports education in both schools and clubs. In essence, it means that sports educators must take every opportunity to provide youngsters with wide-ranging opportunities for both informal and organised competitive play.

six

The *P*s of Perfect Pedagogy

A theory of instruction, in short, is concerned with how what one wishes to teach can best be learned, with improving rather than describing learning.

Jerome Bruner

While it is true that inexperienced teachers and coaches—armed with little more than great enthusiasm and energy, but with a deep commitment to helping young people—can make a real contribution to our field, the craft of teaching at the expert level is a complex, almost intuitive process where art and science are seamlessly melded. As Daryl Siedentop (1991) notes, 'No description fits this picture of complexity so well as Smith's concept of the teacher as ringmaster. Surrounded by a flow of activity, the ringmaster monitors, controls, and orchestrates, accelerating some acts, terminating others, altering and adjusting progress through the program, always with an eye for the total result.'

So while it often appears to be undervalued by the wider community, instruction is a complex task that requires wide-ranging skills and knowledge that can only be gained through intelligent study and reflective practical experience. Consequently, one of the unresolved dilemmas in the preparation of teachers and coaches is the question 'How do you put the wise, intuitive head of the experienced "artist" onto the shoulders of the young?' Since this is clearly an impossible task, the aim of this chapter is to present a model of instruction that provides the foundations

necessary for teachers and coaches to begin to become critically reflective practitioners.

The *P*s model (Launder, 1989) was first developed at the University of South Australia (UniSA) in the early 1970s to provide pre-service teachers with the minimal knowledge required to undertake their initial teaching experiences in a laboratory (lab) school setting. During lab school, pre-service teachers (HPE) engage in the cycle of planning, teaching, and reflection with small groups of 10 to 12 children to begin to develop their teaching capabilities. Since the first of these experiences began early in the program, there was a need for a 'working model of instruction' that simplified this complex process. This would enable pre-service teachers to understand and begin to master some elements of the task of teaching, rather than the traditional approach in which novices are expected to model the master teacher during their teaching practice.

Since no alternatives could be found in the literature of that time, the *P*s model emerged from observation of what teachers, and especially coaches, actually did, and as a result it appeared to have limited theoretical underpinnings as it evolved.

However, it is now clear that the *P*s model is based on the principles that people learn best in the following circumstances:

- They really want to learn something.
- They know that a significant other cares about their development.
- They have a very clear model of the learning task.
- They are not faced with immediate failure.
- They feel that the task is challenging but can be mastered if they make an effort.

The play of beginners can sometimes become a comedy of errors.

HAGAR © KING FEATURES SYNDICATE.

- They have many opportunities to practise in a positive environment.
- They understand the relationship between the practice and the real activity.
- They get useful feedback about their performance.
- They are helped to understand that mistakes are part of the learning process.
- Their efforts, improvement, and successes are recognised by significant others, especially their peers.
- They know that what they have learned will quickly be applied in real situations.

The major advantage of the *P*s model is that it simplifies and clarifies the complex task of instruction and breaks it down into components that can be easily recalled and readily applied so that novice educators can begin to learn their trade. The *P*s model and the lab school model of practice teaching remain the central learning experiences in the preparation of HPE teachers at UniSA. Pre-service teachers from this program report improved pedagogical understanding and growth in instructional capabilities. The model is particularly valuable for guiding the planning of teacher outcomes and informing reflective discussions on teaching and learning (Piltz, 2008b).

It is important to note that the craft of instruction, like skilled performance in sport, is a totally integrated process in which each component interacts with and complements every other. In order to cater for this, the *P*s model, like all working models, can be extended to develop the more

sophisticated, higher-order teaching capabilities and methods outlined later in this chapter.

This chapter details the most significant elements of the *P*s model of instruction that influence student learning.

Plan

Planning is the most critical *P* of effective instruction because youngsters learn best when they understand that someone cares about them and what they are doing. Good planning is manifested in many ways so that learners know they are cared for, even if only intuitively. Proper planning ensures that the principles of safety, inclusivity, engagement, enjoyment, and success are evident. It also encourages participation in aligned activities. Above all, it minimises potential problems while maximising the chances of success.

In some cases the process may only require the planning of the very next session, while for a coach it may involve putting together a detailed program of practices and training extending over weeks or months. The depth of planning involved depends on factors such as the following:

- The nature of the activity
- The prior experience of the students in the activity
- The time available, especially if preparing for a competition, festival, or culminating activity of some kind

Time is almost always limited, so it is important to establish clear priorities. To do this, teachers must decide the following:

- What *must* be introduced
- What *should* be introduced
- What *could* be introduced

The critical issue here, and one that is not always addressed, is the time that is needed to achieve worthwhile improvement in specific elements of effective play. While coaches working with elite athletes have almost too much time, teachers working within the constraints of a school's physical education curriculum never have enough. This has major implications for the content and structure of the curriculum, and it should lead anyone who is serious about developing high standards to consider Daryl Siedentop's Sport Education model.

Prepare the Learner

One of the mantras of Play Practice is that students learn best when they really want to learn something. A strong 'set to learn' is crucial to rapid progress and, indeed, to achieving any learning at all. While many youngsters come to a sport experience with a positive approach, instructors must try to maximise and then sustain this initial motivational set. Often, all that is needed is an enthusiastic teacher, suitably dressed, with a welcoming smile, a positive comment, and the use of each child's name. However, there is little doubt that beginning with a game or a challenge will encourage all youngsters, even those reluctant or resistant learners to be found in almost every class, to make an initial commitment to a session. Teachers and coaches can then sustain this initial engagement on the part of learners by revisiting games and challenges throughout the session and by enhancing the play using ideas presented in chapter 4.

Planning and preparation are the two most critical aspects of instruction, since they minimise the management problems that, more than any other factor, can make the lives of inexperienced teachers miserable. Unfortunately there is a tendency for some novice sport educators to skimp on both planning and preparation, relying instead on personality and an often unjustified confidence in their own ability to wing their way through a session. Whilst this might allow some short-term success in getting on with the class, this approach soon limits the scope and depth of student learning.

Prepare a Protected Learning Environment

People learn best when they feel safe. Two important parts of planning are identifying potential problems and minimising physical and emotional risks. Before any session begins, ensure that all hazards are removed or plan to avoid them: Markings and goals should be in place and balls, bibs, targets, and other necessary equipment should be ready. This minimises time wastage and clearly demonstrates the teachers' or coaches' concern for their students and their commitment to a worthwhile learning experience.

Learners must also feel safe from embarrassment. Establishing a positive class climate and operating structure based on the values of care, responsibility, and respect provides a framework for ensuring emotional safety during all activities. One of the major factors limiting the involvement of many youngsters in sport is fear of failure and the derision and ridicule it can bring. Yet for beginners facing the unknown challenges of new experiences, failure is both inevitable and natural. It is a virtual mantra of Play Practice that without failure, often repeated failure, there will be little or no progress. This is why teachers and coaches must always help students understand this aspect of learning and encourage them to persist and develop the critical quality of resilience that is so important to success in sport.

Present the Task Efficiently

Learning is enhanced when students have a clear understanding of the task. The key to an effective presentation of a technique, or of elements of games sense, lies in demonstrating rather than merely describing. Until learners have seen a demonstration or have been exposed to a game situation, any verbal instruction is often completely meaningless to them.

When introducing a technique, the process can begin by providing an accurate demonstration of the specific technique, ideally in the game context in which it will be employed, so that students understand when and why it is used. The demonstration can be provided by the teacher, by using an appropriate digital image, or by group members, if they are willing and if they can provide a good demonstration. The advantage of the latter method is that class members potentially introduce the 'If they can do it, I can do it' attitude to a class or team. Demonstrate first and then describe what you have demonstrated, not the other way around.

As far as possible, introduce rules and tactics in the context of the game. One strategy is to use a specific signal to freeze play, then rewind the action back to a specific teachable moment. Then, use either a direct or guided-discovery approach to help learners understand the need for a rule or understand the tactical possibilities in that situation. Avoid attempting to describe tactics in the abstract. Always set up a game situation and discuss the possibilities that may exist.

However, students must understand not only what they are to practise but also how they are to practise it. To facilitate this, teachers and coaches can set up the practice scenario, and then clearly and succinctly demonstrate and describe the following:

- How the play practice is to be carried out
- The focus of the specific practice

Remember that poor instructors waste more time when presenting the task than in any other phase of teaching. In essence, they talk too much! This phase of instruction is so important that novice educators should practise key presentations beforehand, even preparing a script when necessary and rehearsing the scene, just as an actor might.

Pre-Test

Learning is optimised if youngsters enjoy early and continuing success. The challenge, therefore, is to structure a series of progressive learning experiences where students can be successful, thus building both competence and confidence. Therefore, except with absolute beginners, it is necessary to establish the entry level of a group: that is, their competence in each of the key aspects of effective performance. Initial play practices and games can then be structured to ensure early success and rapid improvement. Remember, we must always meet learners where they are in terms of their knowledge, competencies, and attitude.

The pre-test can take many forms, from simply eyeballing a game, arranging a series of objective challenges, or, at the elite level, analysing complex statistics. However, this pre-test can do more than merely provide the teacher or coach with a starting point. It can provide the basis for planning subsequent sessions and even the direction the whole unit will take. If the results are recorded or the initial games are filmed, teachers and coaches will have a useful benchmark for judging the level of improvement during the unit. The pre-test can be repeated in subsequent sessions to provide feedback or assess the overall progress.

Other advantages of a formal pre-test include the following:

- It provides a structured introduction to a session, while still allowing students considerable freedom as they test themselves, independently or in pairs.
- It allows the instructor a brief period to undertake some of the housekeeping tasks that must be dealt with at the beginning of every session.
- It enables teachers to define the situation from the outset and so develop the learning experience on their terms.

Novice teachers especially will find pre-tests valuable when working with challenging groups of adolescent boys. For example, in basketball, a simple pre-test in which every player must attempt a 3-point shot three times from each of five hot shooting spots—while a partner records the results—sends the not-too-subtle message that while these youngsters can 'talk the talk', they are not yet able to 'walk the walk'!

Provide Opportunities for Plenty of Practice

This is the key to learning, so educators must create many opportunities for purposeful and pertinent practice in a positive environment. Indeed, the most basic test of effective instruction is how much time learners actually spend playing or practising. This means that strategies for planning, presentation, organisation, and management must all be undertaken with the primary intention of maximising the time that students are actually involved in positive learning experiences.

Practice Should Be Pertinent

In other words, practice must be closely aligned with the ultimate goal. This has many advantages, not the least of which is that players at every level of performance will practice more purposefully when they can see a clear relationship between practice and the real sport. A game, by its very nature, almost invariably leads to purposeful practice. However, purposeful practice, along with persistent practice, is also engendered when the teacher or coach acknowledges effort and commitment, encourages learners to move outside their comfort zone, supports them when they attempt new challenges, and promotes the view that mistakes and failure are an inevitable concomitant of positive learning. The ultimate aim is to help both students and players generate and internalise a mindset that nothing is impossible and that persistence and effort are the keys to improvement.

Practice Should Be Purposeful

Purposeful practice is the only way to help students make progress. The biggest weakness of much of the practice at virtually every level of performance, up to and including professional teams, is that it is aimless, and in fact often pointless. The players simply go through the motions. Indeed, if there is a single quality that distinguishes great teachers and coaches, it is their ability to induce players to practise purposefully. This is captured in the phrase, surely part of every good coach's lexicon: 'Perfection is expected. Excellence will be tolerated.'

If they are to ensure purposeful practice, teachers and coaches themselves must have a clear aim for every session, and they must clearly communicate this aim to every participant.

Practice Should Be Playful

This is the essence of Play Practice, for students, whether beginners or professional players, learn best when they are enjoying the experience. What we have termed the *parallel approach,* with a balance between practising and playing the game, is advocated because it will engage learners and maintain positive learning states. Here, it is important to remember that while youngsters love games they can also be induced to enjoy well-structured challenges that are based on the actual techniques of a game.

Students learn best when they enjoy the experience, so Play Practice uses the parallel approach to maintain a positive learning state.

Practice Should Be Progressive

Learners may be threatened by practices that are too difficult but will get bored if they are not demanding enough. The key is to start with activities that are structured to ensure early success and then gradually increase the challenge and complexity of what is being practised. Ensuring appropriate progression requires a thorough knowledge of the activity and good observation skills. However, the more obvious signs that youngsters are ready to move on—an increase in chatter, a general restlessness, pointed looks at the teacher or coach, and sometimes inappropriate behaviour—all signal a need for progression.

However, it is worth noting the value of going back to review previous practices in activities that are especially difficult or potentially dangerous, such as in gymnastics, diving, or downhill skiing. This gives students the chance to rebuild their confidence before undertaking the next progression.

Practice Should Be Paced

A practice or game that continues for too long may lead to boredom and a drop-off in the quality of performance. Teachers and coaches must carefully define the length of a specific game or challenge in a way that maintains the quality of the practice. This means that they must continually read the group to pick up the subtle signs that some players are not fully committed to the specific task, perhaps because they have already mastered it or because they have found it too difficult. Conversely, it is important to understand that students do not like to chop and change activities too rapidly and, most importantly, that each change bleeds away valuable learning time.

Practice Should Be Personalised

Youngsters vary vastly in their ability, experience, and potential. To the extent that it is possible, teachers and coaches must always attempt to consider differences between individuals and to modify practices to meet every student's needs. This is a higher-order instructional skill that requires deep levels of perception and experience in order to select the range of modifications that are appropriate for diverse groups of learners. However, novice educators can begin to differentiate the range of learning experiences through their planning and by identifying ways that a task can be simplified or made more challenging.

The elements of effective instruction outlined above must rest on a platform provided by good positioning, proximity, and perception, for these allow teachers and coaches to really see what is happening. This enables them to

- assess performance and progress,
- provide feedback,
- modify practices or games where needed,
- provide acknowledgement and praise,
- manage a group and keep them on task,
- decide when progression is needed, and
- ensure good pacing.

Above all, good positioning and perception ensure that the teacher or coach is 'with it', that they know what is going on at all times and can even anticipate problems before they arise. These are vital competencies for any teacher, but especially for those using Play Practice, since this approach requires an interactive teaching style based on the perception of student needs.

Good positioning is a critical facet of effective instruction because it underpins many other aspects of this complex task. Unfortunately, it is easy for novice teachers to get caught in the midst of groups, where they can only see what a small percentage of their students are doing. This can be improved through a conscious effort to position themselves on the periphery of the group and by maintaining an open field of view of all students.

Proximity, or the location of the teacher in relation to individuals or groups, can markedly influence student behaviour. So simply moving closer to students can improve their effort and performance.

However, while it is relatively easy to make good positioning second nature, perception—that is, being able to really see what is happening—is a much more difficult task, especially when working with large groups. Novice sport educators may find the story of the silk scarf valuable. Fighter pilots in World War I began wearing silk scarfs to protect their necks from the inevitable chafing from the collars of their uniforms as they continually twisted their heads to check the airspace above, below, and behind their aircraft. Sport educators have a much less demanding task, but this simple story may remind them of importance of continually scanning the environment so they can stay 'with it'.

Provide Feedback

Learning is enhanced when players get positive and useful feedback about the quality of their performance. Feedback is a critical factor in the learning and teaching process. No matter how effectively the instructor presents the model or task, initial attempts by beginners will rarely be completely successful, and far fewer will be perfect. The task for educators is twofold. First, they must provide a supportive environment where students learn that persistence is the key to success. Then they must provide feedback that will help them bring their performance more closely into line with the required model. This is because practice does not make perfect, it only makes permanent! Practising the wrong thing will only help learners become good at doing the wrong thing!

So, practice alone makes permanent; only plenty of perfect, pertinent, and purposeful practice will make a performance perfect!

Feedback is built into many sporting tasks. For example, in golf, the flight path, direction, and distance of a shot all give players immediate input about the effectiveness of their stroke. This built-in feedback, generally termed *knowledge of results,* is an important aspect of effective learning. To maximise the effects of this simple form of feedback, instructors should first try to help learners understand the relationship between their performance and its result. In effect, instructors are helping them become reflective golfers. Second, they should try to structure situations that provide learners with immediate knowledge of the results of their efforts. This means that they should employ distance markers, targets, and goals of all kinds.

However, while knowledge of the result of a specific performance is valuable, it does not tell the learner why a shot was fluffed or the ball was hooked viciously out of bounds. Even more importantly, it does not tell beginners what to do in the future to avoid these problems. Feedback that helps students understand why a particular result occurred and then suggests a remedy is termed *augmented feedback.*

Providing useful augmented feedback is a difficult task. It is another higher-order instructional skill because it involves many competencies, some of which can only be developed through experience. To begin the process, the instructor needs a theoretical understanding of a perfect model of the activity, along with a clear visual picture of it in their mind's eye. This may be a composite of the visual images of a vast number of performers distilled into a single clear picture of what they believe to be best practice in the activity.

A clear verbal model of the activity is also important. It should include key phrases or cues that can be used to convey a precise meaning of what is required to the student. The best verbal cues convey an effort or rhythm quality, as well as defining the spatial elements of a specific movement pattern. Most experienced teachers and coaches have a fund of such cues, so the enthusiastic novice should make a special effort to acquire as many as possible.

Ideally, a teacher needs the kinaesthetic, or feeling, picture of the activity that can only come from having personally performed at a good level. However, since this is not always possible, they can compensate by developing special verbal abilities and mastering the key progressive training drills and practices.

Next, the teacher must be able to see what the performer is doing. Seeing in this sense implies being at the right place and angle to see, and then knowing what to look for. The reality is that it is not easy to observe a sequence of high-speed movements of different body parts. If they are to be effective, they must do the following:

- Compare what they see with their model of ideal performance.
- Identify the differences between the model and that performance.
- Determine whether the differences are significant or not.
- Decide on the causes of the differences.
- Determine teaching and feedback priorities.
- Ensure transfer of the modified technique into the real situation.

Providing feedback enhances students' learning.

Occasionally, it may be necessary to repeat the initial presentation for the whole group if it is clear that the majority are having problems. Usually, it is only necessary to help individual players or small groups who have not grasped what is required. This can be done in the following ways:

- Restating the cues.
- Trying different cues that contain the same message.
- Demonstrating the task again, perhaps from a different angle.
- Providing intermediate progressions.
- Letting students act as 'feedbackers'.

It is possible to provide feedback visually, verbally, or, in specific situations, through physical manipulation. One of the major problems for teachers is that they have to work with large groups, so providing individual feedback is difficult. As indicated previously, one strategy that has proven successful is to use students to provide feedback whenever possible. Students are assigned a very specific role, one which they can undertake even while participating themselves. Their assignment may be simply to carefully watch their partner and remind them

of one or two of the key teaching cues that were stressed in the original presentation. In this role, they can also encourage and acknowledge their partner, which contributes to a positive class climate. Obviously, if they prove that they can do more than this, their role can be expanded. This process not only develops more reflective participants but also opens up the possibility of having a sport educator's role in the future.

Players also need tactical feedback. This is where the process of focusing becomes vital. However, while it is relatively easy to assess the performance of a single player, it is much more difficult to see the totality of the complex, fast-paced, ever-changing action picture of even a small-sided game. This is definitely a higher-order teaching skill, but it is what makes teaching games such a fascinating and challenging business. It is best to provide tactical feedback by using freeze replays. This ensures that learning is contextual, immediate, and relevant. While indirect teaching approaches seem to be advantageous in these situations, it is also possible to help players understand the tactical implications of a game situation with a direct teaching method.

The critical fact is that instructors can only *see* in this sense if they know what to look for and if they have the capacity to direct their observation to what is really important. To do this, they need a precise model or template of the game to give purpose and focus to their seeing. Effective instruction is therefore based on a thorough understanding of the fundamental nature, strategy, and tactics of a game. For lacrosse, soccer, and other invasion games, these are encapsulated in the 'principles of effective tactical play', which provide the necessary template for intelligent observation and thus help to simplify the process of analysis. Since there is no time during a session to dig out half remembered and undigested ideas on tactics, the concepts involved must continually be revisited and applied if they are to be of real value.

Finally, it is important to remember that while elite performers are ready to accept critical feedback if they know it will help them to improve, beginners are often already anxious because they are attempting something new and so need continual positive reinforcement. If a critical comment must be made, it is important to precede it with some kind of empathetic or moderating statement, like 'That was a really good try. Now, let's see if we can. . .'

Above all, as they deal with the unending and problematic challenges of helping young people strive for excellence, teachers must be masters of the instantaneous response. Here, professional and personal skills must be fused to ensure an immediate and effective response to every one of the interactions with their charges. This is demanding because there is usually little time for reflection and carefully considered responses. It is also crucial, because in that instant of communication, the true values and motives of an individual instructor may be revealed. In a flash, youngsters can discover what their mentor really thinks about them and their performance, no matter what words are spoken.

Praise Performance

Youngsters will practice more purposefully when their efforts, improvements, and successes are recognised and acknowledged by significant others. While praise is enough to motivate many students, rewards for a good effort in a specific attempt or a session that are more concrete can have a dramatic influence. These can range from symbolic awards to small but permanent trophies awarded in a presentation ceremony as part of the culminating activities at the end of a unit or a season. When possible, every student should receive some kind of award. These should be generally positive and related to overall performance, but they can be humorous or even playfully critical. The award of trophies such as the golden ball, racquet, arrow, tenpin, or soccer boot are especially effective because they ensure that successes are remembered for some time, if not forever! If the nature of these awards is announced at the beginning of the unit, they will almost certainly enhance performance right through the end of the unit.

Another approach to providing praise that has been found to have a profound effect on performance is to encourage the development of 'commentators' in a group. These individuals are encouraged to act just like television commentators—naturally, geared to noting the positives—even down to the award of plays of the day.

Project Poise, Patience, and Passion

These qualities on the part of the teacher tend to help learners feel comfortable, thus encouraging positive participation. This is not always easy because teachers themselves often live complex lives, full of stress and occasional trauma. This means that they do not always arrive at a session in a positive, cheerful frame of mind. 'Know yourself' has always been good advice. If these situations arise, it is better to tell the youngsters that you are a little out of sorts and to let them play freely with as little intervention as possible for a while. Perhaps their energy and commitment will revitalise you and bring a sense of perspective to your day! And never underestimate the effect of a teacher's passion on enthusing young people.

Effective Teaching Methods

As suggested earlier, as teachers grow in competence and confidence, they can expand the working model of instruction outlined previously to develop more advanced teaching and coaching capabilities.

In his 1966 book *Teaching Physical Education: From Command to Discovery,* Muska Mosston introduced the notion of a spectrum of teaching 'styles'. Examples of these approaches are outlined in the next sections, providing some information about each instruction method and illustrating how they can be combined in an eclectic way to facilitate student learning. Within any style, it is possible for the teacher to provide information or to use questioning in order to engage learners in the process of inquiry.

Command

At first glance, the command style, with its emphasis on total teacher control, does not appear to have much to commend it. Yet, when teaching activities such as the throwing events in track and field or sports like golf and archery where there is a risk of injury, we recommend its use! With this approach, the teacher can ensure that no one moves into the danger zone until every implement has been delivered, every arrow launched, or every ball hit. Because of the possibility of children making careless and potentially life-threatening mistakes in these activities, the teacher *has* to be in total control.

However, this experience could be preceded by discussion with the students about the dangers involved so they can appreciate why this approach is appropriate and understand the need for personal responsibility. In these teaching situations, it is also possible to integrate other methods, such as peer teaching, within the overall command framework.

Task Approach

The task approach is the most commonly used instructional style in both teaching and coaching. This is because it can be employed in a very flexible manner to present techniques, tasks, or problems. While a problem-solving strategy could be used to help players develop technical ability, the Play Practice position is that the task approach *should* be used where there is clearly one best way of executing a technique, when there is a specific rule that needs to be observed before a game begins, or when youngsters need specific information if they are to play successfully.

Indeed, when activities are potentially dangerous, the approach should be not only direct but also controlled and progressive. This applies to activities such as Olympic gymnastics, skiing, diving, and swimming, but also to many of the disciplines of track and field, even when working models are introduced. However, because it is not as tightly controlled as the command approach, students can enjoy considerable autonomy.

Individualised Instruction

It is possible to use an individualised method to develop technical ability in a variety of activities like personal health and fitness training, weight training, swimming, and some elements of track and field. This method allows students a considerable degree of autonomy and choice, since they are able to contribute to the design of their program, therefore catering specifically to their needs and interests.

A classic example of the value of this approach occurred when a pre-service female student was assigned to teach Australian Rules football with a group of 16-year-old boys. Not only did they believe that they knew more about the game than she did, but when she met the group, they also all towered over her! Of course, she could have had them sit every time she wanted to address them, but she would have risked creating a farcical situation.

Instead, she simply handed out individual cards that outlined the tasks to be completed in the first part of each lesson. These required students to complete a series of interesting technical challenges: for example, kicking at a goal from different angles and distances. Now she was free to interact with individual students as they completed their tasks. She could bring her personality and enthusiasm into play as she built a positive relationship with the boys. During this phase, she allocated playing positions for the game to follow so that the lesson flowed smoothly. She was able to define the lesson on her terms, and the kicking challenge also made it obvious to all involved that improvements could be made. Students enjoyed the freedom of carrying out the challenges and playing in minigames during the lesson. This naturally reduced the pressure on the teacher from that point on.

Reciprocal Instruction

Reciprocal instruction is also called peer teaching. Again, it is better to see this as a method that can be integrated into other approaches within the lesson. Reciprocal instruction can help resolve one of the biggest problems in teaching—that is, the provision of feedback. Here, because of the problems of observing and analysing the performance of 30 students or more once they start practising, the teacher is often unable to provide the support youngsters need at this point.

The method is simple. Instructors can provide up to three specific cues when they present the task. When students move off to practice in pairs, these cues become the focus for their observation and feedback as they watch each other. Because they are forced to think about the key elements of technique as they provide feedback, this process may be as powerful a factor in the learning process as actual physical practice! Whether this is the case or not, students clearly enjoy the interaction and responsibility of this approach. In this role, students do not take on the role of the teacher but are simply feedbackers. However, it is possible to extend reciprocal instruction into a more detailed peer-coaching method in situations with more experienced students where this may be appropriate.

Small Groups

The small-group method is simply an extension of partner teaching. It can be used when it is clear that the activity requires two or more players. An example is the 3v3 cricket sector games that can be set up with one batter, one feeder, and one feedbacker or commentator, with players taking on each role in turn. Meanwhile, the fielders collaborate to solve the problem of how best to cover the fielding space in the game. This method can be used effectively in activities where students are invited to create their own sequence of movement (in dance or gymnastics, for example) or where they work together to design a practice, game, or routine.

Guided Discovery

The guided discovery approach is best used when there are several possible solutions to a technical or tactical problem, especially when it is important for students to understand underlying principles. This method naturally involves questioning. For example, in soccer, students might be asked to work out how to control the ball as it is directed to them. Players quickly identify the fact that they must move towards the flight of the ball and try to catch it with any part of the body except the hands. They also work out that it is best to use larger body surfaces, such as the chest, torso, thigh, and the inside or sole of the foot to control it.

Teachers and coaches could use a similar approach to help young players gain an understanding of the concepts of line and length in both batting and bowling in cricket. However, guided discovery is most valuable when helping players understand tactical principles, since they may be able to generalise this knowledge and apply it to any situation in the game or even to other related games. Here, the teacher can use both clarifying and probing questions to explore tactical options in order to help students develop their understanding of the principles of play.

One of the major advantages of Play Practice is that understanding can be guided by the way a game is shaped. For example, the four-goal play practice detailed in the soccer section not only introduces the principle of width but also gives players the opportunity to immediately begin to exploit it and rewards them when they do! At the same time, it focuses attention on the striking ability needed to play the ball across the field. This both ensures that learning is contextual and saves considerable time.

Problem Solving

Problem solving is a valid and effective method, particularly when there are many ways to complete a task. This is especially true when the movement responses are drawn entirely from the student, as in activities such as educational gymnastics, movement education, music and movement, and dance drama. Here, problem solving allows children to respond to a carefully presented problem or a well-chosen piece of music in any way they like. It is then up to the teacher to extend and improve these early responses through intelligent intervention. In this situation, with process more important than product, the time taken to complete a task is irrelevant. No one way is best.

When problem solving was applied consistently across a range of activities, such as educational gymnastics and dance in the English secondary schools of the 1960s and '70s, it drew amazing performances from children. However, it must always be remembered that the teachers involved at that time had an excellent preparation for using this approach, and they were employing it in almost all of their work. In a sense, the method was the curriculum.

It can be highly effective with responsive students and in the hands of a gifted teacher with the following habits and qualities:

- Really understands the curriculum area
- Creates a positive environment
- Poses problems that children find interesting and challenging
- Has well-developed skills in observation and analysis
- Can assist all children to develop their initial responses

However, the problem-solving strategy has several limitations:

- It demands higher-order teaching skills, especially in observation and questioning.
- Children need to become accustomed to this approach.
- It cannot be used effectively in a single session.
- It will only work with classes of children where there are likely to be few, if any, management issues.
- Unless it is used skilfully, it can lead to a considerable amount of time being wasted.

For these reasons, and especially when time is limited, we believe that problem solving is rarely an effective approach for teachers, especially inexperienced beginners.

Play Practice applies a learner-centred approach where teachers and coaches use whichever methods will best help students become competent and confident players who want to participate in sport and to begin a process of incorporating physical activity into a healthy lifestyle.

As teachers and coaches gain experience, it is possible for them to expand their ability to use a variety of teaching methods in their practice. This can include using an eclectic array of teaching methods within the various learning episodes in a lesson or during a coaching session. For example, when teaching soccer, the following range of methods might be used:

- A task approach to introduce the primary rules of the game
- An individualised method to learning how to run with the ball and control it with the feet
- A partner approach to providing feedback as players learn how to kick and stop the ball
- A command method to introducing heading
- A small-group approach to playing as a member of a team
- A guided discovery approach to examine the rules in play, emphasise the importance of fair play, and help youngsters understand the principles of attacking and defending
- A problem-solving approach to consider the importance of strategy

Summary

Helping young people meet and overcome challenges, even ones as apparently simple as controlling a ball, is a complex process. Sport educators must motivate, encourage, urge, and sometimes even insist that youngsters make a determined effort to master a task, without ever putting them at risk or creating a situation that might alienate them and drive them away from sport and physical activity. This is an art in which both the professional and personal skills of a teacher or coach may be stretched to the limit, where the line between the relative importance of process and product is very fine.

Finally, it is important to understand that becoming an effective teacher or coach is a process of evolution and development that will continue throughout one's career. So perhaps the most important attribute for those who become good teachers and coaches is that they be good learners!

part II
Play Practice in Action

Spoon feeding only teaches one how to recognise a spoon.

Anonymous

While the innovative ideas provided in part I can help teachers and coaches improve their performance, one of the critical elements in effective teaching and learning is what is termed *domain-specific knowledge.* In other words, if you are going to teach or coach a sport, you really need to understand that sport! Shulman (1987) refers to 'pedagogical content knowledge' as a combined knowledge of the specific domain (the sport) together with an understanding of learning and teaching it, and suggests that this is an important form of professional knowing for teachers (and coaches). In fact, the pedagogical content knowledge, along with a clear understanding of how to teach it to young people, should provide the foundation for every course preparing health and physical education teachers and should underpin every program of coach education. Inherent in this is a deep appreciation of learning theory that underpins professional practice.

Unfortunately, what would seem to be a fundamental requirement is not always met. This is particularly problematic in junior coaching where enthusiastic volunteers, often parents, with little experience of the sport are exposed to brief preparation courses lasting only a few hours. These courses rarely deal with the fundamental principles of effective pedagogy and often do not even give participants sufficient depth of understanding of the activity itself.

This would also appear to be an issue in the preparation of physical education teachers in many universities. Here, where practical involvement in physical activity and sport should be central in any program aimed at preparing teachers or coaches, it often survives only on the periphery. It is often outsourced to community agencies, segregated from pedagogy and other discipline areas in sports science, and rarely taught by senior faculty members.

David Kirk (2010) suggests that part of the challenge is to re-think the theory in sport pedagogy so that it is practice referenced and that its subject matter becomes grounded in the realities of life in classrooms and on the playing fields. Unfortunately, as we suggested above, sport pedagogy has gradually been devalued in many physical education teacher education programs in the English-speaking world. As a result, many graduates may lack the depth in pedagogical content knowledge and the relevant practical experience they need to become effective teachers. Indeed they may often be no better prepared for their roles than the original author of *Play Practice* was when he first began his career in 1957.

This problem is exacerbated by the fact that while coaches can usually specialise in one sport, teachers need a sound knowledge of a broad range of physical activity and sports. Clearly, pre-service teachers in HPE would benefit from actively participating in a broad range of sports and physical activities during their professional studies—a process that should continue as a lifelong engagement in physical activity throughout their professional careers.

With minor modifications the book uses the games classification suggested by Len Almond. This makes it possible to group similar activities together and to transfer an understanding of the principles of both tactics and pedagogy. However, it is important to recognise that the principles of pedagogy are constant, and while the tactics of games may be similar, the technical demands can vary enormously from one to another. So, although it is relatively easy to transfer a cognitive understanding of tactical principles between games such as soccer and field hockey, for example, it is usually impossible to transfer the technical element of skilled play from one to another.

Clearly, a book of this kind cannot present a detailed explanation of how to teach or coach every sport. In fact some sports, such as tenpin bowling, offer only limited opportunities to use the Play Practice approach, while others such as those involving intense body-contact or great tactical complexity are dealt with simply by showing how they can be introduced to beginners. Youngsters who then become interested in these activities should be encouraged to move into a coaching environment where they can be taught how to play safely.

The critical fact, often forgotten by those offering advice on how to teach and coach them, is that the major sports are highly complex activities. As a result, the process of introducing them to youngsters can be immensely challenging, even for experienced teachers and coaches. Consider, for example, just three of the possible variables that may affect a lesson:

- *The learning context.* This can vary immensely from one school to another. While the time available is an especially important factor, the quality of the facilities, the amount of equipment, and the size of classes all influence what can be achieved.

- *The specific group of students.* Bear in mind that every class is unique and that the dynamics of even two classes in the same school or in the same grade may be completely different.

- *The experience, skill, personality, and confidence of the teacher.* This is the most critical variable in a learning situation. Unfortunately it is a variable that often appears to be ignored in much of the research in the field of education.

However, both the physical education curriculum and the sport program will also be influenced by the following:

- The value placed on physical education by the school administration

- The socioeconomic status, attitudes, and values of the local community

- The geography of the area and its weather patterns

- The sport and recreation opportunities available in the community, along with the prevailing sport culture

- The relative importance of the physical education program in the school's athletics (inter-school sport) program

- The relationship between the staff of those two programs, especially the philosophy of the head coach in key sports

All of these determine the context in which a physical education and sport program operates. To some degree or another, they will influence the quality of both. However, the critical factor in what can be achieved is usually the competence, energy, and enthusiasm of the physical education staff.

Given the wide range of variables that will impact what can be achieved in any teaching environment, it would be unrealistic to provide specific lesson plans. So while advice on lesson planning is provided below, every teacher must strive to become a true professional, able to assess each group of children and each unique situation they meet, draw together their knowledge of the activity, and then set about creating effective learning situations using their individual knowledge, skill, personality, and enthusiasm. This is no easy task, but it is immensely satisfying when one gets it right!

So after assessing the group and considering the context in which they will be working (especially the time they have available), teachers must determine the priorities for learning and their teaching approach. As we continually restate, while play practices can be used to develop any or all of the elements of skilled play detailed in chapter 2, the initial emphasis with young players should always be on playing fairly and building psychological resilience. Then, depending on the nature of the activity, the critical question to be resolved is whether to begin with games and challenges that help youngsters to improve their technical ability or to focus on developing the components of games sense through carefully modified games. Clearly, this requires a clear understanding of the sport and of the relative importance of the element of skilled play required for initial success. Since this is a critical part of the teaching and coaching process, novice teachers may need to return to chapter 2 to help them to develop their ability to analyse various activities.

It is obviously natural for pre-service and beginning teachers in HPE to feel more comfortable teaching certain sports, usually those they have enjoyed playing themselves. While they must continually try to deepen their understanding of those sports, if teachers are to become really effective professionals, they should try to broaden both their experience and their understanding of sport. Ideally, they should become serious students of all of the major sports and games!

This may take time and focused effort. However, it can be an enjoyable and intellectually stimulating process, one that is thoroughly recommended. In fact actually learning to play another sport (skiing and golf are excellent examples) can be a salutary experience, even for experienced teachers. It can engender a valuable sense of humility in many who may take for granted their skill in sports they have played for years!

We believe that it is possible for all committed teachers to become experts in teaching virtually any aspect of sport and physical activity if they are prepared to grow with their students. For example, Alan, whose only experience of pole vaulting was a 30-minute session at Loughborough College in 1957 (when he cleared only 8 feet, 11 3/4 inches, or under 3 metres), went on to coach athletes to Olympic level and to write the definitive book on the teaching and coaching of this challenging event.

Once the issue of priorities has been resolved, the next challenge is to determine the sequence of learning and, from this, to develop the outline of a curriculum unit. Teachers and coaches should always bear in mind the constraints under which they will operate. It is important to emphasise the notion of an outline, not a detailed sequence of lesson plans. The first lesson should be inked in, the second strongly penciled in, the third lightly penciled in, and so on.

This reflects the reality that every lesson is a happening, a one-off, a unique event that is affected by even more variables. As every experienced teacher knows all too well, a lesson on a Monday morning or a Friday afternoon can be completely different from one with the same class mid-morning on Wednesday. A windy day, the first snowfall of the year, or any week prior to or following a holiday will all alter the dynamics of a group, as will any even minor personal tragedy affecting a class. As a result, priorities may need to be changed over the course of several lessons. This process is based on a revolving, expanding analysis of the needs of students, a process that in turn depends on continuous, perceptive observation on the part of the teacher. Again, this is not an easy task, but when it is successfully accomplished, it helps to confirm that you are truly a professional in your field.

As they go through the process of developing units of work and preparing lesson plans, young teachers should find the recommendations provided in the practical sections to be of value. Fortunately, this process becomes easier every time it is repeated. A lesson plan pro forma has been provided (below) as a possible guide for planning. It has been used successfully by pre-service teachers in HPE at the University of South Australia for many years as a framework for planning opportunities for student learning. The pro forma is connected to key concepts from Play Practice to assist beginning teachers and coaches to develop their professional capabilities. For example, pre-service teachers refer to the elements of skilled play when planning student learning outcomes, and they refer to the Ps of pedagogy model when identifying their teacher outcomes. The back page of the pro forma is orientated to shaping and focusing a sequence of engaging learning experiences to enable student learning.

If you don't know what else to do, play a game! Preferably, begin with a small-sided game of the kind recommended throughout this book and then ensure that it is simplified or shaped to achieve specific outcomes. Here it is important to note that we are not suggesting an approach, long regarded with suspicion by many in the physical education fraternity, where unprofessional teachers simply throw the ball out and allow the students to play the game with limited, if any, supervision. Rather, the 'game becomes the teacher', because if properly 'shaped', it generates a range of learning opportunities. As long as the principles put forward in this work are understood and applied, it is easy to create very positive learning experiences, especially when freeze replays are used to focus attention on either technical execution or elements of games sense.

So this is the process:

Plan

- Consider where the students are in terms of their background, interests, prior experience, and ability.

- Analyse the activity involved, perhaps using the information provided in chapter 2.

- Determine what might be possible to achieve in the context in which you are working.

- Decide what to emphasise with this particular class or group and then develop an outline of what you believe can be achieved.

- Consider which culminating activities to aim for and what prizes, such as the golden boot, to offer.

- Plan the first session.

Teach the lesson

- Begin with a simplified or shaped game, as closely related to the real game as possible, or introduce a challenge involving important techniques. Allow time to observe the situation and note the overall level of performance and participation. Provide encouragement, but only intervene if major problems arise. Make a note of the more experienced players so that they can be used in various roles later.

- Decide what needs to be improved. With beginners this is easy to predict, but with experienced players it may require considerable analysis and reflection.

- Set up specific play practices that will help the group progress most quickly.
  - Shape the learning environment by manipulating key variables.
  - Focus the practice by re-emphasising key concepts, cues, or the key question.
  - Enhance the quality of performance by employing strategies that maximise enjoyment and maintain learner commitment.

- Stand back and observe. Acknowledge effort and participation, and provide feedback. Decide if further progression is needed, and use various methods to facilitate this while catering for the diversity of learners.

- Include an interesting culminating activity for the end of the session. Always try to end the session on an upbeat note.

Reflection is an important process undertaken by teachers and coaches and it is essential for continuous improvement in professional practice. Teaching and learning are highly complex processes, so for novices who are learning to teach or coach, mistakes are an inevitable and important part of the learning process. Novice educators must therefore be supported to facilitate their learning of the reflective process. It is possible to begin the reflective process simply by asking the teacher or coach to review how the lesson went in terms of student safety, individual participation and improvement, levels of engagement, and enjoyment. The reflective process can be completed in a more formalised manner by including a systematic review of both the student learning and the teacher outcomes following the lesson. In this reflection teachers and coaches can include evidence to support their claims and they can begin to link theory with practice. The challenge for novices is to go beyond simply describing what happened in the lesson and to begin to incorporate a deeper level of reflective evaluation. This process includes interpreting what happened and confronting the reasons why this might have occurred before considering what they might do differently next time.

Focus sheets (three examples are included at the end of this section) can also be used to broaden and deepen the level of critical reflection because they contain a range of questions associated with the dynamic constraints associated with learning. The strategies outlined previously have proved to be significant in building personal confidence and competence in undertaking the reflective process with pre-service teachers at the University of South Australia.

With growing experience, teachers can give more time to shaping and focusing specific play practices in order to progress individual student learning. Remember that Play Practice can be used in an ad hoc manner, with ideas presented in this book incorporated into the teacher's normal teaching or coaching pattern. If ideas work, try them again and add another innovative element. In this way, it is possible for teachers to gradually build towards the Play Practice approach without completely throwing away their previous methods.

LESSON PLAN PRO FORMA: Health and Physical Education

The template below outlines an introductory lesson for lacrosse with beginning pre-service teachers. As teaching experience grows the guiding headings in the student learning outcomes and the teacher outcomes can be removed or applied in a flexible way.

Name: **Time:** 9:00-9:50   **Date:**

Activity: Lacrosse session 1   **Class / Year:** Year 6/7

Equipment: Grip pads (16) , lacrosse sticks (16), lacrosse balls (16), cones (16)

Student learning outcomes: **Evidence of learning** *The students will . . .*	Teacher outcomes: *The teacher will . . .*
Aspects of skilful play: Demonstrate the techniques of scoop, carry, throw, and catch in individual and partner challenges. Show games sense by applying the primary rules in the end-zone game. Become familiar with the game structure of lacrosse. **Personal responsibility:** Demonstrate responsibility to play fairly in games. **Social:** Work collaboratively by encouraging and helping in small teams and pairs. **Affective:** Enjoy participation and build resilience by persisting with challenges.	*Ps of pedagogy:* Position self to the periphery of the class. Provide clear demonstration of task. Acknowledge individual students and group at the end of each learning experience. **Management:** Ensure sticks are on ground during demonstration. Acknowledge listening behaviours. **Presence:** Vary the tone of voice.

	Specific learning outcomes *(Students will . . .)*	Activity (shape + method + enhancement)	Organization (shape)	Focus (teaching cues or questions)	Time
Introduction	Engage in and enjoy an active warm-up. Show responsibility for rules. Review key values: effort, fair play.	**Tail Tag** Tuck tag into back of shorts. Avoid losing tail. Protect with body only; no hands allowed. If you get a tail, return. How many tails can you get in 30 s?	Include a visual of the learning task, the dimensions of the space, position of students, etc.	*Keep eyes up.* *Watch out for others.*	9:00-9:05 (5)
	Apply rules (games sense). Demonstrate responsibility to play fairly. Become familiar with the game structure of lacrosse.	**Endzone with grip pads 4v4** One-on-one to free ball No contact (maintain arm's distance) 4-s carry limit Other rules to be introduced in game: scoring, restarting play, rotating goalie Modify rules (possession in each half) if necessary		Key rules emphasise effort and fair play. *How did you show that you were free?*	9:05-9:15 (10)

	Specific learning outcomes (Students will . . .)	Activity (shape + method + enhancement)	Organization (shape)	Focus (teaching cues or questions)	Time
Development	Demonstrate personal responsibility for safe management of the stick. Develop techniques of scoop, carry, throw, and catch.	**Individual challenges:** Control the stick. Hand position apart. Scoop and carry. Lift ball and catch in air.		Carry Hold stick upright near shoulder. Catch Stick target out in front, eyes on ball into the stick.	9:15-9:25 (10)
	Develop techniques of scoop, carry, throw, and catch. Work collaboratively with a partner.	**Partner challenges:** Hand feed + catch Move + catch and carry, then throw over increased distance. **Partner target game:** Scoop, carry to cone, and then throw gates. Combine to score 5 goals.		Throw direct stick head towards target.	9:25-9:40 (15)
	Apply rules (games sense). Demonstrate responsibility to play fairly. Scan the field and run with the ball.	**End zone with grip ball pads or lacrosse sticks (depending on the group):** Prime rules		*What do you do when you get the ball? What were the key rules? What do you do when defending?*	9:40-9:48 (8)
	Review session.	**Acknowledge:** Effort and responsibility			9:48-9:50 (2)

The following chart provides a framework for guiding the process of reflection.

Teacher outcome:	
Reflective evaluation Evidence	Future practice
Student outcome:	
Reflective evaluation Evidence	Future practice

These three focus sheets illustrate the way that perceptive questions can be used to help students reflect on their experience.

> continued

FOCUS SHEET 1: AN OVERVIEW OF YOUR FIRST LESSON

1. What did you enjoy about the lesson?
2. Was there anything that you did not enjoy about the lesson?
   Provide information about this and how you felt.
3. Consider your interactions with students.
   How many individual students did you notice during the lesson?
   What were the reasons that you noticed them?
   Were you able to learn any names?
   Did you encourage and acknowledge the students for their effort, improvement, achievement, or co-operation with each other?
   How did you manage the interactions in the class? Were there any specific incidents?
4. Were there any times during the lesson that you felt uneasy about what was happening? If so, provide the details about the circumstance and why you felt that way.
   Did any of the follow situations apply to your context?
   Insufficient preparation on your part. If so, what happened?
   Selection of unsuitable activities. Explain.
   Poor pacing of the lesson. Detail.
   An incident within the group that you could not have foreseen. Describe it.
   A poor decision on your part during the lesson. Detail.
5. Teaching capability and presentation of the task (refer to handout):
   How did you position the group when presenting the task?
   How did you gain the attention of the group? What strategies did you use?
   Did you use a demonstration? Who demonstrated and how many times?
   Were your instructions to the students clear and concise?
   Can you think of an occasion when they seemed confused about what they were expected to do? Why might this have been the case?
   Were you able to step back and observe the group? What did you do next?
6. Consider student participation.
   Were all of the students actively involved for most of the time?
   If they were not involved, then what were they doing?
   Were you able to provide a physically and emotionally safe learning environment?
   Did you notice any students who appeared reluctant to be involved? If so, who were they and what could be some reasons for this?
   What did you do to encourage participation by everyone?
7. Management of the learning environment:
   In what way did your preparation for the lesson assist with management?
   How did you present the guidelines and procedures for the lesson?
   Were you consistent in the way that you interacted with the class?
8. What were the most important things (1-3) that you learned from this lesson? What will you do differently next time?
   Make sure that you include these in the outcomes for the next lesson plan.

FOCUS SHEET 2: PARTICIPATION

1. Did the learning environment promote safe participation?

   Provide examples of how you promoted physical and emotional safety.

   Were there any issues that arose around safety? If so, what were they and how did you manage them?

   Did you notice any put-downs or harassment in the class? How did you deal with it?

   Were you able to acknowledge individual students for showing personal responsibility for safety or for demonstrating positive support for others in the class?

2. Were all of the students actively involved during the lesson?

   Did you notice different levels of student involvement in particular activities? If so, what were they and why may this be the case?

   What did you do in order to encourage all children to participate?

   Did you notice individual differences in levels of movement competence and self-confidence in your group? Why might this be the case? What did you do to include and accommodate the diversity of students?

3. Were you able to acknowledge the students in your class?

   How frequently did you affirm their effort, persistence, and enthusiasm?

   How often did you affirm their responsibility, helpfulness, and co-operation with others?

   Did you highlight their improvements in technique, thinking, and decision-making skills?

4. Were there any times during the lesson that you felt uneasy about student participation?

   Provide details of the context and the reasons why you felt concerned.

FOCUS SHEET 3: LEARNING EXPERIENCES

1. Were the learning experiences relevant or pertinent to the nature of the activity?

   If so, then provide examples to illustrate this. If not, then provide reasons for including those activities.

   What did you notice about the students' level of engagement in the game-related tasks?

2. Were the learning experiences relevant to the needs and interests of the learners?

   Were any of the learning tasks too easy for the students? If so, what alerted you to this? What did you do about it?

   Were any of the learning tasks too difficult for some of the students? If so, what alerted you to this? What did you do about it?

   How interested were the students in participating in the activities?

   Did you notice any difference in participation within the class? If so, what did you notice and what may be possible reasons for these differences?

3. Self-testing challenges (indirect competition) and direct competition:

   How much time did you spend on tasks that involved direct competition with other students or groups? What did you focus on during this time?

   How did you address the issue of winning and losing?

   Were you able to promote personal success and effort in situations that involved direct competition?

How did the students respond to these activities? Did everyone respond in the same way?

Did you include any self-testing challenges in your lesson (indirect competition)? What type of challenges were they and what was your focus during these tasks?

Were you able to acknowledge all participants in these activities?

Do you think that all participants experienced success in these activities?

How did the students respond to these activities?

4. Did the activity topic favour any individual students or groups in the class?

Identify the students or groups who were advantaged and indicate the reasons why this may be the case.

Identify any students or groups who were disadvantaged and indicate the reasons why this may be the case.

Were you able to include and support the learning of all students in your class? How were you able to do this?

Have you noticed any specific examples of how social or cultural contexts (such as gender) affect individual perceptions and participation in physical activity?

seven

Teaching Field Invasion Games

Soccer, Field Hockey, Lacrosse, and Australian Football

> If an inexperienced teacher or coach is in any doubt about what they should do, they will never be wrong if they get their charges playing small-sided games!
>
> Rinus Michel

This chapter provides an introduction to teaching and learning field invasion games using the Play Practice approach. The focus is directed to the invasion games of soccer, field hockey, lacrosse, and Australian Rules football. However, the principles and the structure of key learning experiences can be applied to other related games including Gaelic football, futsal, and floor hockey.

While elite players in these games must possess all of the elements of skilled play detailed in chapter 2, teachers and coaches working with youngsters should focus on the development of games sense and technical ability while also emphasising fair play and the building of resilience. All of these games can be introduced through small-sided games that are initially modified to reduce their complexity. Soccer is easy because it can be played badly but enjoyably by beginners in 5v5 games on pitches with simple goals and no boundaries. Similar games can be used to introduce Australian Rules football but with tackling eliminated and simplified rules to promote safety and inclusion. Lacrosse can be introduced through the non-contact small-sided end-zone game of mitt-cross or grip ball lacrosse, where the technical demands

are minimised by removing the need to control the ball with the stick. Similarly, field hockey uses the foundations of the roll-ball game developed by Dennis Slade in *Stick 2 Hockey* (2003). The key to introducing all of these games is to ensure that players have plenty of space because at every level of play and especially with beginners, the following equation applies:

$$\text{Space} = \text{Time} = \text{More skilful play}$$

When this approach is used, youngsters can experience the joy of playing a game early on and begin to gain an understanding of the fundamental nature of the game, its rules, its tactics, and its mores almost incidentally as they play. They are then much more likely to make the commitment necessary if they are to progress to the next level. This usually involves the development of the technical ability needed to control and direct the ball.

Here, it is best to use a parallel approach, in which students move from the game into the practice of key techniques and back into the game. In this way, it is possible to maintain high levels of motivation while helping them to improve critical elements of skilled play. However, while games sense can be fast forwarded through the use of freeze replays and the process of focusing, both that element of skill and technical ability can be developed through the methods suggested in chapter 5.

While modified, small-sided games played on relatively large pitches can go some way towards reducing the complexity of the challenge the major games present to young players, teachers must understand the situation from the learners' perspective. Beginners especially are faced with the following problems:

- What do I do if my team has the ball?
- What do I do if my team loses the ball?
- What do I do if the other team has the ball?
- What do I do if the ball is loose?

Of course, this is the most difficult question of all for beginners:

- What do I do if I have the ball?

What should players who receive the ball do? They should try to advance the ball as fast as they can into a scoring position or get it to a team-mate ahead of them who may have a better chance to score. If neither is possible, they should give the ball to a team-mate in the best position to retain possession. This means that they must be encouraged to scan the field of play to decide what to do.

If attackers don't have the ball, what should they do? They should either get ahead of the ball player and into the space behind defenders as fast as they can to receive the ball or position themselves to support the ball player, thus helping their team retain possession.

What should defenders try to do? They should stop the ball from being pushed forward quickly, get on the goal side of attackers, and try to regain possession.

How should attackers react to these defensive moves? They should cut late and fast to the space where they want to receive a pass.

How do defenders counter this? They try to anticipate where the ball is going to be passed and then move to intercept it.

As defenders try to intercept passes, what do attackers do? They precede the cut to receive the pass with a fake move in the opposite direction, and then show where they want the ball delivered, on the side away from defender.

If defenders block the ball player's forward move, what do they do? They look to pass the ball to a player cutting from behind them into a dangerous position. While it can be any team-mate, it is often the player who gave them the ball in the first place. Termed a *give and go,* the *one–two,* or the *wall pass,* this is a very effective tactic in all of these games. The ball is passed

to a team-mate, and as the defender turns to track the ball, the attacker breaks past them for a return pass.

Simple though these questions may appear to be, they have occupied the minds of the greatest players and coaches in the world since games of this kind were first played! Fortunately, while they can give instructors an initial basis for questioning, the answer to each of them and the key to teaching and coaching these games can be provided by an understanding of the principles of tactical play. Anecdotal evidence suggests that this brilliant innovation in thinking about the tactics of a game, developed by English football coaches more than 60 years ago, can even be used by beginners to help them solve the problems they face, not only in soccer but also in the other games in this category. While each game presents its own challenges, our experience suggests that the concepts embodied in the principles of play can be applied to virtually all of the invasion games.

The principles of play begin with attackers trying to play behind defenders and thus penetrate the defence to score, while defenders naturally try to stop them. An application of these principles can best be illustrated by considering the moment when a change of possession occurs. As shown in figure 7.1, O1, who has just gained possession of the ball, must immediately try to penetrate the defence by shooting, passing, or running forward with the ball.

Since this moment of transition provides attackers with a good chance to outnumber defenders and to score, it is important for players in every invasion game to learn how to exploit it. In football other attackers must rapidly move into position to support the ball player and so provide a range of passing options in order to break down the defence. O2 and O3 move close to offer easy options, while O4 and O5 use the principle of width to outflank the defence and O6, O7, and O8 run forward to penetrate the defence or to create space for team-mates by pulling defenders away from critical areas.

Figure 7.1 also shows how the defence tries to counter these moves and stop any penetration. The nearest defender (D1) instantly tries to delay, channel, and pressure the ball so that it cannot be rapidly pushed forward. The time bought allows team-mates D2 and D3 to move goal side of the ball to provide depth in defence, while D4, D5, and D6 ensure concentration to guard important space and prevent easy penetration. Simultaneously, D7 and D8 move to balance the defence so that it cannot be outflanked. All defenders simultaneously pick up, track, and cover potential receivers. Because they are often under pressure, defenders must always play with control and restraint to avoid careless mistakes near the goal.

When faced with a well-organised defence, it may be necessary for attackers to do something unexpected, or improvise, in order to wrong-foot defenders and so create the time and space for a strike at the goal. An example of this is shown in figure 7.2, where O9 runs towards a pass from O7 as though to control the ball, thus drawing defenders to him, but instead allows it to run on to O11, who now has the space and time for an accurate strike at the goal.

The notion of a games player creating space and time may appear to be far-fetched. Yet by using the principle of mobility, they can do just that! Figure 7.3 shows a soccer scenario in which each attacker is marked and the crucial space is covered. However, if O1 and O2 make diagonal runs to the ball side of the pitch and take their defenders with them, they create space for O6 to make a blind-side run from a deep position, arriving unmarked with the time needed to ensure a skilful strike on the goal.

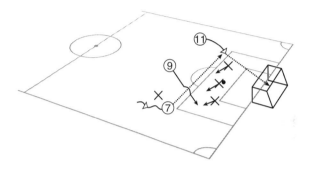

FIGURE 7.2 Attackers wrong-foot the defenders.

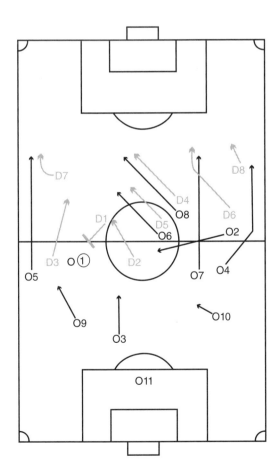

FIGURE 7.1 Penetrating the defence.

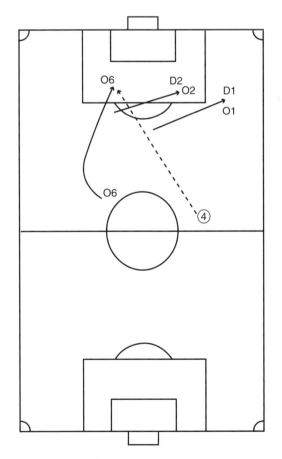

FIGURE 7.3 Blind-side run. O6 makes a strike on the goal.

As suggested in chapter 3, the biggest challenge when teaching these games is to try to bridge the gap between the cognitive play of beginners and the non-conscious, intuitive play of experts. Here, the critical factor is usually the time it takes a player to read the play, decide what to do, and then execute that decision in the chaos of a game. This problem is exacerbated when the execution involves controlling and directing the ball, either using a long stick with a small trapping surface (hockey) or a small net on the end of a long stick (lacrosse). While we can initially eliminate the problems for beginners by using the games of grip ball or roll ball, if they are to go on to play the real game, youngsters must be able to master the techniques involved in each game and use them to solve the problems posed by their opponents. The challenge therefore is to create learning environments where this is possible. Teachers and coaches should continually strive to reduce the demands on young players and to give them more time to execute the skill process.

While the development of the techniques of kicking and stopping, hitting and stopping, catching and throwing, or handballing is relatively straightforward, passing practices in which players combine technical ability with simple elements of games sense are essential. To do this, begin with simple games in the teaching grid shown in figure 7.4. Because the teaching

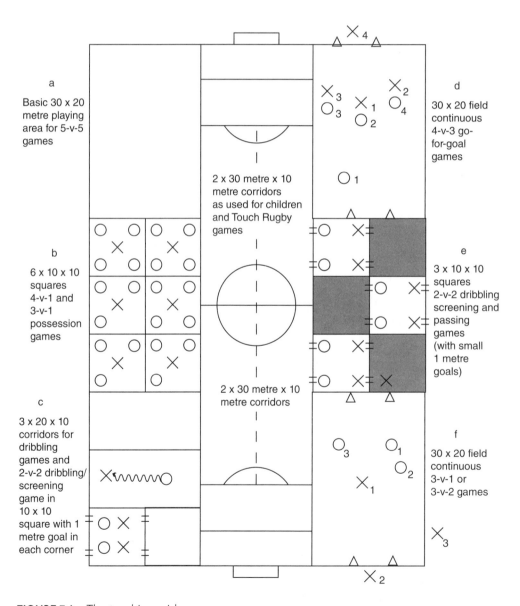

FIGURE 7.4 The teaching grid.

grid is one of the most useful aids in sport education, it is worth detailing this approach.

Indeed, because of the great value of the coaching grid, clubs and schools should mark out as many as possible, preferably on areas not normally used for match play. This may be difficult in field hockey, however, where the quality of the playing surface is very important. Having practice areas of this kind permanently in place can save an immense amount of time in formal sessions. They also provide areas for informal play.

The basic pattern is a 20-by-30-metre (70 by 90 feet) rectangle subdivided into six 10-by-10-metre (35 by 35 feet) squares. However, these dimensions can be modified to suit the specific abilities of any group.

Using cones, it is possible to create the following:

- *One 20-by-30-metre rectangle.* This can be used for 4- or 5-a-side games, which are critical for helping players begin to understand the value of the principles of play.

- *Six 10-by-10-metre squares.* These can be used to introduce the skill of passing through 4v1 and 3v1 games.

- *Three 10-by-10-metre squares, each separated by a 10-by-10 square.* These can be used where the nature of the practice means that balls are not as well controlled.

- *Three 20-by-10-metre corridors.* These can be used for both dribbling and passing practices.

- *Two 30-by-10-metre corridors.* These can also be used for dribbling and passing practices.

The basic 20-by-30-metre rectangle can also be used for the go-for-goal games described in a later section. These games are among the most valuable play practices of all.

Always remember that these dimensions are just a guide. Remember this equation:

$$\text{Space} = \text{Time} = \text{Skilled play (good decisions and good technique)}$$

So, be prepared to adjust the playing area to give youngsters as much space as they need to be successful. Also, ensure that attackers have a numerical advantage over the defenders in the early stages and that the size and nature of the

goal, a critical element in shaping the direction of learning, suits the outcomes for that session.

4v1 Keep-Away Games

Begin with 4v1 keep-away games played in 10-metre squares, as described in the introduction. At this point, use a parallel approach: Youngsters move from a game to practicing elements of technique and then quickly back into the game, where they begin to develop their games sense. In this way, they always apply their newly acquired technical ability in the real situation. This clarifies the link between technique and tactics and underlines the importance of improving technical ability. These games introduce the need to control the ball quickly, read the position of the defender, and then play the ball to the open team-mate. Players stay in position at the corner of the square to ensure good passing angles, which they need to learn if they are to use the principle of support. The aim is to make five consecutive passes. After that, the defender is switched. However, if the defender manages to touch the ball, he switches with the last player to play the ball. All subsequent play practices contain these elements as they gradually increase in complexity.

3v1 Keep-Away Games

This play practice requires players to use games sense to run intelligently to the open corner in order to make an angle for the pass. This is a simple but vital aspect of tactical play.

The logical progression from a 3v1 game would seem to be 3v2 or even 4v2. However, this will not work with inexperienced players. In a 3v1 situation, the ball players only need to play the ball past the single defender, so the pass is usually successful. This is because they can observe the single defender, even if only by watching his feet as they control the ball and direct it to a team-mate without lifting their vision.

However, with two defenders, the situation changes. The novice player must now both deal with pressure from the first defender and look up to see where the second defender is. This is a far more difficult task, so play will repeatedly break down. So when introducing a second defender, move to a 5v2 play practice played without boundaries. This provides more space and time for attackers to deal with the new challenge. Now they are more likely to be successful as they begin to improve their vision and ability to read the display, important elements of skilful play that must continually be emphasised. Teachers and coaches should encourage team-mates to support the ball player and to create triangles, for this is the smallest attacking unit that can ensure both width and depth in attack.

Note that the progression to a 5v2 game is crucial, because it encourages teachers and coaches to really think about the nature of skilled play from a beginner's perspective. It is especially important in soccer and hockey, where the ball is primarily played on the ground. In lacrosse and Australian Rules football, where it is easier to pick up and control the ball while scanning the field, successful progression can be made quickly from 5v2 to 4v2.

Go-for-Goal Games

These games, adapted from the fast-break drill used in basketball, are among the most effective play practices for teaching many games. Played in a 30-by-20-metre area, they provide enough space for small teams of young players while introducing the notion of playing in bounded areas. If the ball goes out of the play, the game restarts from that spot with a kick, throw, or push in.

3v1 Go for Goal

The format is simple: As three attackers (O) go for the goal, they are confronted by one defender (X) (see figure 7.5). Initially, the entire goal line should serve as the goal. To score, ball players must simply take it over the line and control it with the sole of the foot (soccer) or the stick (hockey). In other games, the ball could be directed to an attacker who has moved into an end zone just beyond the goal line. In this game, attackers should begin to apply the first principle of attack, penetration, to move the ball ahead as quickly as possible by running forward with it or passing it to an open player farther along. As defenders learn how to position themselves to prevent this, attackers must use the principle of support in attack to retain possession. They should then employ the principle of width to outflank the defender. In this way, youngsters quickly realise that playing in triangles in attack ensures both depth and width.

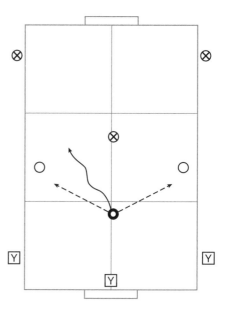

FIGURE 7.5 3v1 go for goal.

In this and in all go-for-goal games, defenders must work harder if the goal is the full extent of the goal line, as it is in the rugby codes. The smaller the goal, the easier the defenders' task, since they can funnel back to cover the area directly in front of a small goal. They cannot do this if the goal is the whole width of the pitch!

As players improve in their ability to control and direct the ball, scoring may become too easy. So to alter the balance between attack and defence, the goal can be whatever the teacher decides it is. Bear in mind that a large goal makes it easy for attackers to score with minimal passing, while a smaller goal forces them to pass more often to set up a shot. In this way, it is possible to use a small goal as a defender. In effect, a 3v1 game becomes a 3v1.5 game. However, a small goal may also encourage the lone defender to drop back and become a goalkeeper. Bring in a rule that if the defender forces the attackers to make five passes, he wins the game! This encourages the defender to work hard to delay the attackers.

After a score or a change of possession, the lone defender is now joined by two team-mates who have been waiting off the pitch. They begin to counterattack against a single player of opposing team Y, whose team-mates are out of play, until the ball is regained. They can then join in as attackers against O. In this way, the game flows continuously, with each player taking on the role of defender, who learns to delay and channel the ball so as to contain the attack for as long as possible.

With large groups, it is possible to have up to four teams playing in turn on each pitch. While this involves some waiting, the time need not be wasted, because teams can be encouraged to discuss how to improve their performance while they wait.

These go-for-goal games are valuable in teaching all of the invasion games, so when the 3v1 game is first introduced it is worth investing the time youngsters will need to begin to understand the sequence of attacking and defending because they can find this confusing in the beginning. However, once they do understand the way the game is played they will respond positively and then find it much easier to move onto the next game in the sequence.

3v2 Go for Goal

Now with a second defender providing the principle of depth in defence, the first defender can begin to pressure the ball player instead of merely trying to delay her (see figure 7.6). This means that attackers must pass skilfully and use the principle of support to retain possession along with the principles of width and mobility to pull defenders out of position and so create space for a score. If the ball is passed across the pitch, the defenders switch roles, with the covering defender moving up to pressure the ball and the other dropping back to cover. Again, defenders win the game if they can force attackers to make more than three or five passes.

4v3 Go for Goal With a Schemer

This is similar to the previous game, but now the third defender balances the defence, making outflanking moves more difficult while also providing additional cover (see figure 7.7). With this cover behind them, the first defender can put even more pressure on the ball player, while the second defender can play more aggressively and look for interceptions. Attackers must therefore be patient and counter this pressure by playing the ball back to the supporting player, ideally a star player designated as a 'schemer,' or quarterback. This player's role is to help the team retain possession while continually looking to change the point of attack. With three defenders to beat, attackers now begin to understand how clever movement without the ball or mobility with the ball (dribbling or carrying) can be used to create space and perhaps a scoring chance for a team-mate. Continuous 4v3 is much closer to the real game, and even experienced players may find it challenging.

The function of the schemer is similar to that of the point guard in basketball: that is, to bring other players into the game. This is often a good way to use better players, particularly with the

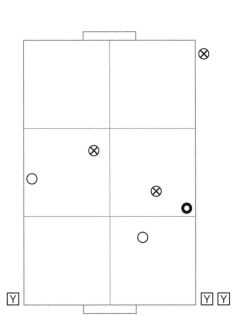

FIGURE 7.6   3v2 go for goal.

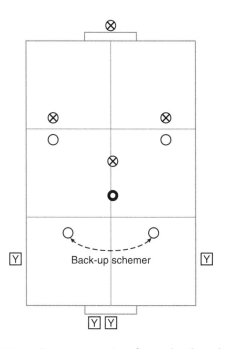

FIGURE 7.7   Continuous 4v3 go for goal with a schemer.

condition that schemers can never move in front of the ball in attack or that, in soccer for example, they can only have two touches of the ball. As players develop, instructors should give all of them an opportunity to take on this role, perhaps in tandem with a more experienced player who can coach them during play.

Although these play practices can be played as continuous go-for-goal games involving up to four different teams, they can also be played as normal games between two teams. Conditions such as taking the ball behind the goal before scoring in lacrosse can also be included to suit the specific features of each game.

Of course, sport educators should continually return to 5v5 games played on pitches that can gradually increase in size from the 30-by-20-metre (90 by 70 feet) rectangle. These are true learning laboratories for invasion games because they give young players the opportunity to apply all they have learned to that point. However, teachers and coaches should be ready to use freeze replays to focus play in order to cope with breakdowns in play as youngsters inevitably make one mistake after another.

Note that while the play practices outlined previously can be used to improve skilled play in all the games listed here, differences still exist between them, especially in terms of the techniques required to play them well. These issues are dealt with in the following sport-specific sections.

Association Football (Soccer)

Like all the great games of the world, soccer is simple in concept but complex in practice. While the aim is merely to place the ball in a goal positioned deep in enemy territory, players at the highest level must possess all of the elements of skilled play outlined in chapter 2.

However, despite this apparent complexity, soccer is a very easy game to introduce to beginners, in part because it is enjoyable even when being played badly! The key is to begin a game as quickly as possible. After outlining the basic rules relating to not handling the ball, kicking or tripping opponents, rugby-style tackling, and so on, instructors should begin

with small-sided (ideally 5v5) games on a pitch up to 30 metres (90 feet) long. They can set up crude goals using cones or even sports bags, but dispense with sidelines and goal lines. Play can continue behind the goals, although it is only possible to score from the front of the goal! In this way, children can play unchecked by any boundaries. This not only extends the playing area, thus providing more space and time, but also eliminates the need to introduce the rules for goal kicks, corner kicks, and throw-ins and ensures a free-flowing game. At this point, the goal should be large, and there should be no goalkeepers! In fact in these early stages, the goal can even be simply for an attacker to take the ball over the goal line.

With very young players these initial games can be played using volleyballs, which are ideal with beginners because they can be booted farther away from the pack. Players are then forced to chase the ball, which naturally causes them to spread out. This creates even more of the space and time essential as beginners attempt to become more skilful players.

As always in the early stages, the focus should be on the development of games sense, technical ability, fair play, and resilience. However, teachers must get used to the fact that with young players, especially beginners, all games and practices will appear absolutely chaotic in the early stages! Never forget Jean-Paul Sarte's comment 'Football is a simple game, only the opposition complicates it.' Let time, practice, and the use of freeze replays bring some semblance of order to the chaos.

Some children are not capable of executing even the most basic techniques of kicking the ball. So while elite players can easily pass the ball from a standing position to a team-mate up to 30 metres away using the inside of the foot, the instep, or even the outside of the foot, young players cannot. This immediately limits their options in a passing situation, since 'What is tactically desirable must be technically possible' and 'What is technically desirable must be physically possible!' This problem is exacerbated in physical education classes where students often do not wear soccer boots, which certainly restricts the power with which they can kick the ball. So, with beginners, teachers and coaches must accept low levels of ball control and kicking ability and remember that young players need much more time to execute the skill process than experienced players do.

As they assess the quality of play in the initial game, teachers can consider four possible options to improving performance. While one group may already know the game, another group may have never even seen it played before. The options shown in figure 7.8 include the following:

- Ball-control activities
- Kicking and stopping
- Introducing the skill required to pass the ball using the 4v1, 3v1, and 5v2 possession games outlined in the introduction
- Considering whether players are ready to move straight to go-for-goal games
- Play practices shaped to improve specific aspects of play

Ball-Control Activities

When groups have never previously kicked a soccer ball, simple ball-control activities can be used to build their confidence and their competence. Children each receive a ball and move around freely, pushing it with any part of the foot. On a signal, they freeze and control the ball with the sole of the foot. On the restart signal, they quickly move away in a different direction, ready for the next stop signal. This practice is simple indeed, but it can rapidly be expanded as players learn to keep the ball under control, using first the inside of the foot, the outside of the foot, then the inside followed by the outside, always stopping with a foot on the ball on the signal. As they improve, they should be encouraged to pull the ball backwards with the sole of the foot on the restart signal and then move off in the opposite direction.

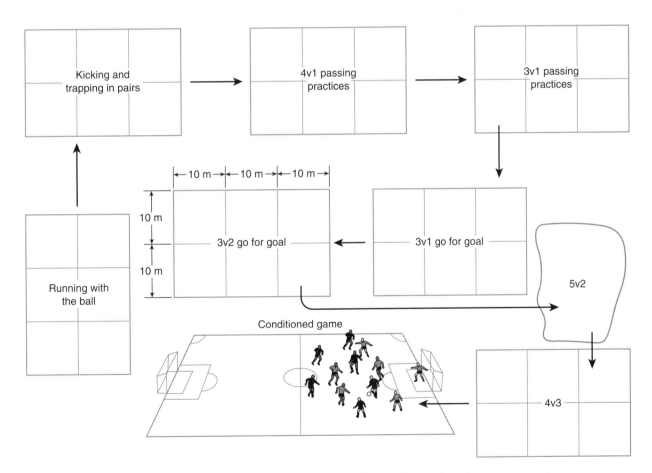

FIGURE 7.8 A possible progression for teaching soccer, depending on the students' previous experience.

Gradually, the size of the practice area can be increased and players can be encouraged to accelerate away after every change of direction. Next, they can work in pairs: One runs with the ball, continually changing direction and speed, while the other tries to follow the partner's movements as closely as possible. Next, they face one another at a distance of 10 to 15 metres (35 to 50 feet). One executes all the moves previously learned and the other must carry out a mirror image of those moves.

Kicking and Controlling Activities

The techniques required to kick and control the ball can be introduced when a group has a basic understanding of the nature of soccer.

In pairs 10 to 15 metres apart, players kick and stop the ball, using the instep or even the toe to kick it and the inside of the foot to control it. As figure 7.9 shows, the technique is simple: Players take a slightly angled approach from two or three steps, keeping the non-kicking foot level with the ball and the head down, then whip the kicking foot through to strike the ball, ideally with the instep. Note that although most texts recommend kicking with the inside of the foot, a technique used extensively by experienced players, many young players lack

the adductor strength to use this technique effectively.

Kicking practices should always involve a challenge of some kind, so use cones to create small goals as targets positioned midway between partners. Improving kicking ability must be an ongoing priority, and giving youngsters a chance to shoot at a real goal always ensures purposeful practice. However, change this activity as quickly as possible to passing practices, where players have to use their technical ability to solve the problem posed by an opponent. It is possible to start these initial passing games in the teaching grid described in the introduction to this section.

Go-for-Goal Games

As suggested in the introduction, these games, adapted from the fast-break drill used in basketball, are among the most valuable play practices for teaching many games. Played in the 30-by-20-metre (90 by 70 feet) area, they provide plenty of space for young players while introducing the notion of playing in bounded areas. If the ball goes out of the play, the game simply restarts with a kick in from that spot. Do not worry about corner kicks or the throw-in at this point.

FIGURE 7.9 Kicking technique using the instep.

Small-Sided Games

Continually return to 5v5 games played in the 30-by-20-metre rectangle. These games are true learning laboratories for soccer because they give young players the opportunity to apply all they have learned in competitive and realistic situations. However, the length of the pitch can gradually be increased; this forces players to lift their vision to read the play and encourages them to make longer passes to get the ball behind defenders and perhaps shoot over them at an extra-large goal 10 to 20 metres (35 to 70 feet) wide. This is important because if young players always practise in small spaces, they never improve their vision. At some point, 'rush goalies', who play as field players but are allowed to use their hands to stop direct shots at goal, can be introduced. This brings these games more into line with the real game of soccer. However, until some youngsters decide that they would like to specialise in that position, change goalies after every score.

Catching the Ball With the Body

As the size of the pitch is increased, the techniques needed to make longer passes and to control high balls can be introduced. In the Play Practice method, players are introduced to the principles of catching the ball with the body, obviously without using the hands. These principles can either be directly taught or drawn from the players using a guided discovery method. In brief, these are as follows:

- Move quickly towards the flight path of the ball.
- Choose a body surface to control the ball: The bigger and softer, the better!
- Present the body and let it give to catch the ball.

Throw-In

Combine ball-control practices with the technique of the throw-in. At this time, the rules and technique of the throw-in can be introduced and used to deliver the high balls needed to improve catching the ball with the body. Figure 7.10 shows

FIGURE 7.10 Throw-in.

the throw-in technique, where both feet are on the ground until the ball is released and the ball is thrown equally with two hands from over the head. This method encourages movement to the ball and the use of any body part to control it.

Thirds of the Field

All of these games, and especially the go-for-goal games, should continually be revisited to emphasise various elements of effective play. At some point it is important to introduce the concept of thirds of the field by marking a pitch as shown in figure 7.11. This instantly clarifies critical elements of games sense. Obviously, it is foolish to risk the ball near one's own goal (i.e., in the defensive third) by trying to beat an opponent in a dribble or by careless passing.

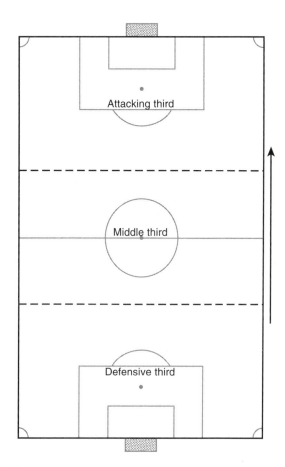

FIGURE 7.11 Thirds of the field.

if it sets up a scoring chance. Gradually other specific elements of technique, such as heading and dribbling, can be introduced as needed in the following manner.

Heading

Because of the possibility of injury if a ball is incorrectly headed, a direct teaching approach should be used. For example, when young players hold the ball themselves, they are forced to hit the ball with their foreheads, punching the head and shoulders forward powerfully while keeping their eyes on the ball. This practice eliminates the problems that occur if beginners are expected to head a ball lobbed to them by a partner. Inevitably in this situation, they lunge forwards and meet the ball with the top of their heads.

Of course, once they have mastered the basic technique using the direct method, they can move to heading a ball thrown by a partner (figure 7.12). From here, it is a simple step to

On the other hand, in the attacking third, it is clear that if there is any chance of scoring a goal, it may be worth risking the ball by taking on defenders in a dribble or by attempting risky but potentially damaging passes. Indeed, one of the critical lessons young players must learn is that few goals are scored in soccer unless attackers are prepared to risk possession of the ball. However, in a real game, tactics in the middle third may depend on a team's strategy for a particular game and the score line at any point. A team playing to maintain a lead or aiming for a draw may well be very cautious in the middle third, while one aiming for a win may take more risks both with passing and dribbling.

This is also an opportunity to introduce the notion of passing the ball into the space behind the defenders. It is easy to forget that while ball possession is important, the aim of attackers is to score goals. So, players must risk the ball if there is a chance of getting the ball behind defenders and thus taking them out of the play, especially

Strike the ball with the forehead

FIGURE 7.12 Proper heading technique.

have players running and jumping to meet the ball with a powerful header.

Once the working technique is mastered, it is possible to move to a game of throw, head, and catch. Teams of 4 or 5 players must head the ball across the goal line on a 20-by-30-metre (70 by 90 feet) pitch for a score. It always takes beginners a few minutes to grasp the sequence. After a jump ball to start, the player with the ball tosses it in the air for one of their team-mates to head forward. Another team-mate should catch it. This process is repeated until a goal is scored. The opposition can only gain possession if they manage to get their head to the ball at any time and if their header is caught by a team-mate.

Dribbling

Dribbling is another word used to describe two different phenomena in soccer. Our view is that it should only be used to describe a situation where the ball player is trying to beat an opponent, not simply running with the ball! For while running with the ball can be introduced in the very first session, dribbling past opponents should be introduced much later, after players understand the advantages of team play based on good passing.

Dribbling past a defender involves a combination of ball control and agility. It involves changing direction, changing pace, or a combination of both. These qualities can evolve naturally from the simple ball-control practices outlined earlier, where children learn to change direction and speed while retaining possession of the ball.

It is possible to play simple one-on-one dribbling games in a grid. Here, the attacker tries to get past the opponent to reach the goal on the other side of the grid. Players change over and repeat, playing the first to three goals. This activity is very tiring, but the necessary breaks give the teacher or coach a chance to draw out the key principles again. By continually changing opponents, a considerable amount of progress can be made.

As we suggested above, it is important for players to understand the purpose and place of dribbling because there is always the chance of losing possession when taking on an opponent. This is where dividing the pitch into thirds helps youngsters to understand that they should only try to dribble in the attacking third, where losing the ball is not going to cause major problems for their team. In this way players can begin to really appreciate the importance of tactical principles and understand why they should and should not do certain things in specific areas of the pitch.

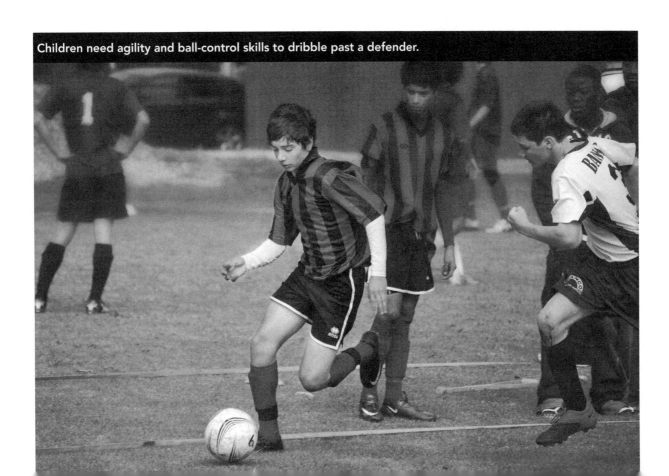

Children need agility and ball-control skills to dribble past a defender.

In essence, players should never risk the ball by dribbling in their defensive third. Instead, playing as a team, they must ensure that the ball player always has many options to pass the ball to supporting team-mates in good positions. Whenever possible, at least one team-mate should be in a supporting position behind the ball player, where defensive pressure is less likely.

So, players should learn to retain possession in the middle third unless they see a clear opportunity to play an early direct ball behind the defenders. They should only attempt to dribble past defenders in wide positions and only then if the dribble will take them into the attacking third.

Finally, in the attacking third, players should be prepared to risk the ball by dribbling or by making a pass which risks being intercepted, but which may lead to a score. One of the great misconceptions in soccer is that the objective should be to retain possession of the ball, that it is good football to string a long series of passes together. While this is sometimes the case, possession is only a means to an end: a chance to strike at the goal. Players must be encouraged to risk the ball if there is a chance of a score resulting because in soccer, there are usually few opportunities to score.

This does not mean that players should not learn how to maintain possession, for there will be times when the only objective should be to keep the ball away from opponents striving to equalise or to win the game. However, this strategy is not recommended in junior soccer, where players should always be encouraged to play positively.

As they improve, players must learn when to try to play behind the defence with early direct passes and when to hold the ball up and retain possession. From here, it is a simple step to learning how to control the tempo of a game by passing the ball in the back two-thirds before releasing it to players running forward with a chance to score.

Another misunderstanding is that the main aim of the defence is to keep the opponents from scoring. While this should be an objective, the main aim should always be to regain possession as quickly as possible. This simple change in thinking turns defence from a passive approach into an aggressive one. So the instant the ball is lost, players should immediately begin to position themselves to put pressure on the ball in order to regain it.

Shaped Games

While the emphasis so far has been on introducing the game to young players, Play Practice can be used to improve performance at every level of play. While it is possible for anyone to create and shape their own games by using the principles detailed earlier, coaches can use the following games to develop specific aspects of skilled play.

5v5 Long Soccer

With experienced players, it is possible to simply divide the normal pitch down the middle to create two pitches of 100 by 40 metres (330 by 130 feet) long. This long narrow pitch with big goals encourages players to make longer passes and to shoot from farther away. This in turn encourages them to lift their eyes to scan play 30 or even 40 metres (90 or 130 feet) away, a crucial aspect of passing in the full game. Note that although the theme is long passing, other aspects of play become important. For example, longer passes mean the ball will be in the air more often, so there will be many more opportunities for players to control high balls.

With 5 to 7 players on a team, long soccer is also an ideal game to help youngsters make the transition to the full 11-a-side game. This is because the additional space makes it possible for attackers to make longer passes and to play behind the defence. While it can be played with rush goalkeepers, there will come a point when some brave souls will decide that they would like to play in goal full-time!

Two-Touch Soccer

Two-touch soccer is a game shaped by the rule that only allows players two touches of the ball at any one time. This eliminates dribbling, encourages good ball control, and forces players to become aware of potential receivers even before they get the ball. Above all, it encourages every attacking player to support the ball player intelligently and to use good calling to tell them how much space and time they have to control and direct the ball. This game, as well as the progression to one-touch soccer, prepares players to inter-pass accurately and quickly in the limited space and time near their opponent's goal. Neither are games for beginners!

Four-Goal Soccer

Four-goal soccer can be used to teach players to use cross-field passes to switch play away from heavily defended areas. With a large goal in each corner of the pitch, attackers facing a strong defence on one side can switch play to the other side for a more open shot at the goal.

2v2 Game

The 2v2 game illustrates the Play Practice approach to the development of dribbling and ball control at the highest level. It is played in 10-by-10-metre (35 by 35 feet) squares, with 2-by-2-metre (8 by 8 feet) goals in each corner. The ball player now has only one potential receiver, who is likely to be closely marked, so passing will be difficult. Pressured by their own marker, ball players must learn to shield the ball as they look to pass the ball to another closely marked teammate, shoot for a goal, or try to dribble past their defender (figure 7.13). This is a very demanding game that is only suitable for experienced players, and even they will only be able to play for short periods. However, it improves their ability to shield the ball under pressure and forces them to lift their vision while doing so.

Remember that it is possible to shape many other aspects of play at the elite level by changing only one condition. For example, if the condition is that goals can only be scored with the head, players will quickly work out that it is far easier to do this when the ball is crossed in the air from the flanks. This in turn encourages the use of width in attack and leads to more attempts by players to dribble past defenders so that they can create the space and time to make a good cross. The coach can then focus play on any of these elements. For example, they might work on near-post and far-post positioning for the header or continually stress the importance of taking on and dribbling past defenders. Instructors must reward every attempt to take on defenders and should never criticise players if they fail to beat their opponent.

Full Game

If youngsters are to play the 11-a-side game, instructors should introduce a basic playing formation. Here, we recommend what is termed the *WM formation*. While it, along with the names of the playing positions, will seem old fashioned to many, this formation (figure 7.14) is perfect for beginners. In its basic form, it illustrates the principles of play, especially width and support in

FIGURE 7.13 Shielding the ball.

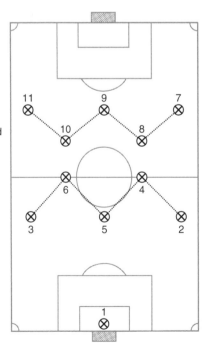

1. Goalkeeper
2. Right back
3. Left back
4. Right halfback
5. Centre back
6. Left halfback
7. Right winger
8. Inside right
9. Centre forward
10. Inside left
11. Left winger

FIGURE 7.14 WM formation.

attack and depth in defence. It helps youngsters understand the importance of effective positioning and enables them to take on roles in the formation depending on their specific abilities. Note that this formation can be used very flexibly to create a range of other formations. For example, by moving one player, it is possible to turn it into the 4-3-3 commonly used by many elite teams.

Goal Keeping

The goalkeeper is a highly specialised position. While all students should be given an opportunity to play as rush goalies, they should never be forced to take on the full role in organised games. However, if youngsters do decide that they want to play in this position, they will need specialised training to improve both their positioning and agility.

Field Hockey

Although there are obvious similarities between field invasion games, certain differences affect the way they are best taught and coached. So while hockey is conceptually identical to soccer, and many of the practices outlined in the previous section can be used to teach hockey, the teacher must be aware of the following differences:

- Potential danger exists from careless stick use and from the hard ball, which can be propelled at up to 160 kilometres per hour (100 mph). Because of this, it is recommended not to include goalkeepers in lessons and to have strategies in place for ensuring safe practice.

- Controlling and directing the small ball with a long lever is a very difficult challenge for beginners, particularly as they control the ball at ground level and simultaneously lift their eyes to scan the field.

- The contact and obstruction rules mean that players must be very conscious of body positioning and control.

- While soccer can be taught on almost any piece of ground, hockey can be a dangerous game unless the playing surface is level and free of obstructions likely to deflect the ball.

- Hockey is a much easier and safer game to learn using small-sided games on an artificial grass or hard court surface.

As play improves, teachers should remember the following:

- While soccer is a game played in three dimensions, hockey is essentially played in only two, especially in the scoring zone. Because lofting the ball is both difficult and potentially dangerous, in hockey it is much harder to play the ball into the space behind defenders.

- The narrower pitch means that it is easier for defenders to prevent penetration by balls played along the ground.

- The small goal and restricted shooting area mean that the ball must be taken much closer to the goal for a shot than in soccer.

These factors make it easier for the defenders to deny space and closely mark attackers, especially in the scoring zone. When space is limited, time is also limited. It is therefore more difficult for players to be skilful. So, attacking play is much more demanding in hockey than in soccer, especially for beginners. The one advantage for attackers are rules that make any defensive infringement in the circle potentially very costly, because the short corners that result from defensive errors can lead to many goals.

The implications of all of this are as follows:

- The fast break is as important in field hockey as in any invasion game: Getting there 'firstest with the mostest' (that is, outnumbering the defense) is a high priority.

- Tactical width must be exploited to provide new angles of attack and to pull gaps in the defence.

- Defensive pressure on the ball must be countered by maintaining depth in attack. This also helps the attackers retain possession and gives players the chance to continually change the point of the attack.

- The ball must be played or taken into the circle by a dribbler as often as possible.

In essence, we recommend that the majority of the practices suggested for teaching soccer should be employed when teaching field hockey. They can also be applied when teaching floor hockey. However, the game can be introduced to beginners using the approach developed by Dennis Slade (2003). Using what is essentially a Play Practice approach, he created a simplified starting game, played without the stick, in which the ball is rolled along the ground to a team-mate. It is advisable to begin 5-a-side games with a softball. Ensure that in all play practices the ball stays below knee height.

With the technical demands minimised in this way, youngsters can immediately play a game that retains many of the characteristics of field hockey. In this game, players can either roll the ball to team-mates or carry it forward in attack. A tag then replaces the tackle, forcing the ball carrier to stop and roll the ball. A carry limit of 4 seconds can be used in place of the tag tackle to eliminate body contact and congestion around the ball.

Scoring is made easier by using the full length of the end line. However, scoring is differentiated by centrally locating marker cones as a small goal. Attackers may carry the ball over the end line or roll the ball to a team-mate, who is behind the end line, to score either 1 or 5 points (through the goal). As players become accustomed to the game, a corner roll can be introduced if a defender plays the ball over the end line.

Once players have a feel for the game, it is possible to introduce the stick and the essential techniques of trap, push, and dribble in a progressive manner. Slade (2003) advocates the parallel approach, where techniques are developed and then immediately brought back into the roll-ball game with a small adjustment to the conditions of play. For example, after the trap technique has been practised using partner tasks, players return to the roll-ball game, where the stick can be used to trap the ball. However, after trapping the ball, players are able to pick up the ball to carry it forward or to roll it on to a team-mate. The pushing technique is added in a similar manner. Finally, players move on to the dribble. They continually return to the game each time with slightly different conditions based on the addition of the new technique. The parallel method continues by moving players from challenges and target games or the practices that improve elements of the skill of passing, back to the small-sided games.

The 4v1 and 3v1 games played in the coaching grid detailed in the introduction can be used to help young players develop their technical ability and their games sense concurrently. With attackers outnumbering defenders, the learner has enough time to control and direct the ball and to scan the play to identify open players. These games can be preceded by individual challenges where the initial emphasis is on the development of the techniques needed to control and direct the ball whilst moving across a space. The simple ball-control challenges outlined in the soccer section can be applied to hockey with an emphasis on moving with the ball, stopping the ball, and changing direction whilst scanning the environment. The games to develop scanning and dribbling in basketball or the heavy traffic activity in lacrosse may also be of value. Challenges that combine techniques and include agility, scanning, and communication can be employed and progressed to possession games in the teaching grid. The techniques of pushing and trapping the ball and the more advanced techniques of hitting the ball and the advanced trap can all be introduced using a similar pattern to that suggested for soccer. They can then be transferred into the 20-by-30-metre (70 by 90 feet) teaching grid described previously. As always, these dimensions are not sacrosanct and can be modified to suit the specific abilities of any group.

Because of the greater difficulty of controlling and directing the ball in hockey, when using go-for-goal play practices to develop passing, attackers may be given an additional advantage. For example, the 3v2 continuous go-for-goal game can become 4v2 where the extra player is a schemer, a position that should usually initially be filled by the best player in each team. This schemer or quarterback is crucial because he provides the depth essential for his side to maintain possession, can switch play from side to side to ensure width, and must be ready to make penetrating passes if defenders leave gaps in the centre of the defence.

These play practices can be used to develop technical ability, to teach the principles of defence and attack, and to introduce or reinforce the rules of the game. As players progress, it is possible to adjust the attacker–defender ratio and to introduce all of the games outlined in the soccer section (for example, long soccer and four-goal soccer) to achieve specific outcomes.

It is also worthwhile introducing the concepts of thirds of a field outlined in the soccer section. As with soccer, players must learn where and when to take on opponents in a dribble. While players should understand the tactical implications of the field being notionally divided into thirds, in field hockey, it is even more vital that attackers understand the importance of using the dribble to take on defenders in the circle. This is because this often forces a defensive error, leading to a short corner and a good chance to score. In this context, players with the ball can learn the importance of exploiting the rules to force defenders into mistakes, which will often lead to a penalty corner.

As youngsters improve, they can move to 5v5 games played on a half pitch. If possible, real goals should be used. As with all play practices for hockey, there should be no goalkeeper. This is a very specialised and potentially dangerous position, so goalkeepers must be carefully prepared and equipped for the role (figure 7.15). Again, this is different from soccer, where rush goalies can be used from the outset.

It must be emphasised again that it is not necessary to understand and apply Play Practice as a complete package. However, when sport educators understand the principles of shaping, focusing, and enhancing, they can apply them in many ways to create enjoyable and effective learning situations. Coaches will find that the more advanced games listed in the soccer section can easily be applied to hockey with little modification.

Lacrosse (Non-Contact)

Lacrosse superbly illustrates the value of the Play Practice approach. Even when played with a soft rubber ball and plastic moulded sticks that make catching, carrying, and throwing the ball easier, it is still a difficult game for beginners to play. However, the Play Practice solution, where players use a grip-ball pad

FIGURE 7.15 Protective gear for goalkeeping.

(or a softball mitt) to catch the ball and throw it with their free hand, makes it possible for beginners to play a game virtually identical to lacrosse from the very start. In this way, they can begin to develop the games sense they need for successful, joyful play. They are then more prepared to undertake the technical practice needed to play the real game.

The non-contact version of lacrosse is an ideal learning game, since it is small-sided game (4 players plus a goalie) with a simplified game structure and easy-to-follow rules that promote safety and inclusivity. The game can be played indoors on a basketball-sized court, on a 20-by-30-metre (70 by 90 feet) area of the coaching grid, or on an outdoor hard-court space of similar size. A unique feature of lacrosse is the potential to use the field space behind the goal. Beginners should play the game without a goalkeeper and can score by making a successful pass to a team-mate in the end zone. When a small goal is introduced, the game can still be played without a goalkeeper by placing a chair or rubbish bin to block part of the goal face. However, if time permits, the goalie position can be introduced. One of the main advantages of non-contact lacrosse is the positive transfer of technical ability and games sense to the more complex field forms of the men's and women's game.

Simplified End-Zone Game

The ideal starting point for learning lacrosse is in a simplified end-zone game, where the technical demands are reduced by replacing the lacrosse stick with a grip-ball pad and a Velcro ball. The three primary rules are introduced. Players have the opportunity to demonstrate games sense by applying the rules in the game and to take personal responsibility for playing fairly. This game provides the context for learning, and it can be revisited at any stage for fun or to introduce new tactical concepts. The coloured Velcro pad makes it easy to identify teams and also communicates an excellent visual catching target for passing (figure 7.16). The simplified game begins with a focus on the three primary rules of the game in order to ensure safety and to maximise learning.

1. No stick contact or body contact is allowed. Players are responsible for safe

participation, so they must learn how to manage the stick safely when attacking and defending.

2. Establish a 4-second carry limit. This rule restricts the time any one player can hold the ball, preventing individual domination of play. Because lacrosse is a running game, players can be encouraged to move with the ball during the 4-second limit.

3. Establish a one-on-one rule for contesting a free ball. Only one player from each team may contest a free ball. Players may not cover the ball with their stick. This rule prevents congestion around the ball, which is common when the ball is on the ground with beginners. It also encourages team-mates to adopt good support positions.

In the end-zone game, a goal is scored when the ball is caught by a player positioned in the end-zone area. This player can move freely in this space, since no other player may enter the end zone. After a score, the attacking player who passed the ball into the end zone switches roles with the receiver in the end zone. The game is then restarted on the court alongside of the end zone, and all defenders move back behind the center line. This allows the attacking team to commence play without defensive pressure.

FIGURE 7.16 Grip-ball pad and ball used in the starting game.

Teaching in the Game

Once the end-zone game is underway, the teacher can step back and observe the play, allowing the learners to participate freely. Teams are encouraged to umpire themselves or to rotate the umpire role. Games can be paused at any time and at a set time interval to clarify the primary rules, provide feedback, ask questions, and acknowledge effort and fair play.

Beginners will possibly need clarification of the non-contact rule, so teachers should remind players to maintain an arm's distance when defending the player with the ball. It might also be necessary to apply conditions to improve the play, particularly to counter the tactic of one long throw at the goal, which will often emerge in the game. An easy way to counter this is to require at least one pass in each half before players can try to score. This condition encourages team play; however, it is also important to acknowledge the tactical thinking demonstrated by the player who initiated the long throw option.

Enhancing Play

These games can be enhanced by playing for a short time (for example, 4 to 5 minutes), by rotating teams regularly, and by changing the focus of play. The structured break between games provides an ideal opportunity to acknowledge fair play, to clarify rules, to reflect on tactics, and to consolidate learning. It also provides time to introduce a new focus, such as showing a target when receiving the ball in attack or moving with the ball before passing, both important aspects of lacrosse.

Developing Basic Technical Ability in Lacrosse

Once students start to enjoy playing the grip-ball end-zone game and realise that it is very similar to lacrosse, hopefully they will be interested in playing the real game and of course learning to use the lacrosse stick. This is a perfect time to introduce the notions of safety and the personal responsibility players have for managing their stick. The teacher can outline the injury potential of the stick and take this opportunity to show how it can best be controlled, with the hands about shoulder's width apart and with the lower hand near the end of the stick (as shown in figure 7.17). Players can then be asked to show responsibility for safe management of their sticks as they engage in a variety of individual challenges to improve their technical ability. The essential techniques for beginners to master include scooping the ball from the ground and bringing it to the carry position, where it is easy to run, dodge, or pass the ball. In addition, players must learn how to catch the ball in the head of the stick and throw the ball from the stick using an overarm action. Individual challenges and partner target games can be used to develop technical ability. Examples of these include the following:

- The scoop and carry challenge is a simple challenge that allows beginners to practice scooping up the ball using the lacrosse stick. They move freely in an open space scooping the ball from the ground using the stick and then lifting the stick up to the carry position with the head of the stick alongside of their shoulder. This position is important because it enables players to raise their eyes to scan the field and to pass quickly if they see an open teammate.

- In the catching challenge the ball is lifted up into the air from the stick using an underarm action and then it is caught in the head of the stick. Beginners will find it easier to catch the ball if they present the pocket of the stick up above their head, and then watch the ball closely into the pocket.

- The techniques of scooping, carrying, and throwing the ball at a target can be combined in the next challenge. Partners share a common target and score points for accurate throws at the target with an added bonus for accurate throws from increased distances. Scores can be individual or collective. This game can be extended by carrying the ball in before taking a shot at the target (figure 7.17b).

These challenges enable beginners to develop a working model of technique and to experience success. Learning is facilitated further by a clear demonstration of the challenge, together with encouragement and simple 'bare-bones' cues such as 'watch the ball right into the stick,' 'hands apart,' and 'scoop under the ball' when needed.

Partner Challenges

Partner challenges involving peer cooperation can also be used to improve techniques such as catching. Here, the helpers assist by feeding

FIGURE 7.17 Lacrosse techniques: *(a)* scoop, *(b)* carry, *(c)* catch, and *(d)* throw.

the ball to their partners, who are ready for the catch with the stick head held up and forward as a target (see figure 7.17c). Co-operating feeders can be positioned 5 to 6 metres (15 to 20 feet) away from their partners. They use an underarm feed to loop the ball to the target because it is easier for their partners to track the ball into their stick. The ball is then thrown back to the feeder using the stick. These 'feeders' may also take on a coaching role by providing feedback and encouragement. A simple extension to this challenge is to increase the distance and have the receiver lead forward, presenting the stick head as a target and calling for the ball. When the ball is caught, the receiver turns and carries the ball back to where she started. She is then challenged to use her stick to throw the ball back over a longer distance to her partner.

Returning to the End-Zone Game With Grip-Ball Pads or Lacrosse Sticks

While some groups may be ready to play the end-zone game with lacrosse sticks, most novices will initially return to the grip-ball version of the game where the reduced technical demands allow players to develop their ability to read the play and improve their games sense. This is particularly important when focusing the play on tactical principles, such as running with the ball, supporting the ball carrier with width, and delaying the ball while retaining goal-side positioning.

Note that when youngsters do become ready to use the sticks in the game, it is important to revisit the non-contact rule and explain how it applies for both attackers and defenders.

Defenders

When delaying or pressuring a player with the ball, the defender should remain a stick's distance away and hold the stick vertically in order to block the pass. Defenders may not move their stick forward of the vertical plane or cause stick contact as they attempt to intercept the pass.

Attackers

Attackers must take care when passing the ball, and they are not permitted to throw the ball at a defender or to cause stick contact with defenders while following through. This means attackers with the ball and support attackers without the ball must try to move into space to create safe passing angles.

Teaching in the Game

Initially the ball will be on the ground much of the time, so players must learn how to contest the ground ball within the rules. For example, they may not cover the ball with their stick or hit the opponent's stick away to gain possession. These rules along with the one-on-one rule for contesting a free ball can be reiterated and clarified when the situation arises in the game. With beginners, it is helpful to award possession to the first player who attempts to scoop the ball during ground-ball contests. This minimises the incidence of stick contact and congestion at the ground ball, allowing the game to flow more freely. With these guidelines in place, the game can be played enjoyably, if chaotically, since beginners will have limited technical ability. However, they can continue to play fairly, safely, and enjoyably by applying the non-contact rules. This game context is an ideal learning setting, especially when coupled with short playing times and the use of freeze replays to focus learning.

In every lesson it is important to revisit the techniques of scooping and carrying along with throwing and catching using individual and partner challenges. These techniques can also be applied in games of low organisation, such as red rover, where players must carry the ball in the stick safely across the area without dropping the ball. Target games, including shooting at goals, are also very popular, and it is possible to extend those students who are ready for the challenge of shooting with their non-preferred hand. The heavy traffic activity described in the basketball section can be used in lacrosse to improve scanning, communication, and technical ability. Here players move across a congested space, keeping their eyes up to avoid other players whilst carrying the ball in their stick. All of these challenges can be differentiated to cater for the diversity of individuals in the class simply by making variations to the distances and size of targets and by changing the techniques used.

Passing and Receiving

As soon as possible, students should be introduced to a variety of passing and receiving games where attackers have the numerical advantage (4v1, 3v1, or 4v2, as described in the introduction). These games can be played with the grip-ball pads initially and then with the lacrosse sticks. However, when playing with sticks, players will need more space so they have the extra time they need to scan the area, read the defenders' position, decide on the best option, and pass accordingly. While supporting attackers without the ball can begin to learn to 'show a target' and move to create a safe passing angle, defenders meanwhile are learning to read the play, position themselves to cover passing lanes and especially the direct route to goal, anticipate and block passes, and develop the resilience necessary to play sound defense.

Go-for-Goal Games

The go-for-goal games outlined previously can be introduced as half-court games or as continuous go-for-goal games using various combinations of attackers and defenders (3v1, 3v2, 4v2). The attacker with the ball is encouraged to read the play and advance the ball by carrying it to goal or by drawing a defender and passing to a team-mate in a better position. Attackers without the ball move to get ahead of the ball carrier and into the space behind defenders. Defenders work on delaying the ball and adopting goal-side positioning to support one another. With a slight modification the continuous go-for-goal game can be converted into a defense transition game suited for more experienced players (see the basketball section). This change increases the intensity of play as attackers respond rapidly to cover back in defense, encourages communication, and creates a more chaotic environment for decision making.

Using the Space Behind the Goal

A special feature of lacrosse, as with ice hockey and korfball, is that play can continue in space behind the goal. Moving the ball behind the goal cage offers advantages for the attacking team primarily because it creates a difficult situation for defenders who are tracking their player and have to turn their heads to also keep vision on the ball. The ball may be carried by a player to this area or passed to a team-mate who has moved to receive the ball behind the goal. From here the attacker with the ball has several options. Because they are relatively close to the goal, they could drive quickly around the circle

to the goal face for a shot. If this drive to goal draws an additional helping defender, then the attacker can pass the ball over to the open team-mate for a shot. The area behind but to the side of the goal is also known as the 'prime feeding position' because it is a key area for passing the ball to attackers cutting from in front of the goal. An accurate pass to an open cutting player often results in a goal from this position. This is because the keeper has to turn quickly and reposition themselves to cover the shot coming from the opposite side of the goal.

Players therefore need to learn to use this space effectively, and the shaping process is used to encourage them to do this. This shaping can take several forms, but one of the most effective methods to shape the play is to simply turn the goal to face the rear for this makes it obvious that attackers should get into this position to score. The go-for-goal games mentioned previously can also be shaped to ensure that the attacker with the ball works from behind the goal. This helps players decide what to do if they have the ball and they are attacking from behind the goal, and it also challenges the attacking players without the ball to adjust their support positioning. Bonus points can then be allocated in the game for using the space behind the goal or for goals that are scored in attacks from this position.

Goal Keeping

Depending on the length of the unit of work and the group of students, it may be appropriate to introduce the specific role of goalkeeper. In this case, the goalkeeper must be equipped with the appropriate protective equipment, including a helmet or face mask. Once a goalkeeper is introduced, the rules associated with the goal circle and goalie, as well as the defending restrictions for the immediate space in front of the goal, can be clarified. Teachers and coaches should help players understand how to position themselves and move as a goalkeeper to cover key spaces and reduce possible shooting angles. In addition, they require information and practice of the techniques required to cover high and low shots from set-ups that occur in the game. The introduction of the goalie gives the defense an opportunity to focus on communication and clearing, while attackers can direct their attention to shot placement and tactics to create scoring opportunities against the goalkeeper.

Australian Football

Australian football and Gaelic football are both descendants of the primitive football games played in Britain in the early 19th century. Aussie Rules, as the game is usually called, is the most popular male sport in Australia. It is administered by the Australian Football League (AFL), which organises a national professional competition for men, a non-contact 'Auskick' game to introduce children to the sport, competitions for women, and a recreational form of the game.

The full game is played on a large oval space, approximately 150 metres long by 135 metres wide (490 by 445 feet), with 18 players per side and with complex rules that always seem to be in a state of flux. Players maintain possession of the ball by passing it using various techniques, including kicking and marking (catching the ball), handballing (punching the ball off the hand holding it), and by gathering the ball from the ground. Players can run with the ball, but they must touch it to the ground or bounce it approximately every 15 metres (50 feet) as they run. Points are scored by kicking the ball through the goal posts located at either end of the field. A goal (worth 6 points) is scored when the ball passes through the central posts, and 1 point is earned when the ball passes through the side posts. In this vigorous and physically demanding body-contact game, both tackling and bumping the ball carrier are permitted, as well as restricted blocking off the ball. These factors all contribute to the complexity of the game, especially the pressure of physical contact at the contest for the ball, the large number of players involved, and the oval-shaped ball with its unpredictable bounce.

When introducing this game to beginners, the physical contact demands must be eliminated and various other aspects of the game structure simplified to provide a safe and enjoyable starting game.

Australian Rules football can be introduced using a parallel approach similar to the other sports described in this chapter, in which there is a blending of play in simplified games together with individual and partner challenges to improve technical ability. Many of the play practices outlined in the introduction can be easily adapted for Australian Rules, especially the partner target games involving kicking for goals, which is a key feature of the game. As always with Play Practice the initial emphasis should be on playing fairly, developing games sense, improving technical ability, and building resilience.

Here it is important to modify the rules with beginners to provide the framework for an enjoyable game. However, these modifications must allow the game to retain its essential feel while providing a safe, inclusive, and challenging game environment that maximises learning opportunities. This is achieved by reducing playing numbers, adjusting the field size, minimising physical contact, and applying rules to reduce player congestion around the ball and restrict potentially dangerous play.

Modified Game Forms

Footy nines, originally developed by Jenny Williams (2008), is a modified game structure for Australian Rules football. It provides a clear and progressive rule package for introducing and developing the game, including three levels of rules to suit the diversity of participants within any class or community. The rules for levels 1 and 2 promote inclusivity and foster enjoyment for participants of all ages and experience levels. However, while the beginning game eliminates contact, the level 3 version of nines closely resembles the full game, with bumping and tackling. This rule package has been used successfully in school physical education classes with boys, girls, and co-ed groups, as well as in community sport with participants of varying ages and levels of experiences.

Footy nines' rules for beginners shape the game for safety, inclusion, success, and learning. Some of the key rules are included here:

- The non-contact rule is initially used with beginners to promote safety and participation by eliminating tackling and bumping. This allows players to build their confidence to contest, gather, and move with the football. Once players gain a feel for the game, a two-handed touch on the ball carrier can be included to represent a tackle, resulting in the ball having to be moved on quickly with a kick or hand pass.

- The 5-second carry limit restricts the time that any one player can have the ball, and this promotes inclusive play and teamwork. Again, once players gain confidence, they can be introduced to the option of moving further with the ball by touching it to the ground or bouncing it after five steps.

- Only one player from each team can contest a free ball. This rule reduces congestion around the ball when it is loose on the ground. It also encourages players who are not contesting the ball to move into good support positions ready to receive it.

- The ball may not be kicked off the ground. This rule promotes safety and encourages players to gather the ball from the ground rather than kick it.

These key rules can be applied in small-sided teams with playing numbers ranging from 4v4 up to 9 a side in the formal nines game on an appropriately sized playing area. The 9-a-side game is well suited to be played across the football field or soccer-sized pitch. In this game, the pitch is divided with a halfway line, separating 3 forwards from 3 backs. The 3 midfield players can move freely to either end. This enables a structured rotation of players to each zone. With beginners, the games must be played with plenty of space, no boundaries are needed, and portable plastic goal posts can be located at either end. In these small-sided games, the players can be encouraged to take ownership of fair play and apply the key of rules in their own games. One of the advantages of using the halfway line to divide the field of play is that it accommodates a diversity of playing experience within one team and allows even matching of players. This can be achieved with playing numbers as small as 4 a side. The rules can be differentiated according to the experience of the players in each half of the field.

First Lesson

A novel way to begin a unit on Aussie Rules football is to use an action fantasy game. The teacher adopts the cameo role of a visiting AFL coach who will be preparing the class to participate in an official AFL-sponsored school carnival at the culmination of the unit. Beginners can each start with a smaller, softer football and begin to experiment with ways to control and redirect this ball with its unpredictable bounce. A variety of individual challenges (similar to those presented in the early sections) for gathering the ball, moving with it, handballing it, and kicking it can be practiced before progressing to partner kicking challenges and then to a small-sided game using the rules outlined previously. As usual with Play Practice, students spend a lot of time playing games; however, they may come out of the game for a short time to focus on improving particular techniques as needed. The action fantasy theme can be continued during the unit and integrated with the sport education approach to bring in specific roles, team selections, allocation of uniforms, trial games, practices, and dream team points.

Developing Technical Ability

The challenge approach is well suited for developing the technical ability needed to gather and run with the ball, kick, mark, and handball it in the early stages of learning to play Aussie Rules football. Many of the individual and partner challenges and target games outlined in the earlier sections can be applied to Aussie Rules, and a reciprocal learning environment is recommended. Partners can help each other to focus on the bare-bones cues, such as 'hold the ball over the kicking foot,' 'move in line with the ball when gathering it,' or 'hands up early for the mark'.

Self-testing kick-for-goal challenges provide an engaging experience for developing the important technique of kicking. The practice can be set up so players kick from predetermined distances and angles and record their performances. This task can be extended to cater for more experienced students by combining techniques, such as gathering the ball followed by a snap shot at goal by using left- and right-foot kicks, and encouraging different kicking techniques.

Improving the Ability to Read the Play and Further Develop Games Sense

The heavy traffic game and variations (outlined in the basketball section) can be used to practice handballing technique, moving with the ball, communication, and scanning. The handball technique can also readily be applied in 3v1 games, since it is easier to scan the field when holding the football in the hands. This allows players to learn to read the play and to improve the tactical aspects of games sense. The 3v1 groups can be combined to play a 4v4 end-zone handball game in the 20-by-30-metre (70 by 90 feet) teaching grid. In this game, teams look to move the ball using handball techniques and score with a handball into the end zone. Increasing the space to 50 metres (165 feet) and adding a new condition allowing a kick to be taken after five consecutive handballs build up other aspects of game play.

Go-for-Goal Games

The go-for-goal games outlined in the introduction can also be applied to Australian football. As always with beginners, attackers are given a numerical advantage with the attacker-to-defender ratio depending on the type of techniques to be emphasized. The complexity can be increased by introducing specific conditions for the game, by restricting space, or by adding numbers. In this way games can be shaped to cater for the specific needs of the group of players. One example of this is a game called dream-team footy, designed by Phillip Ward, a pre-service student at UniSA during his final teaching placement in 2011. This game worked well with his year-10 boys' class at a school with a strong Australian-Rules culture. It can be played on a half field (or within the 50-metre arc, depending on numbers) with 7 to 9 players per side. Similar to other half-court games in basketball and lacrosse, the defenders and attackers play in the one half of the field and use the one goal. Defenders must clear the ball beyond the 50-metre arc before changing roles to then attack the same goal. The game rules can be set according to the group, and in this instance contact was restricted to a two-handed touch. After the touch, the ball had to be played immediately. The other rules included no kicking the ball off the ground and a one-bounce option to allow players to move with the ball using a bounce after taking five steps. An additional condition was that the attacking team must have three touches before attempting to score. At any phase in this game, when a double whistle is blown, play must stop and a shot for goal is taken from that point. The game is enhanced by the allocation of points for team contributions by players from both teams where they were awarded 5 points for kicking, handballing, and marking, 10 points for a running goal, and 50

points for a goal from a set kick. A key feature in this game is the role of dream-team captain, a role which various players (who wear a brightly coloured bib) in each team may take on. When these players gain possession of the ball, they can gain double points for their team. This means team-mates are always looking to bring these players into the game.

Shaped Games at the Elite Level

Play Practice has been accepted in professional coaching within the Australian Football League. David Parkin, a triple premiership coach, was one of the earliest coaches to embrace Play Practice principles. In recent times, of particular note is the work of Mark Williams, an innovative master coach and former premiership coach at Port Adelaide whose expertise in the design of creative play practices is becomingly increasingly recognised within the sport.

An example of one of Mark's play practices, called 'should I go or should I stay?' is presented as an example below.

The game is played with two teams (blue and white) of 10 players. However, the game is shaped to create a situation where the forwards outnumber the backs at each end of the field (4 backs versus 2 forwards). The midfield have 4v4, with an additional 2 midfield players wearing red bibs who play on either team depending on who has the ball.

4 backs (b) vs. 2 forwards (w)

4 mids (b) vs. 4 mids (w) (+ 2 red mids)

2 forwards (b) vs. 4 backs (w)

The unique feature of this game is that it can be started at different source-point situations over the ground, including centre bounce, free kick, a throw-in, a stoppage in the forward area, or deep in the back line. The percentage of play starting from particular source points can be based on the data analysis of the previous game.

When the game commences, the additional 2 midfielders join the attack and try to kick to the outnumbered forwards. The weighted numbers create pressure on the ball as it is delivered into the 50 metres, which means the backs should gain possession and exit kick from the area. The mids who have turned over the ball must immediately respond in defensive transition to find a man and pressure the ball to keep it from exiting the area. Those players who can't directly influence the play need to find an attacking player quickly or recover back into defensive 50 metres.

The opposition midfielders now attack, running hard to assist in moving the ball forward. The additional 2 red mids (who change roles and are now attackers with the opposition) link up with their extra numbers and try to hit their outnumbered forwards at the opposite end. The forwards may mark and kick for goal. If the backs gain possession, they then spread, quickly identify the spare man and space, and try to kick to the free player on exit. The 2 red midfielders now return to the original side. This game continues with either of the two groups coming in for three movements and then swapping, or with the interchange (additional 2 red mids) rotating at will.

Mark has shaped this game so that it is aligned with the reality of what happens in the game. It is specifically focused to improve decision making in the transition phase of the game. The intelligent weighting of numbers allows players to develop their games sense, since they are constantly challenged to read the play and respond accordingly, particularly as the ball rebounds from the 50-metre area. In addition, this play practice can be personalised to meet the specific needs of players or adjusted to suit the particular team. For example, players who need to build their ability to work hard in attack both on and off the ball can be allocated to the red-midfielder position. Other teams may decide to add another player in the forward contest (3v4).

Mark's expertise and familiarity with the Play Practice process enable him to teach productively in the game. He makes especial use of freeze replays to stop the play at relevant times in order to question players, reiterate key points, or refocus their efforts. In addition, because this practice is filmed from different angles, the learning for players continues off field as the video is viewed and analysed.

Another example from coaching at the elite level in Australian Rules football is from David Parkin, who designed a centre-clearance game that focused on rapidly moving the ball forward after gaining possession at the centre bounce. The centre bounce is a critical phase of the game that represents a perfect moment of transition where both teams must be ready for instant attack or defence. In this contest, 2 ruck players run in and compete to knock a high-bounced ball down to 4 members of their attacking team. An equal number of defenders try to harass and pressure them as they try to bring the ball clear of the centre area and deliver it with an open kick into the 50-metre zone. Players in this game wear suitable body protection and use padding to apply game-like pressure without the risk of injury. The attackers score 1, 2, or 3 points depending on the zone in which they receive the ball. Although defenders cannot tackle the ball players, they must make it as difficult as possible for the attacking team to advance the ball by blocking and bumping opponents. Because play is initially in a confined space, it is difficult for defenders to generate the momentum that can lead to serious injury. Teams change roles and try to score more points than their opponents. It is possible to manipulate the ratio of attackers to defenders to focus this game closely to the group's needs.

eight

Teaching Court Invasion Games

Basketball, Netball, Korfball, Handball, and Futsal

I love the feel of the pebbly leather on your fingertips; that moment of neo-religious purity when your eyes lock on the front rim and you release the ball and it backspins and there is nothing else in the entire world.

A character in the Harlan Coben novel
Long Lost

Basketball, netball, korfball, and team handball can all be introduced through lead-up games, such as end zone or line ball, bench ball, and skittle ball. These games can be played indoors or outdoors with small-sided teams from 5 to 7 a side on a court 20 to 30 metres (70 to 90 feet) in length. The basic rules are that the ball can only be thrown, not kicked or punched. Initially, no dribbling is allowed and the ball cannot be taken away from the player in possession, although if it is held by two opposing players at the same time, the appropriate method, such as a jump ball, can be used to resolve the situation. Dealing with this situation presents teachers with a good opportunity to have a discussion about the need for an understanding and acceptance of the rules to ensure enjoyable and fair play.

In line ball or end zone, a goal is scored by passing the ball to a goalie, who can run anywhere behind the goal line. This makes scoring easy, which is an important factor in games for children. The passer who scores the goal changes places with goalie, and the ball is then given to the other team to start an attack.

Bench ball is identical, but now the goalie stands on a gym bench behind the goal line. Mat ball is the same, but the goalie is positioned on a gym mat. Each progression makes scoring just a little more difficult, so passing must become more sophisticated. In all of these games, the rules dealing with the ball going out of bounds, held balls, and restarts can be introduced as and when needed. This approach makes the rules relevant so that children are more likely to both remember them and abide by them.

In these lead-up games, players can be introduced to the idea of attacking and defending a goal as well as the concepts of teamwork and supporting the ball player. The simple attacking tactics such as passing and moving for a return pass, together with the basic defensive principle of goal-side positioning, can also be introduced. Gradually, the notions of the fast break and of covering attackers can be dealt with.

While throwing and catching are important, they can be developed fairly easily with simple partner exercises. Teachers should not spend too much time working on these techniques in isolation but quickly move to passing practices. With beginners, the key to rapid improvement is the use of simple 2v1 and 3v3 passing games.

2v1 in Free Space

Here, a defender tries to prevent an attacker receiving a pass from the ball handler O1, who is not allowed to move. Without pressure from a defender, O1 has the time to decide where, when, and how to deliver the ball to O2, who must learn to cut late and fast to get open and to clearly show where he wants the ball delivered (see figure 8.1). To ensure that players focus on passing, no dribbling or running with the ball is allowed. The game is won if the receiver takes two consecutive passes or if the defender intercepts the ball. Players change roles then or after four attempts. In this simple game, attackers can also learn the following:

- To fake a cut and change direction
- To use different techniques of throwing the ball
- That passing the ball is the first step towards teamwork
- The travel law or stepping rule in the game (for example, in basketball, the law that allows a player to take two steps after catching the ball in the air and then to use either foot as a pivot on landing)

Meanwhile, defenders learn to cover their opponent's moves and work to improve their footwork. To prevent this game becoming a pointless game of piggy in the middle, the defender must always try to cover his direct opponent! To maintain their commitment, players should continually change roles; however, this is where every teacher must assess the group and decide how best to keep them on task.

3v3 in Free Space

Here, the 2v1 groups can join together to become a team playing against another group of three. Now the ball handler must decide between two potential receivers while preparing to deliver the ball and dealing with pressure from an opponent (see figure 8.2). The same basic elements of moving and passing can be stressed, along with the technique of pivoting to protect the ball. When commencing this game, defenders can be required to remain 1 metre (3 feet) away from the attacker with the ball, similar to the obstruction rule in netball, in order to reduce the pressure on the player who is passing the ball.

Defenders have to improve both their positioning and their vision as they try to watch the ball handler, the ball, and their direct opponent. In these games, the attacking team wins by making five safe passes, while the defenders naturally win if they intercept, or even merely touch, the ball. Again, defenders must learn the specific rules of each game with regard to allowable contact and the use of the arms in defence.

For young players, this increase in complexity is huge, so play will continually break down as a team tries to complete three passes to win the game. Teachers must therefore be very patient and should be prepared to go back to the 2v1 game

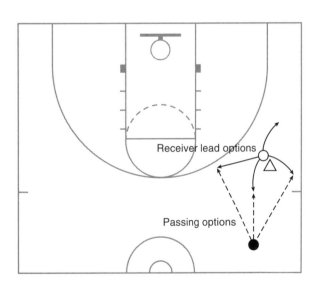

FIGURE 8.1 2v1 in free space.

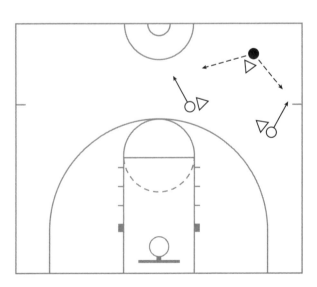

FIGURE 8.2 3v3 in free space.

or even to a badly played version of one of the lead-up games detailed in the basketball section!

Because all this takes time, with young players it is important to maintain motivation by continually changing opponents and rebalancing teams when necessary. Teachers and coaches can always complement these simple games with the original lead-up games to allow students to develop other elements of games sense, such as passing and cutting in attack or tracking and marking in defence.

It is possible to use a grid approach similar to that detailed in the introduction to chapter 7, with court markings and marker cones. For example, in netball, the court space can be divided into thirds to play 4v4 or 3v3 end-zone games across the court or divided in half to play 4v3 or 4v4 half-court games. Other games that can be played in the teaching grid are outlined in the netball section (see figure 8.9).

Basketball

Basketball can be introduced through lead-up games such as line ball, bench ball, and skittle ball. See the preceding section for guidelines and rules for these introductory games. With beginners, the key to rapid improvement is the use of simple 2v1 and 3v3 passing games, which are outlined earlier and shown in figures 8.1 and 8.2. These can be used either in parallel with lead-up games or to prepare very young children for those games. They introduce the idea that passing the ball is a team activity that requires skill from both the passer and the receiver. However, to play even the simplest of these games, youngsters must be able to throw and catch the ball, often while they are on the move. If children cannot throw and catch even while standing still, they are not ready to play the lead-up games outlined previously, far less the complex game of basketball. In this situation, teachers should focus on tag and chasing games to improve agility until youngsters are developmentally ready to throw and catch a ball on the run.

Basic Techniques

To play this great game, in addition to being able to pass the ball under pressure from defenders, youngsters need to be able to dribble and shoot the ball. In a strong basketball culture, they acquire these techniques through a process of mimicry as they model what they see older players doing. However, where this is not the case, mastery takes considerable practice. The Play Practice approach therefore is to introduce shooting through a series of challenges and dribbling through a range of enjoyable play-like activities.

Shooting

The challenge of shooting the ball is one of the great attractions of basketball. Begin by introducing the set shooting technique shown in figure 8.3. Youngsters start within 1.5 metres (5 feet) of the basket for an individual shooting challenge, moving back 30 centimetres (1 foot) every time they score. After three consecutive misses, they must begin again from 1.5 metres but at a different angle to the basket. This challenge gives every child the opportunity to develop an effective technique. It can be even more valuable and interesting if players are encouraged to 'coach' their partners.

At the beginning of a unit with more experienced players, it is worthwhile challenging them to find out how many baskets they can score from three attempts from any of five selected spots at 3-point range. Players work around these spots in pairs, with a recording card. The results, once evaluated, may convince a group of 'superstars' that they are not quite as good as they think they are and ensure that they are more likely to take practice more seriously. It will also confirm how difficult the task can be, even without a defender trying to stop them. This opens up discussion about the importance of getting the ball to the player in the best position to score.

This experience may also encourage players to use the more advanced technique shown in figure 8.4, with a greater drive from the legs. This challenge will not only establish the performance level of each student but also allow the teacher to identify any exceptional players in the group who can be enlisted as assistant coaches. This approach allows teachers to define the initial encounter with a group on their own terms and may be a career saver for inexperienced teachers working with a difficult group of adolescent boys who feel they're already great players!

FIGURE 8.3 Set shooting.

FIGURE 8.4 Increased knee bend in preparation for a more advanced shooting technique.

This game can be followed by a team shooting competition, with 5 to 7 players at each basket working as a team and shooting from a range of 5 metres (15 feet). On a signal, free shooting begins. The first team to score 11 baskets wins. Teams must call out each successful shot (i.e., *1! 2! 3!* and so on). When teams reach 11 scores, they must sit down in position, holding the ball above their heads. Clearly, the teacher must stay with it to ensure that enthusiasm does not turn into cheating!

It is now possible to use this shooting technique in a game of goal ball, which is played exactly like line ball except that the ball is returned to the player who made the original pass in to the goalie. That person gets a set shot at the real basket from the free throw line. An alternative is to play 3v3 at half court. Here, any team that makes five consecutive passes is entitled to choose to take a set shot from the point of last reception or from the free throw line.

In a basketball culture, the layup shot is taken for granted, but youngsters who are not immersed in the game find it difficult to master. The problem is that beginners cannot control the ball in a dribble while simultaneously organising their footwork to produce the right foot, left foot take-off to jump up and lay the ball in off the backboard (for right-handers). Nor are they able to take advantage of the rule that permits two steps when the ball is caught in the air; in fact, the complexity of this apparently simple element of technique is not always understood.

The bounce-one-two layup shown in figure 8.5 resolves the dilemma that while the layup needs to be introduced early on, many youngsters cannot dribble the ball well enough! The bounce-one-two method allows players to execute a layup even if they cannot dribble the ball! Here, right-handed players start by standing with feet together. As they step forward onto the left foot, they push the ball forward and down firmly with both hands (figure 8.5a). Next, they do a small forward jump off that foot so that they are in the air when they catch the ball as it rebounds from the floor. This allows them to exploit the two-step rule, and they now have the ball in their hands during these two steps and can transfer their attention to the hot spot on the backboard as they prepare to jump up off the left foot (figure 8.5b). Initially, players can shoot the ball from both hands, but they can gradually transfer the emphasis to the right hand (figure 8.5c).

As figure 8.5 shows, good players can cover a considerable distance with just one bounce. Using an aggressive bounce-one-two movement, even a beginner can travel from the top of the key to get close enough to shoot a layup.

As dribbling ability improves using the practices outlined next, it is possible to add two or three bounces until children have the timing required to dribble the ball and go in for a layup. Once they have mastered this working model of the layup, youngsters should be encouraged to test themselves with build-up challenges. This means that after they have scored one basket, they try for two in succession, then three, and so on. Any time they miss, they drop back to their previous score. They repeat this and try again.

FIGURE 8.5 Bounce-one-two layup.

This can be followed by a challenge in which teams of 4 to 6 players try to build up to the highest number of consecutive baskets or play first to 11 baskets against each other.

3v1 Half-Court Game

Attackers try to score using only a set shot or a layup. Each student will have plenty of opportunities to be involved if—and this is often a big *if*—there are enough courts available. At this time, rules about personal fouls can be introduced. In addition, the basic concepts of positioning are introduced in the form of spread and balance with a focus on continually building the triangles.

1v1 Game

Players are set up at a range of 5 metres (15 to 16 feet). The attacker can shoot from outside to score 20 points for a basket or 10 for hitting the ring. The attacker can also fake the shot and drive to the basket for a 5-point score. This differential scoring encourages defenders to play honest defence rather than dropping back to stop the layup. Partners should be changed frequently.

3v2 Half-Court Game

This is organised as for the 3v1 game, but with two defenders to make life more difficult. Scoring is only through a set shot or layup.

Dribbling

Dribbling a basketball is automatic for children who have grown up with one, as is the case in places like Kentucky and Indiana where basketball is a vitally important element of most communities, but it takes time for novices in other environments to master. However, with clever use of variety, progression, and pacing, it is possible to keep youngsters involved in the purposeful practise necessary for mastery for long periods of time. Eventually, players must be able to dribble competently with both hands while keeping their heads up so that they can see open team-mates. The following sequence of practices is recommended:

- Begin by kneeling and holding the ball close. Treat the ball like a friend, so do not slap it! Move the hand with the ball and not against it. Use your fingertips. Gradually, move the ball around your body and then farther out. Change to the non-preferred hand.
- Close your eyes and repeat.
- Repeat the sequence standing.
- Repeat the sequence moving slowly, using your free arm to feel the way when your eyes are closed.
- Run freely and fast, keeping eyes open and maintaining open space.
- Gradually compress the space from full court to half court, to one quarter, to the keyway only.
- In pairs, move freely, following and copying a partner, who continually changes hands, the height and speed of the bounce, and the direction of movement.
- In pairs, face each other and mirror a partner, who varies the movement and speed as much as possible.

Players should practise in groups of 3 or 5, as shown in figure 8.6*a*. As the first player in the group dribbles across, he calls out the number of fingers player 2 is showing and continually changing on one hand. When 1 arrives, 2 dribbles towards 3, who shows fingers for 2 to count and call. All players must keep the ball bouncing throughout. When they are stationary, they must use their non-preferred hand. The teacher or coach may add a stop signal that means the dribbler must stay in place dribbling the ball until the signal is changed to numbers and they can move on. Signals can be added to indicate turning, changing hands, going fast or slow, backing up, or dribbling behind the back or through the legs, and so on.

The formation can then be changed to the 'heavy traffic' activity shown in figure 8.6*b*. Students must now be aware of players coming at right angles and try to avoid the collisions that their guides are deliberately trying to create.

Note that it is also possible to use simple games of low organisation, such as dribble freeze tag, at any point. In this game, everyone has a ball, and the group is divided into two teams.

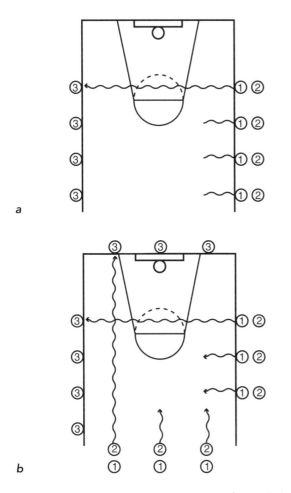

a

b

FIGURE 8.6 Practicing (a) in groups of 3 and (b) in heavy traffic.

When touched by an opponent, players must freeze to the spot but keep the ball bouncing until released by a team-mate.

At any point, it is possible to return to the bounce-one-two layup. Players then progress to bounce-bounce-one-two, and then on to the half-court dribble and layup, maintaining the rhythm and two-count gather and shoot. From here, it is possible to progress to a full-court dribble with little pressure where defenders begin to learn how to delay the dribbler using only their heads and their feet, not their hands. This practise can then be extended to a full-court dribble against real defensive pressure, where for example the dribbler must practise two rear turns before trying to beat the defender and go in for the layup.

Of course, the 1v1 practice outlined earlier can be revisited but this time from 6 metres (20 feet). The dribble can also be incorporated into the classic fast-break 3v1 and 3v2 games. At some point, players can be introduced to how the dribble can be used tactically in order to create a better passing angle to a potential receiver or to draw defenders away before passing in the opposite direction. At an even higher level they can begin to exploit the dribble in moves such as the 'penetrate and pitch out' and the 'drive and dish.'

3v3 Half-Court

The sequence of games continues with 3v3 half-court. Along with the fast-break game outlined in the next section, this is the fundamental play practice for basketball. This game, or one played 4v4 depending on the numbers in a group, can be used to introduce virtually all the tactical concepts of the half-court game, including screens on and off the ball, clear outs, give and go, back door moves, court balance, and the basic principles of rebounding. These games are also ideal for focusing on defensive tactics. The 3v3 and 4v4 games can be shaped to accommodate the experience level of the players. For example, the inclusion of a rule that restricts defenders from taking the ball out of attackers' hands has advantages for novices. It reduces the pressure on the ball carrier, allowing them space to dribble and pass the ball. Defenders are forced to maintain a good defensive stance, holding position and anticipating the pass. Combining this with a four-bounce dribble restriction creates a fairly balanced contest. The half-court games also can be shaped to focus on specific aspects of tactical play—for example, allocating bonus points for baskets scored from a back door or give and go tactic.

Fast Break

The fast break can be introduced through the classic 3v1 drill, which is converted into a game. This produces what we have termed a go-for-goal game, a valuable play practice to develop effective play in many games. Begin with 3v1 (figure 8.7). As soon as the Os get the ball, they break downcourt to attack. This game is continuous and it focuses on the transition into attack.

As the players' offensive skills improve, gradually introduce more defenders. One way to do

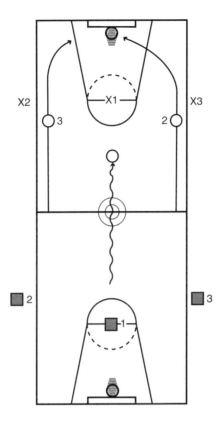

FIGURE 8.7 Fast break.

this and make the situation even more game-like is to specify that the second defender can join in after the attackers have made two passes. The third can join in after three passes. With only three teams of 3 involved, this play practice will challenge the fitness of young players. It may be best to use four teams to give players time to recover. Teachers and coaches should discuss their defensive tactics before outlining how they will go about the next attack. If enough courts are available, the number of teams should be kept to a maximum of five. If there are too many children to do this, the instructor may have to balance maximum individual participation against alignment and settle for half-court games.

The go-for-goal games can be adjusted slightly to focus on the transition into defense. Two of the three attacking teams must quickly retreat to play defense as soon as they have attacked and attempted a shot. The next attacking group are waiting behind the baseline, ready to break into attack as soon as the ball hits the floor. They must respond quickly, using the dribble to progress the ball into the front court and working hard to catch

the defenders out of position. The rapid response by the new attackers leads to an increase in the tempo of this game, which in turn challenges the reactions, communication, and games sense of defenders. The trailing defender may be brought into play from the halfway line after attackers have made one pass. The defensive transition game provides an excellent example of game-specific endurance, particularly if two groups of three players are located at each end of the court, allowing only a short break between bursts up the court to score and then back to defend.

Jump Shot

The jump shot (figure 8.8) is an advanced technique, but it can be mastered by youngsters who are willing and able to practise in their own time. Two tactical applications for this technique exist. The first is when it is used instead of the set shot. The second is as a pull-up jumper, where the player starts a drive to the basket, senses that the defender has retreated a fraction too far or too soon, and simply stops and pops up to shoot.

While experienced players can shoot the jump shot from a standing position, young players can master this technique more rapidly if they use a one-bounce dribble to build the rhythm of the shot.

Introducing the Full Game

While all of the elements of basketball can be introduced to classes of up to 30 students, it is difficult to introduce the full game. There are two reasons for this. The first is that few schools enjoy the luxury of more than one basketball court, so it is not possible to play more than one game of 5v5 at a time. The second problem is player density. With 10 players operating in a semi-circle 8 metres (25 feet) from the basket, things become very congested until players understand the importance of positioning and structured movement. The problem is that the relatively small playing area means that beginners can easily run around the whole attacking zone, something that is impossible in soccer, for example. Inevitably, every player tries to get close to the basket, hoping to receive a pass and score. The keyway becomes jammed with attackers and their defenders, so no one is open to receive a pass.

FIGURE 8.8   Jump shot.

In a basketball culture such as that of the United States, youngsters may be able to move to a full game with hardly a pause. However, this is not the case with children who are introduced to the game in a country where it is not so developed, such as England. While it is relatively easy to introduce the techniques of basketball and to begin to develop elements of games sense, it is difficult to put all of these elements together in a short period of time. The limited space in this game means that beginners cannot rely on reading and reacting to the fast changing environment. They just do not have enough time to be skilful.

The great American college coach van Breda Kolff liked his offence free form: 'Just go fast, stay out of one another's way, pass, move, come off guys, look for one on ones, two on ones, two on twos, three on threes.' That is, in fact, the substance of basketball, which is almost never played as a five-person game anymore but is rather a constant search conducted semi-independently by 5 players for smaller combinations that will produce a score. 'One on one is the basic situation of the game: one man with the ball trying to score against one defensive player, who is trying to stop him with no one else involved' (McPhee, 2005).

However, it is completely impossible for inexperienced players to play this way because freedom can rapidly lead to chaos. With such a small playing area, confusion and congestion are inevitable, since beginning attackers run everywhere trying to get their hands on the ball. So if inexperienced players are to be prepared for competitive 5v5 matches, teachers and coaches must provide a basic structure for offence.

Our experience suggests that the only way to resolve this problem with beginners is to introduce a zone defence. Here, the five defenders are in relatively fixed positions, operating as a single unit to guard the critical space close to the basket. A 2–3 (can easily become a 2–1–2) zone is the easiest for beginners to understand and use. Young attackers will find it intimidating when faced with a zone defence because it appears to close off almost all scoring opportunities except a long outside shot. This is especially the case if defenders learn to play with their hands up high and move to block passing lanes through the zone. Gradually, they will learn to move rapidly to put pressure on the ball. Note that we are aware that most coaches want young players to immediately begin learning player-to-player defensive principles, and in a coaching environment this is certainly what we would recommend!

Attackers will find their task infinitely more difficult if they do not employ some very simple offensive principles, and especially if they allow the zone to match their attacking formation. Here, defenders can easily cover the key scoring areas, move into position to guard their immediate opponent, and also pressure the ball wherever it goes, without having to continually adjust their position!

However, if attackers use games sense, they can create problems for defenders and get many opportunities for open shots, often close to the basket. Here are the two most important tactical principles of attacking a zone:

1. Split the seams of the zone. This positions the attackers in the gaps between the defenders. Against a 2–1–2 zone, this automatically produces a 1–3–1 attacking formation.
2. Overload the zone. Again, this simple tactic ensures that the attackers outnumber the defenders in specific areas of the court, giving attackers open shots.

As defenders improve and begin to move quickly as a unit to pressure the ball, the attackers must learn to use quick and intelligent passing to force the defenders to move. Invariably, this creates gaps inside the zone while allowing open shots from outside. Gradually, young players can learn all of the following elements of games sense:

- Reverse the ball to change the direction of the attack.

- Use the skip pass to pass the ball over the defence to open players on the other side of the court.
- Use the dribble draw to pull defenders out of position, since they must respond to ball movement.
- Make inside cuts to exploit gaps left inside the defence.
- Use replacement cuts, an advanced tactic where one attacker cuts through the defence and draws a defender so that a team-mate can cut into the space created.
- Pass to an open team-mate.
- Take the open shot.
- Ensure at least 2 players move to rebound every shot taken, while at least 1 player moves into position to cover a possible fast break by the opponents.

As always in games, attack and defence are balanced. So while these tactics can help youngsters deal with zone defences, as defenders begin to improve their one-on-one defence and transfer it into the team defence, the balance can swing back towards them. Only when the offence can be certain to hit a high percentage of 3-point shots will the balance again swing back to the attackers.

One of the major issues that must be addressed when teaching basketball to adolescent boys is the need to develop the kind of teamwork that leads to good shots. This is important because almost inevitably, if a lad is open, he will usually launch the ball at the basket, whether or not he has any chance of scoring or even if team-mates are open close to the basket. One of the strategies that our student teachers have used with considerable success is to carry out the 3-point shooting challenge suggested at the beginning of the unit.

Once players have learnt the importance of careful positioning when attacking a zone defence, they will be better prepared to accept the need for a similar method when dealing with player-versus-player defences. So, it is possible to introduce a 2–1–2 attacking formation. With an emphasis on the give-and-go moves, this can be very effective for young players. The shuffle cut introduces the importance of maintaining set positions as the guard uses the set screen provided by the centre to lose their defender.

An additional advantage is that a single give-and-go cut from the guard, along with slight adjustments in the positions of the other attackers, converts the formation into the 1–3–1 set suitable for attacking the zone.

At the next level, the problem can be solved by running set plays or *shuffles,* structured offensive patterns that ensure that all attackers know their role, their movement patterns, and their court position at all times. Our experience suggests that if, and only if, the teaching context is favourable, it is possible to introduce youngsters to a simplified version of what has been termed the *Drake shuffle.* The first cut of the shuffle both provides a simple scoring opportunity for any defence and helps attackers identify whether it is a zone or man-to-man defence. If it is a zone, the first cutter simply stays low. The attackers automatically fall into a 1–3–1 formation, as shown previously.

Note that the best way to beat a zone defence, indeed any form of defence, is to get there 'firstest with the mostest'. In other words, fast break and get the ball downcourt before the defence is set up. However, in the early stage of introducing basketball, this may lead to a helter skelter form of the game, with lots of action but little learning! Leave the fast break until youngsters have learned the essentials of good positioning, teamwork, and intelligent movement.

Remember that the full 5v5 game is much more complex than 3v3 or even 4v4. It should not be used until students have made a commitment to the game or unless enough courts and time are available to ensure they can deal with the greatly increased complexity. One solution to this problem is to play a form of basketball that was once common with girls in the Midwest of the United States. Here, teams of 6 play, with 3 students from each team in each half of the court. This is infinitely easier for youngsters to cope with, since it reduces both the complexity and the endurance demands. It can be structured so that players are defenders for one period of the game and attackers for the other period. We recommend this game, or even its extension, 8 players on a team with 4 in each half, unreservedly for young players. Because it reduces the cardiovascular demands, we believe that it would also be an appropriate game option for some divisions of masters play.

Netball

Netball is major game in many of the Commonwealth nations, which include Australia, Canada, England, Northern Ireland, Scotland, Wales, New Zealand, and some of the West Indian nations. It is predominantly played by females, but there are also both male and mixed competitions. It is a popular social game for players of all ages because it is tactically quite a simple game with minimal demands on endurance because of zone restrictions.

Netball is a relatively simple team passing game with a rule structure that promotes safe and inclusive participation. The game is played with a medium-sized ball that is caught with the hands. The 3-second rule allows players just enough time to scan the environment before passing. In addition, defenders must allow 1 metre (3 feet) of space to the attacker with the ball. Players are restricted to areas on the court, which, as we indicated earlier, minimises the endurance demands and reduces the player-to-space ratio on the court. Because of these factors, it is possible to start with small-sided passing games to gain an appreciation of the key rules while also developing games sense. The continued use of a variety of shaped games, focused accordingly, will generate the dynamic learning conditions in which all aspects of skilful play can emerge.

In netball, the ball can only be advanced by passing and receiving—no dribbling or running with the ball is permitted. However, the 3-second rule restricts the time a ball handler can hold the ball. This means players with the ball are always under pressure, since they have limited time to select their target and pass the ball to a receiver, who is usually tightly guarded. All players must therefore quickly improve their ability to 'go late and fast' and to time their lead as receivers. When they have the ball, players must learn to quickly read the play and pass accurately to closely defended receivers. The keys to successful play in netball include agility, especially quickness over 2 to 5 metres (8 to 15 feet), and simple elements of games sense.

Netball can be introduced using many of the ideas presented in the introduction to this chapter with the focus being on developing games sense and promoting fair play and resilience. Simplified games feature as key learning experiences together with 2v1 games for improving the skills of passing and receiving. For beginners a variety of individual challenges and partner target games can be used to improve throwing and catching technique. This is particularly important when players move as they catch the ball because they must learn the footwork patterns to land without stepping.

The netball court is a natural teaching grid that can be easily divided for participation in a variety of challenges and games. The court thirds and the goal circle provide working spaces on the court. This space can be further divided into half-courts or into corridors from goal to goal. Figure 8.9 illustrates the grid and a variety of learning activities that can be undertaken using these spaces.

Games of Low Organisation

Simple tag games of low organisation such as 'high-five tag' or its variation 'dunny flusher' are excellent introductory activities for netball. They are easy for the teacher to organise using either the full netball court or two-thirds of it (depending on numbers), fun to play, and provide instant activity. In the class, 4 to 6 students are identified with a coloured sash as the 'chasers,' and they move to tag the other free class members. Once

a player is tagged, she must stand still and hold up either her hand (high five) or a clenched fist (dunny flusher). Other free players can release the players who are caught by either giving them a high five or by bringing the clenched fist down using a 'shh' sound to replicate the flushing toilet (dunny flusher). These games can be played in short time intervals with chasers changing frequently, and they are ideal for promoting fun, scanning, agility, and fair play.

4v4 or 3v3 End-Zone Games

End-zone passing games (3v3 or 4v4) played across a third of the netball court or on a half-court area are ideal starting games for assessing the level of the learners. In these games the primary rules are introduced, and players can only pass the ball to progress it down the court. They score by making a successful pass to a player standing unguarded in the end zone space beyond the sideline (see netball grid). This game allows the teacher to observe the players' understanding of the primary rules, including no contact, obstruction (1-metre distance), 3-second possession, and no stepping with the ball. Depending on the

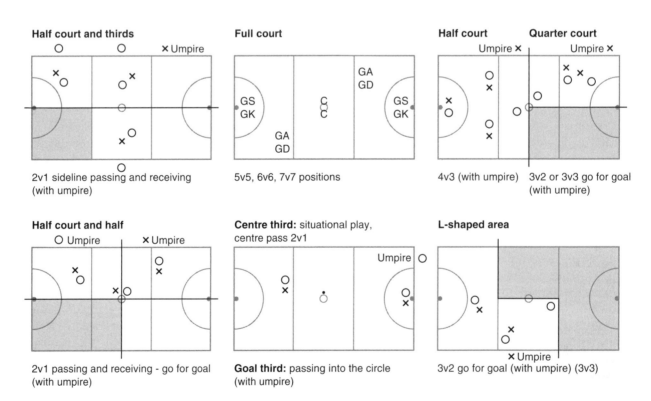

FIGURE 8.9 Netball learning activities and teaching grid.

experience of the group, the rules can be introduced and clarified in the context of this game. With beginners, the rules can also be slightly modified to increase success. For example, allowing players more time (5 seconds) when in possession of the ball and some leeway on the strict stepping rule will assist the flow of the game.

These games can be enhanced by applying the following strategies:

- Use short play-time intervals with reflective breaks for questioning and clarification. For example, the teacher's observation of the game might suggest that the obstruction rule requires attention. The 1-metre distance (approximately an extended arm's distance away) can be clarified and then focused on in the following play interval.

- Rotate opposing teams frequently, encouraging personal responsibility for abiding by the rules and fair play. Allow students to adopt the umpiring role and use in action fantasy games (such as World Cup games).

- Differentiate the shape of games to cater for the diversity of learners in the class. It is easy to personalise game play by applying different conditions of play to teams. For example, teams may decide if they wish to use the 3-second or a 5-second possession rule.

Agility is a key aspect of skilled play in netball.

Individual and Partner Challenges for Basic Techniques

Beginning netball players often struggle with their footwork to avoid stepping as they receive the ball. They must be able to catch the ball on the move, land without stepping, and then pivot using the grounded foot to either adjust their body position or transfer weight forward to assist their throw. Confidence to do this can be developed using individual challenges. Each player works with his own ball, throws it up into the air, and moves to catch it. As players catch the ball, they first try to land with both feet touching the ground at the same time. This allows them to select which foot is the 'grounded foot' and to practice pivoting by moving the other foot around the grounded one. Next they repeat this challenge but land on one foot first in a right-left or left-right fashion. The grounded foot is the first foot to land, and the player can then pivot around the grounded foot. Teachers and coaches can help to improve players' understanding of the stepping rule by relating it to the concept of the grounded foot and how it can be lifted but not re-grounded before the ball is released. Players can move from one end of the netball court to the other, catching and landing without stepping, and once they enter the goal circle they can shoot. The goal circle can be divided into two zones with a challenge of scoring three goals from close to the ring before moving back into the outer part of the circle.

Partner challenges that combine throwing to a moving target as well as maintaining the emphasis on footwork and pivoting can be used. The player with the ball positions herself at the sideline of the netball court with her back to her partner, who is on the court. When the player with the ball pivots to face the court area, her partner makes a quick lead to the side and shows a target (hand). The throw is directed to the target hand. Points can be scored for throwing accuracy, and bonus points can be added for correct footwork. This activity also can be set up around the goal circle area to include goal shooting.

Goal shooting in netball is limited to specific positions; however, it is important to provide opportunities for all participants to improve their shooting technique and to be able to adopt these positions in the game. Shooting challenges similar to those outlined in basketball can be used for

125

netball, and the reciprocal teaching method with which partners help each other to improve their technique is advocated. Differential scoring can be applied so that shots hitting the ring score 1 point whilst shots through the ring score 2 points. Similar differential scoring can be allocated to the distance from the ring. Goals scored from the inner zone gain a 1-point bonus whilst longer shots from the outer zone gain 2 bonus points.

2v1 Passing Games

It is very easy to progress from these simple challenges into passing and receiving games, which form the foundation of netball.

The 2v1 passing game can be applied to a range of specific situations as indicated in the netball teaching grid. In this game, the attacker with the ball improves his ability to read the positioning of both his teammate and opponent, and learns to choose when and where to deliver the ball. Potential receivers learn how to time their lead, moving late and fast to get free of the defender, as well as how to make a target with their hands when looking to receive a pass.

The playing space in these 2v1 games can be adjusted to suit the agility and passing skills of the players. A wider and shorter space promotes lateral leads by the receivers, while a narrow and longer space focuses the receiver on moving quickly forward in a sharp lead or holding her position and then dropping back into the open space behind the defender (illustrated in the netball teaching grid). When the space is shaped in this way, it allows the passer to improve the lob technique as she passes the ball over the defender. This is an important passing option for moving the ball into the goal circle. Defensive positioning can also become a focus for learning by considering how to hold front position and to cover the attacking lead.

The 2v1 games with an umpire can be set up in specific areas of the netball court, such as the centre pass situation, sideline or baseline throw-ins, and especially play around the goal circle. This allows rules to be clarified, such as the positioning of players and starting rules for the centre pass, and specific tactics to be developed, such as passing in and out of the goal circle to gain a closer position to goal. Extra players can observe play and begin to adopt the role as umpire or coach.

Half-Court Games

Half-court games are ideal for developing passing and receiving skills within the game context. In addition, they also allow players to adopt the positional roles in netball—an important aspect of skilled play in this game. Players should rotate positions frequently to allow them to experience each of the playing roles and to discuss the particular rules and playing responsibilities of each position. Freeze replays are ideal for teaching in these half-court games, particularly to clarify positional play and decision making in relation to free passes.

Half-court 4v4 games with an umpire (see netball teaching grid) start with a centre pass, and just as in half-court basketball both sides attack the same goal. After a goal is scored, the game is restarted with a centre pass, and the other team now have a chance to attack. If there is a turnover, the defending team must clear the ball to the centre third before restarting the game with a centre pass. It is possible for additional players from each team to rotate into the umpiring role. Teams can be adjusted after a short playing time to ensure even competition and rotated to play other teams when five goals have been scored.

With beginners this game can be simplified by playing 4 attackers against 3 defenders, again with an umpire. This reduces the pressure on the attack centre pass by providing an easy outlet support pass. For more experienced players, an additional defender can be added to increase the pressure on attackers, forcing them to sharpen their agility and passing skill.

The court can be divided into halves from goal to goal, creating a corridor along each side of the court. Novice players can play 3v1v1v1, where the 3 attackers attempt to pass the ball and move from one end of the court to the other, confronting a defender in each third. If defenders intercept the ball they gain a point, but the attack still tries to progress down the court to the end line and gain 3 points. The number of interceptions is then subtracted from the 3 points to work out the attackers' score. Defenders and attackers then change roles, with each team aiming for 3 points. These games help players develop games sense as they read the play, apply tactics, and make decisions, while all the time improving the quality and range of their technical ability and movement skill.

The game can be progressed by allowing the defenders to cover two-thirds of the court, creating a 3v2v2 game. In this game players can focus on how they can control the pace of play by playing for a short time with the condition that the attacker receiving the ball must land and stop before passing the ball. This can then be compared to the pace of the game where players are permitted to use a run-on step as they pass. This corridor passing game can be further adjusted by including the full goal third into the playing space. This allows goal circle work and goal shooting to be included into the game (see the netball grid).

Working in Thirds of the Netball Court

The goal-circle third of the netball court is ideal for passing games involving 3v2, 3v3, or even 3v4 defenders that focus on tactical play in and around the goal circle, including goal shooting and defending.

The 3v2 game can be played with a group of 6 students to include an umpire role. Two attackers take on the roles of goal attacker (GA) and goal shooter (GS), with the third attacker as the wing attack (WA). The two defenders adopt goal defence (GD) and goalkeeper (GK) roles (see the netball grid). Play starts just inside the goal third with the WA making the pass. The attackers work to pass the ball into the goal circle for a shot. The game can be conditioned so that a shot is not permitted until the ball has been passed in and out of the goal circle a set number of times. For more experienced players this might be 3 or 4 times. This forces the GA and GS to work together in the small goal circle space, timing their moves to get open, indicating where they want the ball, then repositioning themselves as the ball is passed out of the circle. This game generates interest because every player can take on a central role that includes goal shooting and defending.

Full-Court Game Play

Full-court games can involve 5, 6, or 7 players a side. The 5-a-side game is recommended because it provides an increased opportunity for each player to pass and receive the ball in a less congested space. This can be set up by removing two positions from either wing attack, wing defence, or goal shooter. These games provide an authentic context for developing all aspects of skilled play, and they can be enhanced in a variety of ways, including the following:

- Employ short play-time intervals with set time-outs to allow players to rotate into different positions and to discuss aspects of game play.
- Use fantasy games such as world championships and game simulations. This can include dream-team players who have specific responsibilities and draw bonus points for possessions.
- Allocate bonus points for particular tactics and introduce players to zoning across the centre third.
- Use the sport education model, which encourages individuals to take on specific roles such as scouting, umpiring, coaching, and reporting on game play.

Korfball

Korfball was developed in the Netherlands as a game for both male and female participants. It has a great deal to commend it as an educational and recreational game because the rules have been structured to specifically emphasise co-operative teamwork, equity, and fair play. Unfortunately it has to compete for numbers with the more well-known sports of basketball and European handball, which are all played professionally, and so it has been unable to reach the audience it deserves. However in recent times the game has grown internationally, with world championships being held since 1978 and world games participation since 1985, and there are pockets of enthusiastic players in many countries.

The game can be played indoors and outdoors, and a beach version of the game has emerged. Indoors it is played on courts 40 by 20 metres (130 by 66 feet) and outdoors on fields with a maximum size of 60 by 30 metres (200 by 90 feet). The large baskets with no backboards are set inside the court. This has a major advantage because this setup encourages passing and shooting from anywhere around the goal. This emphasises good passing and agility while minimising the importance of rebounding and the need for tall players.

The following are the key primary rules:

- Players cannot move the ball with a dribble. Therefore, they are forced to pass the ball to open team-mates; this encourages tactical team play.

- Teamwork is also encouraged by the rule that players cannot shoot at goal if they are guarded and so must pass the ball to a player who is open.

- Note that a player is seen to be guarded if the defender is in a position between the ball and the goal, is facing the opponent, and is within arm's distance of the attacker.

- Teams must have equal numbers of male and female players. Teams of 8 are divided into two parties of 4, consisting of 2 male and 2 female players. Players can only defend one person of the same gender (this can be modified).

- Each party is allocated to one half of the court (zone) as defenders or attackers.

- After every two goals are scored, the parties change zones. The defensive quartet switches with the attacking foursome.

- It is essentially a non-contact game. Defenders may closely defend their opponent in order to block or intercept passes, but they may not take the ball away or knock the ball out of an attacker's hands.

Because of the great similarity with netball and basketball, it is possible to use all of the play practices recommended earlier for developing elements of skilled play for Korfball.

Novices especially will benefit if the netball rule that restricts defenders to a 1-metre (3 feet) distance from the player in possession of the ball is applied. This reduces the pressure on the ball handler. As players improve their passing and pivoting abilities, this restriction can be removed.

The critical point, as in all of these games, is that participants must be given many opportunities to play in small-sided games. This allows them to develop games sense, particularly in coming to terms with the rules and the tactics that underpin this interesting game. Fortunately, the game structure allows the two zones to be used independently for most of the small-sided games.

With beginners, playing numbers should be reduced and weighted to the attackers (3v2, 4v3) to give them the time they need to read the play, make good decisions, and so ensure passes are completed. As they improve, the 4v3 game is ideal for focusing on shot selection and shooting, using both long shots and the running-in layup technique.

Conditions can be applied to focus on particular aspects of play, especially in 3v3 or 4v4 game play. For example, a condition that the ball must move behind the goal before a goal can be scored can be introduced to encourage players to use this space and to open up tactical possibilities around the goal. Bonus points can be allocated for particular tactics, such as goals being scored from shots taken from behind the goal or from a give-and-go move.

Of particular note when teaching korfball is the promotion of the explicit philosophies of co-operative team play, fairness, and equity. These can be celebrated and developed within any unit of work on this topic through culminating games, action fantasy games, or a sport education approach.

Team Handball

This game is often called European handball because of its popularity in central Europe, where there is a professional league. Unfortunately like korfball, a game with enormous potential for children, it has been largely ignored outside Europe even though it is an Olympic sport. Played on a 40-by-20-metre (130 by 66 feet) court space with a small soccer goal at each end, the game combines passing, dribbling, and shots on goal.

It is possible to play basic and advanced versions of the game. At the elite level, the game is mainly played around the shooting circle, with defenders dropping back to defend that zone as soon as the ball is lost. With the defence packed into this crucial area, scoring depends on very clever passing and on powerful, driving one-on-one moves as the ball handler tries to jump through or over the defenders to get a shot at the goal. This introduces a degree of complexity that beginners cannot cope with.

However, at the basic level, team handball is much simpler and more enjoyable because it combines passing, dribbling, and throwing to create a simple open game that is easy to play with defenders guarding on a one-on-one basis. One of the keys to success and enjoyment of this game is the size and nature of the ball because players are allowed to hold it for 3 seconds and to take three steps with it in their hands. However, the regulation ball is just too large to be gripped by the smaller hands of children, so it is important to use a smaller ball that can be bounced in the dribble and thrown easily, especially when shooting at the goal.

Because of its great similarity to basketball, it is possible to transfer all of the play practices recommended for the development of passing and dribbling in that game to the teaching of team handball. The go-for-goal games are particularly relevant for developing games sense, especially in developing an understanding of the rules and the tactics of the game.

Futsal

Futsal, a court game of soccer, is rapidly growing in popularity around the world. This is not surprising, since it has many of the characteristics of a pick-up game. It evolved in South America, where there are many more football enthusiasts than could ever be accommodated on full-sized pitches. In those countries, people love to play soccer so much that they play anywhere there is a remotely flat piece of ground. In fact, this is little different from the small-sided games that were played with any available ball, usually a tennis ball, in the English school playgrounds and streets in the 1950s and 1960s.

With teams of 5 a side, futsal can be played outdoors on almost any piece of level ground or indoors on basketball courts or on specially created courts. While it is increasingly being recognised as a major game in its own right, with leagues and championships developing rapidly, it has major advantages as a preparatory or supplementary game for soccer.

Apart from the small team sizes and playing area, the major difference between the two games—and one of the greatest strengths of futsal—is the small, low rebound ball that can only weigh between 390 and 430 grams. This has a major effect on the game because it means that, as with field hockey, it must be predominantly played on the ground. This, along with the limited space available and the likely proximity of opponents, means that quick ball control and accurate passing are critical. Since passing is a team skill, all team-mates must continually move into good positions to offer the ball player a range of passing options.

In this game, players may enjoy up to 12 times as many opportunities to control and direct the ball. Games sense, especially the application of tactics, is of critical importance. While players gradually drift into certain areas to suit their specific abilities, it is possible for everyone to play in every position. This is a great advantage with youngsters.

The rules for futsal are as follows:

- Five players should be on the pitch, but instructors should use rolling substitutions.
- Play to the lines, with the ball returned to play with a kick in.
- The goal is 3 by 2 metres (10 by 8 feet), but clearly, this can be varied with young players to meet specific outcomes for the group.
- All players are allowed to enter the penalty area.
- The ball can be played to any height in the air, although this is not to be encouraged.
- Each player is allowed to foul only five times, as in basketball.

nine

Teaching Rugby Codes

Touch, Rugby Sevens, and American Flag Football

> Soccer is a game for gentlemen played by hooligans, rugby is a game for hooligans played by gentlemen, American football is a game for hooligans played by chess pieces and Australian Rules football is a game for hooligans played by hooligans.
>
> Anonymous

Rugby union and rugby league are complex games in which games sense, especially the ability to use an understanding of the rules, is a critical element of skilled play. American football, which evolved from an early version of rugby union, is an even more complex game. However, coaches have done their best to simplify the game by eliminating the need for decision making and, therefore, the need for games sense on the part of the players.

The crucial thing about all of these games is that, unlike soccer, they are not much fun to play when played badly. Every time a mistake is made, the game stops. While this is not a problem for experienced players who understand the nature of these games, it can be a major issue with beginners. This means that play practices must be carefully structured to ensure progression and enjoyment. They must also reduce the complexity and thus simplify the challenges beginners face. Indeed, the one-on-one practices used to introduce these sports are the simplest form that any such game can take!

One of the major issues with all of them is that in the rugby codes, a player must actually take or receive the ball over the goal line. This means that agility, physical toughness, and resilience are critical factors in skilled play at the elite level. This clearly raises issues when these games are introduced to beginners, and the biggest problem is how to deal with the inevitable physical contact that can occur as ball players attempt to carry the ball over the goal line and defenders try to stop them.

For these reasons, it is inadvisable to move beyond the simple format offered here unless the teacher or coach has a thorough understanding of the real game and the time to teach all of the elements of skill related to tackling.

As suggested previously, the rules create tactically complex games in which well-developed games sense is often more important than technical ability. In the case of rugby union, for example, both the scrum and the lineout introduce complex tactical and technical issues that must be understood and mastered before the full game can be played. Therefore, the Play Practice approach is to reduce both rugby union and league to their simplest possible forms.

This means introducing the non-contact version of touch first and then progressing to rugby sevens. Input from John Davies (an experienced teacher and coach formerly of University of South Australia) for the development of the rugby sevens section is gratefully acknowledged. We begin with one-on-one games, where a ball carrier tries to advance the ball against a single defender, and then gradually expand the number of attackers. Next, we increase the number of defenders until youngsters can play modified

5v5, 6v6, and 7v7 versions of the game. It is important to note that touch is a popular game in its own right in Australia and not merely a lead-up to rugby sevens.

Although it has similar roots to the other rugby codes, American football has diverged so much from them that it must be given separate attention. The tactical complexity, potential for injury, and expensive equipment requirements all mean that it is not possible to introduce anything approaching the real game except in a highly structured coaching environment. In fact, teaching the real game of American football presents so many problems that it is rarely if ever taught in physical education programs, even in the United States. As a result, we recommend teachers aim to introduce flag football, a considerably modified version of the real game that is a very popular recreational activity in American universities.

Touch

Touch has grown rapidly in popularity in Australia since evolving from a training game for both rugby codes. It is now a major game in

its own right. This non-contact running game is safe, inclusive, and suitable for all ages. It can be played by single-sex or co-ed teams of 6 players. It is easy to organise since it requires little equipment and an open playing space. These characteristics have enabled touch to be marketed as a popular social game, providing fun and fitness for families and friends of all ages while also developing as a competitive sport.

The Play Practice approach to teaching touch was originally developed at the University of South Australia after it became clear that the traditional methods being used to introduce the game were based on a flawed analysis of the elements of skilled play. In essence, these approaches focused on the isolated practice of techniques instead of developing the more important element of games sense and especially an understanding of how the rules determine successful tactics.

The objective in touch is to score a touchdown by moving the ball through the defence. Since the ball cannot be thrown or kicked forwards, it is only possible to gain ground and to score by carrying the ball forward. So touch is fundamentally a running game, not a passing game.

Touch is a running game.

An analysis of touch indicates that skilful play is based on the following:

- Agility, especially running in all its forms (forwards, backwards, diagonally), accelerating, stopping suddenly, varying speed, and changing direction to dodge opponents. It is an essential part in both attack and defence.

- Games sense, particularly a clear understanding of the rules and how they influence game play. In touch, more than in any other ball game, the rules determine successful tactics, although players must also quickly learn to assess their own abilities against opponents. Therefore, tactical possibilities are often only limited by the ability of individual players.

With this in mind, the ball player must first try to gain ground, while team-mates must provide support behind the ball carrier. Mobility with and without the ball is therefore important to create space and generate scoring options. Meanwhile, defenders must try to delay the forward movement of the ball while working as a team. They must maintain a consistent line to cover attackers across the field and continually adjust their positions as the attack develops. Clearly, communication between defenders is essential.

- Technical ability. While the ability to catch and deliver the ball is less important than traditional approaches to teaching the game have assumed, players do need to improve their ability to carry, throw, and catch the ball, often while moving at high speed.

One of the most important things for beginners to learn, especially if they have played other invasion games, is that it is often better for the player with the ball not to try to pass it to a team-mate. This is because any mistake such as a forward pass or a dropped pass turns the ball over to the opposition, while an intercepted pass often leads to an easy break-away touchdown for their opponents. In addition, players can also try to catch the defenders offside and so gain the 10-metre penalty that results from this mistake. They can do this by running hard at the defender, making a touch on them, and then quickly playing the ball and moving it forward before the defenders can retreat back 5 metres.

Players must therefore learn not only how to pass the ball but also when to pass it or—and this is of critical importance—*if* they should pass it. More than any other invasion game, touch illustrates the vast gulf that exists between the tasks of mastering the simple techniques of throwing and catching the ball and developing the games sense needed to pass the ball effectively. Teachers and coaches must therefore teach passing in the context of game situations that simultaneously develop all the important elements of play, rather than through isolated throwing and catching practices or unrelated minor games.

Teachers and coaches can also use a teaching grid, where a 90-by-60-metre (300 by 200 feet) space can be separated first into three mini-fields and then into a series of corridors of varying width and length. They can then use these spaces for the progressive build-up games advocated in the Play Practice approach. The advantages of teaching and learning touch in this way include the following:

- The small numbers of players in each game promote positive participation and inclusivity and maximise the rate of learning. Small-sided games also enable differentiation and progression, based on individual needs, as well as evenly balanced teams for tournaments to further encourage purposeful play. The progressions gradually introduce players to the notion of taking and making a touch. This is crucial for youngsters whose past experience with contact sports may be limited. They will also grasp the principles of skilled play because all practice takes place in a game context, making the relationships among techniques, rules, and tactics easier to understand.

- The similarities and differences between touch and other invasion games can be considered within the game context, making it easier to minimise the problems of negative transfer from these games. For example, it is easy to show the importance of taking or effecting the touch to hold ground already gained, instead of running backwards away from the tackler, as participants may have learned to do in other invasion games.

- Players quickly learn the importance of carrying the ball forwards and of only delivering a pass when they are certain it will go safely to a team-mate. They also learn to retreat quickly in defence to avoid penalties.

• This approach to introducing touch gives all players the chance to take on officiating roles. This not only builds their understanding of the rules but also confirms the importance of officials in promoting fair play.

Rule Modifications

With Play Practice, teachers and coaches usually minimise or even eliminate either the tactical or the technical demands of a game to make it easier for beginners to understand and to play. The tactics of touch are virtually driven by the rules, so they must be modified if beginners are to have any chance of playing enjoyably. This is because in touch, the normal rules penalise errors in both attack and defence so heavily that play continually breaks down as a result of even simple mistakes. For example, in the real game, if a defender is offside, it can cost the team a 10-metre penalty, while a dropped ball by an attacker automatically turns the ball over to the other team.

As a result, the following rule modifications must be made in early play practices:

• Reduce the penalty for a dropped pass (along with other rules that would normally result in the loss of the ball) to the loss of two possessions from the six attempts normally allowed.

• Eliminate the offside penalty against defenders by ensuring that the ball cannot be played at the mark until they have retreated the required 5 metres. This slows the game for novices and allows both defending and attacking teams the time to get ready for the next phase of play.

These modifications still penalise errors but allow the game to flow without the continual turnovers caused by the simple but inevitable mistakes that beginners will make. Naturally, as players become more competent, the official rules and their penalties can be phased in. This will occur as players progress through the 3v2, 4v3, and 5v4 mini-games. The secondary rules can also be introduced when appropriate within the context of the game.

Teaching Progression

Tag games are an ideal introduction to any touch session. These games promote scanning, agility,

tagging, and fair play while ensuring enjoyment. Simple modifications such as carrying a ball add in the techniques of running with the ball, and this can be incorporated into a game of red rover to include scoring a touchdown.

Game 1: Run, Carry, and Make Ground

The Play Practice approach begins with a simple running game played in a 10-by-30-metre (35 by 90 feet) corridor, shown in figure 9.1. Coloured markers can be set up every 5 metres (15 feet) within the grid to help both players and referees judge this crucial distance.

The ball carrier (O) runs forward and tries to dodge a defender (D) to get to the score line. If D touches O, the spot is marked with a bib or flag. Players change roles, and the new ball carrier D tries to make more ground than O managed in her attempt. This 1v1 game continues until both players have had three attempts in each role, and then each player challenges a different opponent.

In this simple game, players learn the following:

• Ground can only be gained by the attacker carrying the ball forward.

• In defence, a touch stops the attacker's forward run.

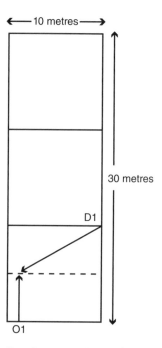

FIGURE 9.1   Running game in touch.

- The touch must be made safely.
- How to carry the ball safely.
- How to use a change of pace or direction to dodge the defender.

With a slight addition, this game leads into game 1b (see figure 9.2).

This game is identical to the first, except that after a touch, the attacker places the ball on the ground at the point where the touch was made (this point is known as *the mark*). The defender then moves back 5 metres from this mark. This retreat distance can be determined by the players and can vary from 5 to 10 metres to create a fair contest. Now the attacker picks the ball up from the mark and tries to run past the defender to the try line. Each attacker has five more attempts to gain ground and score. Meanwhile, the defender may only move forward to initiate the touch once the attacker has picked up the ball. After each touch, the defender must retreat the nominated distance.

After the sixth attempt or after a touchdown is scored, the attacker and defender change roles. So player D then becomes the attacker for six attempts and works to score a try or at least to gain more ground than O did. This game restates much of what was learned in game 1, but players also learn the following:

- The rules and concepts associated with the touch, the try line, and the touchdown.
- The attacking sequence in which the ball is played at the mark after a touch.
- The attackers have a total of six attempts (possessions) to carry the ball forward or to score a touchdown.
- After the sixth attempt, attack and defence roles change. The ball is automatically turned over, and play commences at the mark where the final touch was made.
- After a touch is made, the defence must quickly move back 5 metres from the touch mark in order to be onside. Players who have not retreated the 5-metre distance are offside. They cannot interfere with the play until they are back at the correct distance. For beginners, the 5-metre offside distance may be increased to allow the attackers more time to get organised.

Game 2: 2v1 With Referee

In the second game, player numbers are increased so that attackers must now cooperate to make ground past a defender within the 10-by-30-metre (35 by 90 feet) corridor. The number of players can be further increased to 3v2 and 4v3. This game builds on previous learning and brings in the role of the supporting attacker.

O1 picks the ball up from the ground and passes it to O2, who is positioned on an angle behind O1. O2 receives the ball and runs it forward to try to beat defender D1 and reach the score line (figure 9.3a).

If a touch is made on O2 by the defender, O2 must stop and place the ball at the mark. The defender retires 5 metres, and then O2 restarts the play by picking the ball up and passing it to O1, who moves to carry it forward. This pattern continues as the attackers try to make ground in the six attempts or until they score. D2 acts as the referee, making sure that the attackers play the ball at the mark and that the defender retreats the correct distance (figure 9.3b).

Now the teams change roles after the sixth attempt or when a touchdown is scored. So D1 and D2 now become attackers, starting where the final touch was made on their opponents or at the try line if a touchdown was scored. O1 and O2 take up the roles of defender and referee.

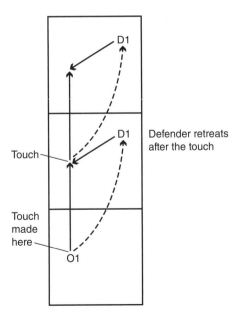

FIGURE 9.2 The defender retreats back from the gain line, and the attacker waits to play the ball.

The support attacker receives the ball wide and moves forward to gain ground.

FIGURE 9.3 Second stage of touch played in a 30-by-10-metre corridor.

This game is aligned with touch and is shaped using play conditions to encourage success and progression for novice players in specific ways:

- The ball must be placed on the ground at the mark after each touch. This rule ensures the attacker returns to the mark before playing the ball. Once in position, the ball is passed to the receiver, who moves to catch the ball and carries it forward. This encourages the attacker to return to the mark before playing the ball.

- The attacker must wait until the defender has retired the 5 metres (or a specified distance) before playing the ball. This allows all players to become familiar with this pattern of play, and it also gives supporting attackers time to reposition themselves behind the mark.

- The loss of possession rules are modified to give attackers more time with the ball and ensure greater continuity in play. So with novices, a dropped ball or a forward pass is only penalised by the loss of two possessions, not the loss of the ball, as is the case in the real game.

Other rule infringements, such as not returning to the mark to play the ball, also result in the loss of two possessions, not loss of the ball.

This game focuses on the key concept of the gain line and how to make ground as the support attacker (figure 9.4).

The concept of the gain line is crucial in touch and in all the rugby codes. This imaginary line drawn horizontally across the field indicates the

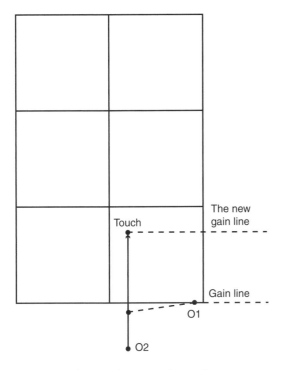

FIGURE 9.4 The gain line in rugby codes.

position of the ball at any instant, and in these games, the ball may not be passed forward of the gain line. This primary rule ensures that the ball can only be advanced safely by a ball carrier taking it forward, and this means the player with the ball and the potential receivers must work together to maximise the ground gained.

Clearly, the gain line continually moves forward and back with the position of the ball, so when a touch is made, players must return to the mark on the new gain line, where the touch was initiated. The ball is placed on the ground at this mark, and the new gain line extends though this mark across the width of the field.

Because the ball cannot be passed in front of the gain line, the ball carrier must quickly judge the position of a potential receiver and accurately time the delivery of the pass. Meanwhile, potential receivers should begin running from well behind the gain line to give themselves time to accelerate so that they can gain ground after receiving the ball. This requires good timing of the forward run to take the ball close to but not in front of the gain line. Verbal calls, such as 'on your left,' from the receiver to the passer will assist this process. The crucial concept here is that while the ball cannot be thrown forward, it should not be thrown backward (behind the gain line) any more than is necessary!

Co-operation is also required once the pass has been made, because the new supporting attacker must immediately reposition themselves to receive a possible return pass. This sequence of pass and support, repeated every time, is an important aspect of skilled play in touch. At any time, teachers and coaches can change the game's shape to make it more complex by increasing the number of players (3v2, 4v3) and the playing space (20 by 30 metres [70 by 90 feet] or 30 by 50 metres [90 by 165 feet]).

Game 3: Running the Ball Up + 3v2 With Referee

In this game, the corridor is extended to 20 by 30 metres and can be played with 3v2 and then with increased numbers (4v3 and 5v4). However, because it requires some specific techniques and several new rules and concepts, a simple practice situation is necessary before starting the game. The concept of rucking the ball as a specific tactic for running the ball forward with minimal risk of turnover can now be introduced together with key roles and then practised in the corridor (as shown in figure 9.5).

Teachers and coaches must explain the basis of this pattern of play and why it is important in the game. This will help players understand and establish an automatic pattern of taking the ball behind the gain line, running straight with the ball, initiating the touch, placing the ball quickly on the ground, and stepping forward over the ball, so the acting half can play it. The acting half then passes the ball to the receiver, who begins the sequence of taking the ball behind the gain line again. Players can gradually speed up the rucking and running process, using this quickness to gain ground and to increase the chances of catching defenders offside if they are not able to retire quickly to 5 metres. This is an ideal time to discuss the offside law and the penalty for infringements, because it provides a clear rationale for using the tactic described above. In this play, the first receiver takes the ball after one short pass and drives straight up the field as fast and far as possible without risking the ball by attempting a second pass. This allows the ball to be advanced quickly and safely away from a dangerous position near the opponent's score line. In addition, if attackers are quick, they can easily catch their opponents offside and gain 10 metres without risking the ball at all. This tactic

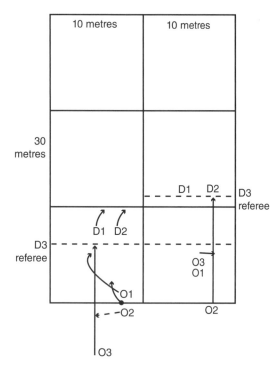

FIGURE 9.5 Running the ball up using a rucking pattern to gain ground.

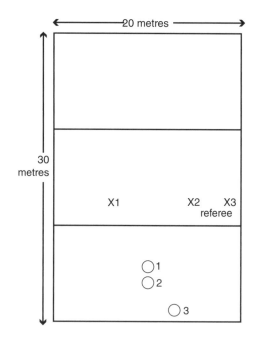

FIGURE 9.6 3v2 with referee.

can also be used to settle play after a change of possession or simply to safely gain distance towards the score line.

O1 executes a roll ball to O2, who is the acting half. The roll ball must be played at the mark by placing the ball on the ground and stepping forward over it. The ball may not roll over a 1-metre (3 feet) distance. The acting half (O2) makes a short pass to O3, who is set up diagonally behind the team. O3 then bursts forward, moving close to O2, to take the pass while still accelerating. As always, good timing is important in order to maximise the speed when receiving the ball close to the gain line.

Next, O3 runs the ball directly up the field to gain ground. If O3 cannot burst past the defender (D2), he may instigate the touch before quickly executing a roll ball to O1, who has again been trailing O3 in a good support position. O1, who is now the acting half, passes to O2, who has been moving into the support receiving position. Now O2 accelerates forward, takes another short pass, runs forward to gain as much ground as possible, and then quickly instigates the touch. In each case, the roll-ball player follows on to become the next acting half.

The rucking pattern is introduced into the 3v2 game, shown in figure 9.6, where the attacking team has six attempts to score a touchdown before turning the ball over to their opponents if they are unsuccessful. The referee now becomes increasingly important, focusing on the rucking pattern, observing the mark, and checking if the defence has retreated the correct distance.

In this play practice, players will learn the following:

- To ruck and run the ball efficiently so as to catch defenders offside
- The offside rule and the penalty
- The importance of not over-running the touch, since this wastes time coming back to the mark
- To roll the ball quickly
- To communicate with the acting half as the receiver

Players will also have many opportunities to practise the techniques they have previously learned.

Teachers and coaches can further shape these games to achieve specific outcomes—for example, by introducing a play condition restricting the movement of the acting half with the ball. This condition, which may be introduced for 4 to 5 minutes of play, forces the acting half to work on passing the ball to supporting team-mates rather than running with it before passing. This condition also encourages the support players to position themselves in relation to the acting half and to time their movements to receive the pass. Another condition to consolidate the use of the rucking and running play pattern is to mandate that attackers must use this pattern for at least two attempts whenever possession is gained. Shaping the play by applying conditions for a certain length of time in the game is a productive way to focus attention on particular aspects of tactical play.

Figure 9.7 shows the 4v3 game (with a referee) played on a pitch 30 metres wide by 30 metres long. It follows the same pattern as the 3v2 game, but the extra player provides more opportunities for teamwork in attack, while the extra width may make scoring easier. As always, the object is to score a try by advancing the ball to the score line 30 metres away within the six allowed possessions. Now the 'real rules' can be introduced. For example, rather than simply imposing a loss of two possessions for an error in attack, referees must emphasize the actual rules, which now means any infringement results in either a loss of possession or a penalty. Referees play an increasingly important role in this game because they enforce the following rules:

- Defenders offside = Penalty: This is a tap taken from where the defender should have retired to, with all defenders moving back 10 metres.
- Passing after touch = Penalty
- Forward pass = Penalty
- Ball not played at the mark = Penalty
- Obstruction = Penalty
- Acting half touched with the ball = Loss in possession and the attack commences with a roll ball
- Dropped ball = Loss in possession and the attack commences with a roll ball
- Acting half fumbles the ball = Loss in possession and the attack commences with a roll ball
- Roll ball travels more than 1 metre = Loss of possession and roll ball to opponents

In this next game, the starting tap can be introduced. It is used when the game starts, after a touchdown is scored, and also after a penalty. Here, the player with the ball places it on the ground, taps it forward a short distance with the toe, then picks it up and carries it

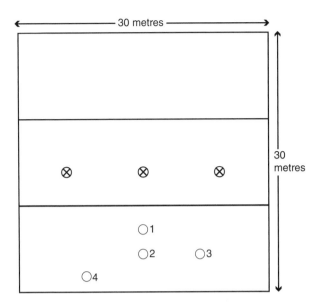

FIGURE 9.7 The 4v3 game.

forward. The defending team are positioned 10 metres back from the gain line where the tap is initiated. They may only move forward once the ball is tapped. In the 4v3 game, for example, when O1 has the ball, she begins play at the opposition score line with a tap.

When the real rules are enforced, the attackers must ensure that they do not turn the ball over carelessly, because if they do, their opponents will take over at the point where the ball is lost. Attackers must also take care not to pass the ball after the touch is made, since this also leads to a turnover and a penalty. In turn, defenders must learn to move back quickly to avoid being caught offside and giving up easy ground through penalties. This forces them to consider how to solve the problem of moving forward to make the touch without being caught by the attackers, who run the ball quickly at them. Teamwork and good communication can be used to improve defensive cover in this situation.

If team O score, their opponents begin their offense from the score line, using a tap to start play. If attackers (team O) make a mistake that results in a turnover, their opponents (team D) begin their first attempt at the point of the turnover. If team O fail to score in the six attempts, team D gain possession and begin their attack at the mark of team O's final attempt. The new attackers can now choose to employ the rucking and running tactic with short passes to advance the ball safely away from the danger area close to the opposition's end zone. The extra player in attack makes it easier to use intelligent running both with and without the ball to create an overload of attackers and so generate scoring opportunities by drawing defenders and then passing to the open player. In this situation, attackers must read the play and use mobility to either outflank the defence or cut through gaps as defenders respond to cover the width of attacking moves.

In this game, players will learn the following:

- An intercepted pass usually results in a score by the opposition.

- An unsuccessful interception that is knocked to the ground results in another six attempts by the attackers to score.

- A dropped or missed pass results in a change of possession turnover.

- Over-running the mark results in a penalty.

- An illegal roll ball results in a change of possession turnover.

- A pass after the touch results in a penalty.

- If the acting half is caught with the ball, it is a change of possession.

- Defenders who do not retire quickly and are caught offside will draw a penalty.

Clearly, understanding the rules is a critical part of effective play in touch, so the primary and secondary rules must be introduced at appropriate moments during play.

However, players will also have the chance to do the following:

- Improve their agility as they carry the ball forward using a change in pace or a change in direction to dodge and evade defenders

- Improve their passing skill, especially while moving into good support positions

- Learn how read the play, move into space, and draw a defender before passing

- Learn how to fake a pass and continue running

- Improve the positioning, timing, and acceleration of the support run to receive a pass

- Learn how to use mobility to wrap around team-mates, creating overload situations

- Learn how take defensive positions along the line and respond to attacking moves

Extending Game Play

Once the attacker team begins to score relatively easily, it is time to even up the numbers and play 4v4, 5v5, or 6v6 games. In these games, it is still possible to differentiate the shape of the game to cater for the diversity of individuals in the class.

While 4v4 or 5v5 games can be played on a 30-by-40-metre (90 by 130 feet) playing space, with the 6-a-side game, the playing area should be increased to 40 by 50 metres (130 by 165 feet). This ensures enough width to encourage a range of attacking moves to stretch the defenders and to create openings in the defensive line, as well as to make ground through the safer tactic of rucking and running the ball up field.

In these games, without the advantage of an extra player, attackers must learn to use tactics such as the overlap or wrap, the switch, reverse, and double overload to create—if only for an instant—a situation where the defender is faced with two attackers. The defenders must communicate with each other and move quickly to respond collectively to the mobility of the attack. This is a difficult task, since defenders must be aware of the position of attacking players and then shift cooperatively to cover any lateral movement of attackers. They also must work together when moving up as a line to help delay the ball, which ensures no easy spaces are left for the attack to easily cut through.

By using limited-time games and rotating teams, player motivation will be enhanced. Time between games can be allocated for reflection, coaching, clarification of rules, and also improving tactical understanding. Players can also design their own patterns of play and practice them before trying them out in the next game. At any point in time during the touch unit, teachers can revisit the earlier corridor practices but with a change in the focus of play. For example, the original 2v1 game played in a 10-by-30-metre (35 by 90 feet) corridor can be quickly extended into a 2v1v1 game by simply adding a second defender and allocating space for each defender. The first defender works in the first 15 metres; the second defender is located between 15 and 30 metres. The challenge is to see if the attacking pair can move the ball down the full length of the 30-metre corridor without being touched by the defenders. Attackers score a point for making it safely across each 15-metre zone without being touched, and the defenders score 2 points for any touch they make. The attacking pair move up the corridor to the 30-metre line and then come back again. The score is then calculated by adding the attack points and subtracting the defenders' points. Attackers and defenders then change roles. This shaped game provides additional opportunity for the attackers to improve their games sense as they solve the problem of getting the ball past each defender by drawing the defender, then either faking and running with the ball or passing it to the support attacker, who then carries it forward.

This Play Practice approach to teaching touch is recommended as the basis for introducing both rugby union and rugby league.

Rugby Sevens

Rugby sevens, like touch, is primarily based on running with the ball and passing. However, in the former game kicking the ball forward is also permitted, which influences the tactics and strategy used in the game. When a stoppage occurs in rugby sevens, the game restarts with a set play. For example, if a handling error occurs, such as the ball being knocked to the ground or passed forward, a scrum is used to restart the play, with possession transferred to the non-offending team. The ball can also be kicked forward from within the defensive 25-metre zone into touch. If the ball lands in the field of play and then bounces out of bounds, play is restarted with a lineout at the spot where the ball crossed the sideline, with possession going to the team that did not kick the ball into touch. If the ball is kicked directly out of bounds, play is restarted with a lineout; however, this is now taken at the sideline in line with where the kick was initiated.

In rugby sevens, body contact is allowed in the form of tackling the opponent who has possession of the ball. Following a tackle, players from both sides may attempt to secure the ball in a *maul*, when the ball is held off the ground, or in a *ruck*, when the ball has come into contact with the ground.

Kicking tends to be a less significant skill in the game, but it can still be important. The game starts in each half with a drop kick from the centre. After each try, a drop kick is used to attempt to convert the try and add 2 extra points to the score. Kicking directly to touch can be used from possession in the defensive 22 metres. In attack, a deep kick from outside the defensive 22 that bounces into touch can be used to gain an attacking position. In general play, an attacking team sometimes uses a variety of kicks to overcome an aggressive defence.

Set Plays

Teachers and coaches can introduce the scrum and lineout in small practice situations, emphasising technique and the role of the individual player or group in the set piece. This can progress from simplified partner challenges, building up gradually by increasing numbers towards the more complex pressure in the game.

Scrum

Players work in pairs to establish the correct body position. This is an ideal warm-up activity that can be expanded to a partner challenge once players have mastered good body position. Players position their feet wide apart to establish a solid base, flex their knees, flatten their back, and tuck their head under the shoulder of their partner. Both partners should hold on to each other's trunks. One partner pushes against the other, sharply extending the knees and attempting to move the stationary partner back. The other partner resists by splaying the feet and locking the legs in position (figure 9.8).

Instructors can build up this technique using a 2v2 practice, in which players bind their inside arms around their partner's trunk and their outside arms around an opponent.

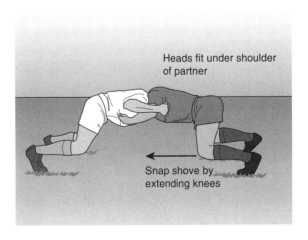

Heads fit under shoulder of partner

Snap shove by extending knees

FIGURE 9.8 Scrum.

3v3 Practice

The 3v3 practice is the scrum used in the game. The middle player is the hooker, who uses the right foot to push the ball back through the legs of the left-side player (loose-head prop). The right-side player (tight-head prop) supports and stabilises the scrum (figure 9.9).

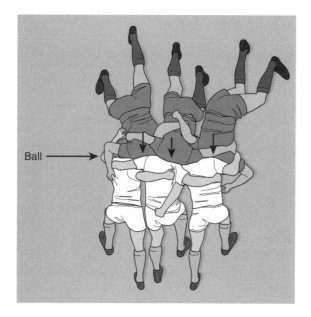

FIGURE 9.9 3v3 practice.

Small-sided games of 4v4 or 5v5 can be played with only 2 players in the scrum (1v1), where the ball is fed into the left side by the halfback and the hooker uses the right hand to push the ball back between the legs. The halfback collects the ball and passes it to the backs, who attempt to get over the advantage line.

This is a simple extension of how the ball is played from the mark in touch, so it can be easily adapted into the progressions outlined in the previous section.

Each scrum can be enlarged from 2 to 3 forwards. With 3 forwards and 4 backs, you have a 7-a-side game. Initially, the game can be shaped so that the side putting the ball into the scrum is allowed to win it. Each side has six attempts to score. The scrum is used to restart play after a breakdown in play, such as a forward pass, a dropped ball, or an offside position.

Lineout

Since there is little kicking in sevens, lineouts occur far less frequently than scrums. When the ball is kicked over the sidelines and into touch, the non-kicking team throws the ball between the opposition forwards, who line up at right angles to the place where the ball entered touch. They attempt to catch the ball and retain possession for their team.

Basic Lineout Practice Working in Grids

The ball is thrown by X1, who faces the jumper (X2) standing 5 metres away. X2 jumps, catches the ball, and passes to X3, who returns the ball to X1 (figure 9.10a). Players rotate roles frequently. A round ball could be used initially for the throw-in with a two-handed under-arm lob to ensure success, followed by a two-handed over-arm lob as in the soccer throw-in. Eventually, a rugby ball should be introduced.

This practice can be progressed further by adding an extra player (X4), who stands behind X2 and assists the jumper by grasping him around the waist and lifting. This is a novel aspect of the lineout. Players will learn to time and coordinate the jump with the throw. By adding another player, the halfback (X4) can then pass to a player running to the ball and practise the linking of forwards and backs. Both of these techniques can be introduced into the game using groups of 5v5, 6v6, or 7v7 (figure 9.10b).

In early games, sport educators should allow the side throwing in the ball to win possession so that the opposition lineout remains passive. As technique and understanding improve, the lineout can become competitive, with both sets of forwards attempting to win the ball. This should lead to the development of tactics by the team throwing in the ball in an attempt to win possession, such as moving forwards or backwards quickly to surprise the opposition.

Rugby sevens can be played enjoyably without tackling by simply using a two-handed touch on the hips of the ball carrier to replace the tackle. This simulates the correct body position and ensures that the ball is passed on immediately. Depending on the context, it may be appropriate to introduce tackling into the game. This can be undertaken using the following progressions.

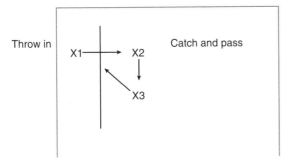

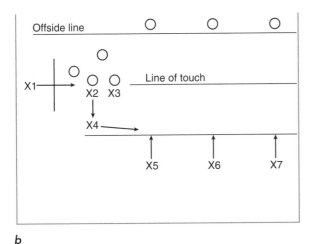

a

b

FIGURE 9.10 Practise working in grids.

Body Contact

Body contact can be introduced initially using small-sided games, such as end ball. In this game, teams are selected and matched for size. This can be done quickly by having the players pair up according to size and number themselves 1 or 2. All number 1s form one team and 2s form another, so that there is an even spread of sizes across the teams.

Two teams of 5 or 6 per side play with four or five balls on a small area with a scoring zone at each end. The equipment is placed in the centre of the area. The aim of the game is to secure a ball, carry it, and hold it in the score zone. Defenders can attempt to retrieve the rugby ball from the attackers by grabbing the ball from their hands and carrying it to their score zone. Conditions can be applied in this game in order to accommodate individual needs. For example, restrictions on the pace of the game and the type of contact can be applied according to the

experience level of the group. The game can be allowed to proceed for 4 or 5 minutes, and the team who secures the most balls in their score area wins.

Walking rugby is another useful introduction to body contact using small-sided games of 3v3, 4v4, or 5v5 played in corridors as indicated previously in touch. Players walk and pass the ball in an attempt to score while defenders grab or hold the attackers. In these games attackers are given a number of attempts to gain ground or score before changing roles after the final attempt or when a try is scored. However, this is a very artificial game, and boys especially may find it difficult to restrict themselves to walking, especially if there is a chance to score! Because of this, short play-time intervals, a rotation of teams, and an emphasis on these games as lead-up trials only are recommended strategies to assist the groups in maintaining a walking pace.

The teacher or coach can observe the players to assess their involvement and confidence with physical contact and can then reorganise teams accordingly. As indicated earlier, they should also match players for size in the early stages of introducing body contact.

Tackling

Safety is of utmost importance when teaching this technique. Factors such as matching players for size and playing on soft surfaces are both very important.

The tackler places the head behind the opponent's hips, with his arms grasped firmly around the other's legs between the knees and hips. The tackler's legs are used to drive the weight forward through the movement. The body position needs to be low, with the eyes focused on the area of contact.

Practice 1: Introducing Tackling

Players should use tackle bags, if available, and work in small groups of 3 or 4. One player supports the bag while the others take turns tackling it. Starting from a squat position, the tackler drives with the legs into the bag, hitting it with the shoulder, holding the head to one side, and throwing the arms around the bag to knock it over. The group rotates so each player gets to tackle. This can be another warm-up activity.

Practice 2: Kneeling Tackling

Players work in pairs of similar size. Both assume a kneeling position within touching distance of one another, with the tackler to the side of and perpendicular to the partner. The tackler drives the leading shoulder into the partner's hip and thigh area, placing his head behind the partner's hips and his arms around the legs. In this way, he attempts to knock the partner over.

Practice 3: Walking Tackling

Players work in groups of 3, with the tackler in a kneeling position. The attacking player to be tackled walks in a straight line past the tackler, who attempts to tackle while driving from the knees. The attacker must not deviate from the path or resist the tackle and should be shown how to relax and fall to the ground. This can be progressed so that the attacker is carrying the ball, and after he is taken to ground in the tackle he learns to position the ball so that a supporting player can pick it up.

Practice 4: Walking and Tackling Small-Sided Game

Players can return to the small-sided game of 5v5 or 6v6 introduced earlier; however, in this game tackling is permitted. The attacking team attempts to score by walking and passing. The defenders can tackle, but the focus is on safety and correct tackling technique. Again this game will have to be carefully monitored and conditions applied to ensure the walking rule is observed.

The attacking players focus on the tactic of keeping the ball 'available' by passing it as the tackle is made or by placing it on the ground in the direction of their team, usually backwards, so that a support player can pick it up and continue the attack. Similar to the earlier game, the attackers are given a set number of attempts to move the ball forward before changing roles. This condition enables both teams more time and practice in the attacking and defending roles. In this game, any turnover or error by the attackers results in an additional loss of one play attempt with the ball (as used in touch).

Contact After a Tackle: The Maul and Ruck

When a tackled player is held and other players join the tackler and the tackled, a 'maul' is formed to contest the ball. Attacking players should attempt to stay on their feet and present the ball to a support player. The defensive players also try to gain possession of the ball.

If the tackled player goes to ground and opponents come into contact over the ball, then a 'ruck' is formed. The tackled player should immediately place the ball back towards the support players and release it. The defence are allowed to step over and attempt to secure the ball. The tackler must immediately release the tackled player and quickly get to her feet in order to attempt to regain possession of the ball.

These techniques can be practised in small-group games. Working in groups of 3, the attacking player with the ball walks into a defender, who effects a standing tackle. The ball carrier anticipates the tackle, lowers the body, and drives in with a leading shoulder, holding the ball back on the opposite hip. The support attacker drives into the ball carrier with the opposite shoulder to seal off the ball and secure it. Groups can be enlarged to 4 attackers against 2 defenders. The attacker with the ball makes the ball available when tackled; the support attacker seals off the ball, secures it, and then passes it to a halfback, who passes to the fourth player acting as a back. These patterns can then be introduced into the 5v5 games of slow-pace walking rugby initially and then without the restriction of walking. The attacking team are once again allowed a number of attempts to score before changing roles. Finally, games can be played using the real rules in which possession of the ball is evenly contested by both teams. The tackler's side are now also attempting to win the ball, which generates a more authentic learning situation. In this context, attacking players learn that not everyone joins in the maul; some players maintain their support positions. The teacher or coach may need to limit the number of players who can enter the maul in order to focus on this tactical concept.

The same process can be used in developing the technique and the tactical understanding of the ruck. Since both the tackling and tackled

- A quarterback delivering the ball
- A receiver catching the ball
- A running back carrying the ball
- Direct involvement in a defensive role, such as covering a receiver or stopping a ball carrier

From there, it was a relatively simple step to develop a series of small-sided games that gave every student a chance to take on each of the preceding roles and progress to playing flag. These games provide the context for learning, and they build up a working knowledge of concepts, roles, rules, and playing capabilities in a sequential manner. Using a series of 10-by-30-metre (35 by 90 feet) corridors in the teaching grid is ideal for organising the learning environment.

The first problem was teaching students the specific technique of throwing the football. Many American youngsters can throw a perfect spiral with the regulation ball. However, children from different cultures, even those with natural throwing ability, can find this task challenging. Fortunately, tough foam black max footballs are now available that are smaller than the regular ball, with finger indents that guide how the ball should be held and improve control as the ball is released. These balls not only make it easier for more participants to throw properly but also are easier to catch. This means that students can throw the ball farther and with greater accuracy, which immediately opens up a wider range of

tactical possibilities for every player taking on the role of quarterback.

Developing Technique: Challenges and Target Games

The sequence begins with a throwing and catching challenge, where partners co-operate to throw the ball with a spiral action. Partners work in the teaching grid 5 to 10 metres (15 to 35 feet) apart initially, and then each pair is encouraged to see how far apart they can move, throwing the ball accurately and with a spiral. For participants with a less-experienced throwing arm, 10 metres might be the maximum range, so in this case, points can be allocated for the perfect spiral plus accuracy in the throw to the target.

This activity can be extended into a challenge of throwing for distance and accuracy by placing distance markers or tape measures. In this challenge, each student practices the spiral throw and keeps an individual score based on where the ball lands. The actual distance of the throw—minus the distance the ball lands away from the tape, so that accuracy is factored in—can be recorded on a class or individual chart. They can use this challenge regularly at the beginning of lessons, with the students working in pairs or small groups. They can also include throwing a vortex ball as a novelty variation to this task.

Partner throw–catch challenges can also be varied simply by including throwing to a moving partner. To do this, the receiver takes a few steps away from the thrower before turning and bursting back, showing their hands clearly as a target to receive the ball. This variation progresses nicely into the hook-play pattern that follows.

Passing Patterns

These partner challenges enable students to develop a working model of technique for effective game play. This is only ever a quick session, since the group should be introduced to the hook pattern shown in figure 9.11 as soon as possible.

The potential receiver snaps the ball back to the quarterback and then runs downfield approximately 10 to 15 metres (35 to 40 feet) before suddenly checking and hooking back towards the quarterback, who delivers a pass to the target's hands in front of the chest.

Smaller footballs can be used to make them easier for students to throw and catch.

Because the receiver is moving back towards the ball, this is the easiest pattern for novices to employ.

Each player has between three and five attempts in each role. At this point, the concept of the line of scrimmage can be introduced, along with the notion of the quarterback's signal cadence. This is where the quarterback calls out a signal for the ball to be snapped. A typical cadence might be 'Down, set, hut,' where the ball is snapped on 'hut'. However, in the real game, the quarterback may choose to change the play at the line of scrimmage before the ball is snapped by including additional signals to team-mates. This is a more advanced concept addressed only with more experienced players.

Players change partners for another sequence of passes. Partners can also be given a card with all of the play patterns so they can set them up and try each of them.

The other basic passing patterns shown in figure 9.11 can be introduced in this sequence:

1. Down and out
2. Down and in
3. Post pattern
4. Flag pattern
5. Down, out, and up

In the final slant pattern, the quarterback moves along the line of scrimmage before passing.

With absolute beginners, it is helpful to use ropes or coloured marker cones to indicate the exact path of the pattern to be run. As each pattern is introduced, teachers should explain or ask the students when and why each is used. Cards illustrating all of these plays can be provided as a valuable teaching resource, and the back of the card can include further information or questions relating to these plays. It is important to help students understand the way these different passing patterns interact with each other and how one play, even if unsuccessful, can be used to set the defender up for the next. Working in a co-operative manner encourages students to help one another and to develop resilience as they persist in mastering and understanding the passing patterns.

Building Attacking Numbers: 3v1, 2v1

Teachers can create a 3v1 game any time after the players have learnt a couple of the passing patterns. The quarterback tries to get the ball to two potential receivers, who are faced with a single defender (figure 9.12a). The defender

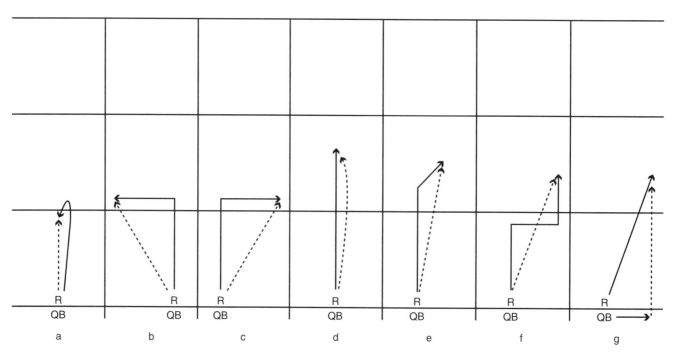

FIGURE 9.11 Flag football passing patterns.

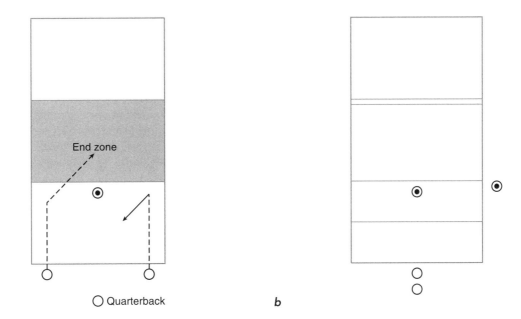

FIGURE 9.12 *(a)* 3v1: Quarterback and two potential receivers are faced with one defender; *(b)* 2v1 with official: Adding pressure on passing and receiving.

attempts to intercept any pass. This encourages quarterbacks to improve their games sense by early scanning and reading the play. The 3v1 task is a game in name only because receivers are not allowed to run on with the ball after making a catch. The game is simply to beat the defender to the ball. However, to introduce some more interest, it is possible to treat the second square in the teaching grid as the end zone so that any catches here become touchdowns. Naturally, players should rotate positions on a regular basis to ensure that everyone takes on each role.

The next progression is to the 2v1 game (figure 9.12b), with the single receiver breaking downfield to receive the ball as the defender tries to intercept. Now both the quarterback and receiver are under far more pressure. The challenge for the quarterback is to read the defender's position and to attempt to pass the ball accurately to the receiver. The fourth member of the group can take on an official's role to determine where the catch was made. Once again, the receiver stops after making the reception but can score a touchdown by receiving the ball in the end zone, which may simply be a zone in the teaching grid. As before, players rotate through each position, including that of the official.

Rules associated with pass interference can be introduced during these practices. In flag, the no-contact rule applies, so defenders must understand the meaning of pass interference. A defending player may not interfere with a receiver's ability to make a fair attempt to catch a forward pass. Pass interference may include tripping, pushing, pulling, or cutting in front of the receiver or pulling on the receiver's arms. It does not include catching or batting the ball before it reaches the receiver. In the game, pass interference results in a penalty, gaining 10 metres.

3v2 With an Official Role

As soon as it is clear that players can cope with a more realistic situation, a 3v2 game can be played with an official (figure 9.13). Now, two receivers are faced by two defenders and the quarterback is allowed only 5 seconds from the snap to release the ball. However, they can move along the line of scrimmage to improve the passing angle. Because they are now under time pressure and must read a more complex display involving two potential receivers and active defenders, both their games sense and their technical ability will be challenged. In these games, receivers must also learn to anticipate defenders' reactions and alter the set play pattern if necessary.

This game can be extended to allow attackers four attempts to score a touchdown (worth 6 points), either by receiving the ball in the end

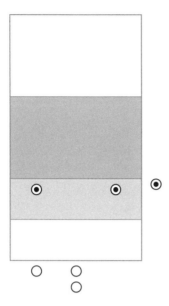

FIGURE 9.13 3v2 game with official role. The quarterback can move across the line of scrimmage, and four attempts to gain ground or score a touchdown are allowed.

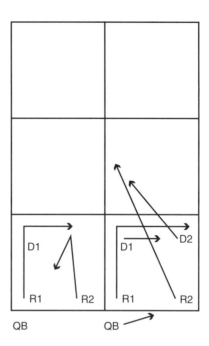

FIGURE 9.14 Football play card. Player R1 goes down and out to pick up 8 metres (25 feet). Player R2 uses a slant pattern, crossing in front of R1, looking for a touchdown pass. QB can move behind the line of scrimmage.

zone or by gaining points for clean possessions ahead of the gain line. A 5-metre gain of ground can be worth 1 point, while a 5- to 10-metre gain is worth 2 points. Teams rotate after four attempts, keeping score of the distance gained and marking any touchdowns. This game introduces scoring, new rules, and game concepts that the official can focus on. It is also possible to introduce tags during this game so that the defenders get used to taking the tag from the receiver when they catch the ball. The tag confirms the ground gained.

Play cards of the type shown in figure 9.14 can be introduced to save time and prevent unending arguments! A range of up to 10 laminated play cards randomly drawn from a box can introduce an element of chance into the game without disrupting its essential purpose. While it is possible to simply call the attackers by their usual names, young players will be happy to take on the names of great receivers from the history of football. Photographs of these players will make the cards even more attractive and interesting, as will a brief history of their playing record or descriptions of the great catches they have made during their career. These can be expanded by students and compiled into a playbook as an extension project.

3v3 Game Play and Movement With the Ball

Next, it is possible to move to the more complex 3v3 game played in a 20-by-30-metre (70 by 90 feet) corridor. The object is to score a touchdown—that is, to move the ball 30 metres in four plays. The previous mini-game becomes a real game, and appropriate rules are introduced in the context of the game. An additional player on each team can take on the umpiring role and then rotate in to play.

The quarterback still has only 5 seconds to throw the ball but is allowed to run forward with it for the first time. If the quarterback moves over the line of scrimmage, he is not allowed to throw the ball forward. The quarterback can choose to carry the ball forward or else throw the ball back if options are available. In addition, receivers can run with the ball after taking a catch. The position where a defender takes the flag (or touches the receiver with two hands if not using flags) becomes the next line of scrimmage.

Each team of three rotates through the quarterback position on the first three plays. If they do not score a touchdown, the farthest point they reach is marked. Their opponents begin their offence from that field position, moving towards their end zone. Ties are resolved with an extra play by each team: The team that gains the most ground on that play is awarded the win. Play cards can be used in this game for the first three plays of a sequence. The fourth play is determined by the offensive team to suit the situation.

Building to 5v5 Game Play

With the essential principles of the gridiron game introduced in this way, playing numbers for flag football can increase to 5, 6, or 7 a side. Combinations may also be used in a class, the size of the playing area can be adjusted, and more detailed play cards can be used.

Once the game is extended in this way, teachers can introduce the tactic of a 'hand-off' from the quarterback to introduce running plays. Students can then be further engaged in the process of play making and creating their own signature moves in these games. This further develops their games sense as they apply tactics, strategy, and an understanding of themselves and their team-mates in challenging game contexts. Mini-tournament play and action fantasy games such as the Super Bowl series can be used as culminating events to extend this game play. The Sport Education model can also be employed to ensure an extended unit or season of play.

ten

Teaching Court-Divided Games

Table Tennis, Badminton, Tennis, and Volleyball

> Table tennis lowers expectations and teaches you to live with disappointment as a necessary function of human engagement.
>
> Howard Jacobson in *Everything You Know Is Pong*

As chapter 3 shows, one of the biggest problems for youngsters learning to play any ball game is the time it takes them to carry out the skill process. By their very nature, racquet sports exacerbate this problem. While students in team games can play skilfully without the ball for much of a game, in racquet sports they must focus directly on the ball or shuttle for the entire game and must be prepared to play it every time it comes over the net!

They must therefore learn how to track a fast-moving object, predict its flight path, move into position to intercept it, and then strike it so well that it will be returned to the other side of the net! This is a far more difficult task than is generally realised, and while these games can be grouped together as racquet sports, each presents unique problems for beginners.

In tennis, students must be able to move quickly around a relatively large playing area to reach balls that may be travelling in any direction and at any height, angle, or speed. Multi-directional agility is critical just to get into position to play the ball, far less to hit it effectively.

In table tennis, the speed of the very light ball means that simply tracking it and finding the time to prepare for a stroke is difficult for beginners. Youngsters often try to resolve this problem by employing a dead-end technique that will interfere with or even prevent further progress.

Badminton brings the special problem of a target that, unlike a ball, can decelerate rapidly from high speed and drop suddenly in a way that makes prediction very difficult, especially for inexperienced players. In addition, the shuttle must be volleyed, increasing the demands for multi-directional agility, particularly the lunge and recovery, to cover all areas on the court. This presents a particularly difficult challenge for youngsters in the early stages.

Since there is little fun to be had from continually smashing the ball off the table, hitting the shuttle into the net or missing it completely, or trudging to the back of the court to retrieve tennis balls, students must be helped to develop the technical ability required to keep the ball or shuttle in play, as rapidly and efficiently as possible. However, this is not easy, and mistakes are inevitable and frequent in the early stages of learning any of these games. They are also obvious, so it is therefore critical to help youngsters, especially beginners, to understand that errors are a natural and inevitable part of the learning process. This is important in any sport, but it becomes especially so in racquet sports.

The Play Practice solution is to create learning situations in which beginners can initially focus totally on the development of technical ability. Therefore, teachers and coaches should attempt to do the following:

- Eliminate the tactical demands
- Minimise the perceptual demands
- Reduce the movement demands of the practice task

Even this process must be broken down into a series of small challenges and achievements so that youngsters can enjoy the feeling of success when they can do the following:

- Make solid contact with the ball or shuttle
- Get it over the net, at least some of the time
- Maintain a rally

It is important for teachers and coaches to understand that in all of these games, tactics are completely dependent on technique. A corollary of this is that it is futile to introduce tactics before players can control the ball or shuttle well enough to direct it where they want it to go. To make this easier, where possible the technical demands are reduced by the introduction of working models of technique (that is, techniques that are stripped back to the bare bones).

In essence, while some authorities recommend a tactical approach to teaching racquet sports, we take the view that if a youngster cannot consistently return the ball or the shuttle over the net, an understanding of tactics will be wasted! Indeed, even at the highest levels, tactics and strategy are always based on the player's specific technical ability. Put simply, tennis players cannot rely on serve and volley tactics unless they possess a powerful serve and sound volleying technique! On the other hand, the tactical game of some tennis players is based on athleticism, endurance, mental toughness, and solid ground strokes. This method can provide a steady income for many players on the professional circuit; indeed, these qualities have enabled players like Nadal and Federer to dominate men's tennis through the early part of the 21st century. It is certainly an approach that will work for many youngsters!

Shaping Court-Divided Games

Table tennis has been a major influence on the evolution of Play Practice. In this game, it is clear that technical ability is the critical factor if players are to be able to keep the light ball in play on a small table. For this reason, Play Practice focuses on innovative ways to help young players improve their technical ability from the very beginning of the experience!

To do this, we simply change the game. First, we eliminate the regulation service action in tennis and table tennis. In the first case, the serve in tennis is a difficult movement that requires shoulder-girdle strength and a degree of coordination that many children do not have. In table tennis, introducing the correct service action too soon may interfere with the development of effective technique in the key strokes that beginners must master if they are to play effectively. However, in badminton, the service should be introduced from the very beginning, since it replicates one of the basic techniques of the game.

In addition to eliminating the serve in table tennis, we change the nature of the game by placing a target on each side of the table. The challenge is now to hit the target and score a point using a designated technique or stroke. Points can only be won by hitting the target. They cannot be lost even if the ball is hit off the table or into the net. Now there is no reason to create problems for an opponent by continually changing the angle, direction, or even spin of the shot while there is every incentive to develop a consistent, accurate stroke.

Players can only win a game, of perhaps 3 or 5 points, by hitting the target more frequently than their partner. As both players strive to score points by hitting their target, the line and length of shots will inevitably become more and more consistent. This in turn reduces the perceptual and movement demands of the task and gives both players more time to position themselves and then prepare for the specified stroke.

In a sense, this creates the ideal Gallwey (1976) game in which the performance of an opponent can help a player improve. The better the opponent, the greater the improvement. In target table tennis, competition indeed becomes true co-operation, for as players strive to win a point, they in fact make it easier for their opponents to do the same thing.

In tennis, a whole range of horizontal targets can be used. But even a game played in the tram lines—that is to say, the lines that differentiate the singles and doubles court—will quickly improve the line of shots, thus reducing the need for lateral movement to the ball, which young players especially find difficult. Readers will be interested in the ideas of Chris Deptula, a University of South Australia graduate who is now a professional tennis coach based in Adelaide. He has contributed to parts of the tennis section with ideas on coaching young children and developing players of different abilities.

In badminton, target games with both horizontal and vertical zones can be used to develop technique and to encourage the forward–backward agility needed in this game. A play practice in which points can only be won when the shuttle is hit over a net 5 metres (15 feet) high has successfully improved the ability of students to consistently hit overhead clears. For absolute beginners balloon badminton is a novel way to introduce the game so learners experience success.

Volleyball is included in this section because technical ability is also a vital aspect of skilful play in this game and it directly affects tactical possibilities. Whilst volleyball is a team game, the players are separated on either side of the net and cooperative team play is based on individual technical ability. Successful play is determined by the ability of each individual to put the ball into play and then to be able to control and redirect it once it travels over the net. Consequently, many of the learning challenges faced by beginners in volleyball are similar to those experienced by beginners in the racquet sports. In volleyball, the starting games are simplified by removing the impact of the serve and minimising the importance of agility just like the introductory games in table tennis and tennis. This allows players to focus on improving their technical ability and games sense within an enjoyable game context. The selection of a softer, lighter ball is critical when introducing the game with beginners because it helps promote success as well as increase player safety by minimizing the discomfort experienced

when learning to control the ball using the forearms. Games should also be shaped to maximise opportunities for individuals to play the ball and to combine with other team members. This can be done by reducing numbers per team and by playing on a smaller court. Mini-courts (using the badminton court with an elevated net) provide opportunity for beginners to play in 4v4 games, and the playing number can be decreased to 3v3 or even 2v2 to cater for more advanced levels of participation. When these conditions are in place it is possible to develop technical ability, games sense, and other aspects of skilled play concurrently in engaging game settings.

These ideas are further expanded in the volleyball section, which includes ideas from David Eldridge, a UniSA graduate who is a master teacher and the most successful high school volleyball coach in Australia.

Co-Operative Learning With Experienced Players

In all of the preceding games, teachers can use the more experienced players in a group as assistant coaches. Their primary task is to put the ball exactly where their partner needs it in order to play a particular stroke. However, under the right conditions, they can also provide information as feedback givers. To keep them motivated, these coaches can be challenged to perfect their own ball control or to improve some other aspect of their own technique while helping their partner. However, this strategy must be used sparingly. The best players in any group want and need opportunities to play and practise with partners of their own standard.

Action Fantasy Games

Anyone introducing racquet sports will find the action fantasy game concept detailed in chapter 4 to be invaluable. These games initially evolved to solve one of the major problems of teaching these sports—that is, engaging children of widely varying abilities and talents in the persistent and positive practice necessary to develop a sound technique. These laminated (or electronic) game cards with practice tasks on the reverse side can maintain the motivation initially developed through target games.

Table Tennis

Despite the fact that table tennis is played by hundreds of millions of people around the world, it is undervalued in many countries, including the United States, where it is usually seen as a mere recreational activity. This is unfortunate because at the elite level, table tennis demands high levels of technical ability, athleticism, endurance, and mental toughness. However, the greatest advantages of this game are that it does not require size or power and can be played competitively at any age from 8 to 80 and even beyond!

Table tennis has much to offer in the physical education setting. With modern wheeled tables that can be quickly moved into position, it takes less time to set up than other popular indoor games, while making effective use of the available space.

Another major advantage is that because only 3 or 4 players are needed to make up a team, it is easy to organise a range of intra- or inter-school competitions or to develop community leagues based around youth clubs, church halls, or even private facilities, as long as they have a good table and sufficient lighting! This ease in setting up a competitive structure is important because one of the primary aims of Play Practice is to help youngsters develop a level of performance that will allow them to begin to play any sport competitively, if they want to do so. The motivation inherent in this process begins to drive the desire to practise so that both performance and commitment spiral upwards.

Although table tennis can be played using ordinary pimpled rubber bats, it becomes a much easier game if modern bats, made with the sandwich construction, are used. It is also important to select good quality balls because they track more consistently through the air and off the table. Any ball with a three-star or three-crown rating is suitable. Because balls of this quality are relatively expensive, students must learn to treat them with respect.

While the light ball and small table may initially present problems to beginners, with good instruction, it is relatively easy for them to develop the technical ability necessary to play successfully and enjoyably. This is partly because it is possible to play table tennis up to the Olympic level with a tactical method based on a powerful topspin forehand that is supported by a limited range of other strokes. If limited time is available, the forehand topspin, the backhand push, and the block, along with the serve, become the focus for teaching and learning. However, we have included information on other important techniques because once youngsters do become hooked, they will inevitably want to improve their technical range and, in so doing, broaden their tactical options. Some may even decide to adopt a defensive strategy and the techniques that are required for that strategy simply because of their psychological profile!

Basic Techniques

As in all of the racquet games, players must learn how to track a fast-moving object, predict its flight path, move into position, and then strike it so well that it will be returned to the other side of the net. In table tennis, the small playing surface and light ball create their own unique problems for beginners if they are to progress beyond mere ping pong. In the original Play Practice work, we suggested that it was necessary to increase the size of the ball to make the game more accessible and enjoyable for beginners. Whether or not the authorities took any notice of this recommendation, they have indeed increased the diameter of the ball from 38 to 40 millimetres! Small though this difference may seem, anyone who has played with both ball sizes recognizes the difference immediately.

Spin

So the first priority is to help youngsters develop the technical ability needed to control the ball and to keep it on the table, even when it has been hit very hard. Here, an understanding of the effect of spin on the flight of the ball is invaluable because the key elements of technique in table tennis are determined by the aerodynamics of the spinning ball. In fact, spin is so important that until their use was banned early in 2009, elite players used highly toxic glues such as toluene to improve the stickiness of their bats. This enabled them to impart as much as 30 percent greater spin to the ball for a given bat speed.

Topspin, or forward spin, makes the ball drop rapidly. Even if it has been struck very hard, it will still come down to hit the table (figure 10.1a). Backspin causes the ball to rise slightly after contact, and then rapidly slows it down so

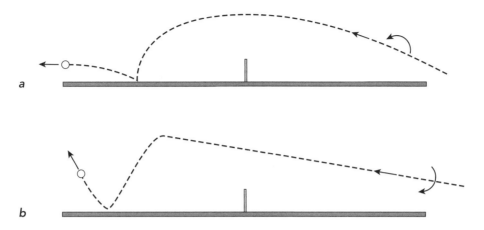

FIGURE 10.1 Typical flight path of a ball hit *(a)* with topspin and *(b)* in chop strokes.

that it will drop under the influence of gravity to land on the table (figure 10.1*b*). Sidespin causes the ball to veer in the direction of the spin. This happens because the spin causes low-pressure areas in the air surrounding the ball, which then moves towards that low pressure.

Of course, players also need to know how to combat a spinning ball when it hits their bat. Topspin makes the ball climb up the bat, while backspin drags the ball down. This means that when blocking or hitting against topspin, the racquet must be closed—that is, angled slightly forward—and when dealing with backspin, it must be more open, or angled slightly back.

While young players may initially experience success against their peers using sidespin strokes, the use of sidespin should be discouraged from the outset. It is a dead-end approach that prevents players from developing the topspin and backspin strokes necessary for success at the next level. Of course, experienced players do combine sidespin with topspin or backspin, especially in the service action.

Grip

The easiest way to hold a table tennis bat is to shake hands with it, as shown in figure 10.2. Players must always maintain this positioning, because any major changes in the grip will make it difficult for them to play both forehand and backhand strokes. In spite of this, anyone who follows this game knows that some of the best players in the world use what is called a pen-hold grip, with the bat handle positioned between thumb and forefinger. However, this is because

FIGURE 10.2 How to grip the table tennis bat: shake hands with the bat.

the players in question are from Asia, and they have spent their entire lives manipulating two chopsticks between forefinger and thumb as they eat! So, the pen-hold grip is natural to them. Despite this, many of the better Asian players do in fact now use the shake-hands grip.

Working Technical Models

This concept of working technical models is important because the advanced techniques used by elite players are based on the use of special high-spin bats and the fact that they can take the ball early—that is, before it reaches the top of the bounce when playing attacking strokes. This advanced technical model becomes a fast, flat sweep through the top quarter of the ball with the racquet angled forward, as shown in figure 10.3*a*. However, beginners rarely have access to ultra-spin bats and, most importantly, they can almost never take the ball early (i.e., soon after the bounce). This is because it takes them longer to track and compute the flight of the ball and then move in to position to execute the stroke. They are forced to hit the ball later, after the top of the bounce (figure 10.3*b*). This means that when beginners play attacking strokes, they must use a more open bat face and employ a working model of technique, which involves a simple lifting swing up through the rear of the ball.

Although there are sound reasons for teaching the forehand topspin stroke first, experience suggests that it is better to begin with the backhand push stroke. This is the easiest stroke for beginners to master because it involves a simple arm movement to push the bat through the ball, which is played in line with the players' eyes and so makes tracking it easier.

The first session begins with a demonstration of the correct stance, as shown in figure 10.4. Standing slightly offset to the backhand side, with feet apart and legs flexed, and holding the bat so as just able to touch the centre line of the table, the player is ready to play any stroke. Now the backhand push is introduced, along with a quick explanation or discussion of why it is important in tactical play at every level.

This simple stroke not only provides a valuable method of keeping the ball in play under any conditions but also ensures a solid foundation for the development of the backhand block, the backhand topspin drive, and the defensive chop stroke.

With the feet positioned parallel with the table and the shoulders slightly turned, as shown in figure 10.4, the player angles the bat slightly backwards and then pushes it forwards through the back of the ball from just in front of the left side of the body, almost extending the arm fully.

The first practice is simple. The player drops the ball onto the table and pushes the rebound across the net to be caught by the player on the other side, who repeats the exercise. Then, perhaps with 4 sharing a table, players drop and hit 10 shots each. Next, the first player drops the ball on the table and pushes it over the net. The partner plays the ball back to make two consecutive shots, and then goes for three, and then four, and so on. If play breaks down, they go back to the score they had reached previously. The first pair to reach 10 consecutive strokes is the winning team in the class. Naturally, this exercise can be repeated several times, changing partners to enhance the practice. Build-ups of this kind are very valuable in motivating youngsters to develop consistent technique.

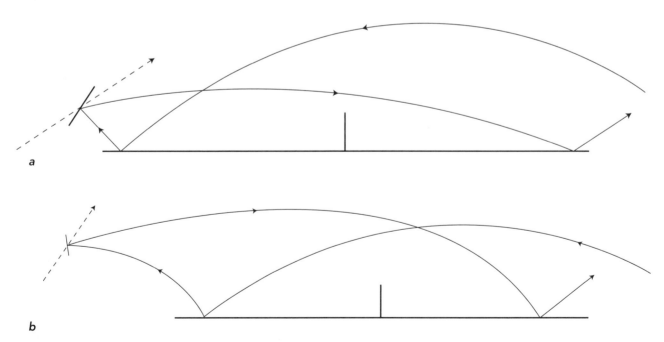

FIGURE 10.3 *(a)* The expert can take the ball early before the top of the bounce; *(b)* the beginner, who needs more time to track the ball's landing, hits it late with an open racquet face.

FIGURE 10.4 The correct stance: Player is slightly off-set to the backhand side, with the feet apart and the legs flexed, holding the bat so as just able to touch the centre line.

Target Games

However, introducing target games really raises the intensity and commitment of players. Here, a target—ideally the size of a video cassette—is placed on each side of the table. The challenge is to hit this target and so score a point using the designated stroke, initially the backhand push. Players can win points by hitting the target. They cannot lose points even if the ball is hit off the table or into the net. So, players can only win a game, of perhaps 3 or 5 points, by hitting the target more often than their partner.

This modification naturally shapes the whole character of the game. There is no reason now for a player to create problems for their opponent by continually changing the angle, direction, or even the spin of the stroke. As both players strive to score points by hitting the target, the line and length of their shots will inevitably become more

and more consistent. This in turn reduces the perceptual and movement demands of the task so that both players have the time they need to prepare for and execute the chosen technique correctly. Above all, this game gives beginners the time they need to work through the technique cognitively.

Another major benefit of target games is that young players can watch the movement of their opponent's racquet throughout the stroke. This is an element of skilled play that is at best underestimated and at worst completely ignored in the teaching of racquet sports. However, it is only by watching the racquet as it is prepared for the stroke, the angle as it strikes the ball, as well as the effort qualities of the whole swing, that players can begin to predict the speed, flight path, and degree of spin on the ball as they prepare to receive it.

This is especially important because of the rule that permits high-spin rubber on one side of the bat and anti-spin rubber on the other. To help players cope with this problem, the two faces of the bat must be of different colours. This means that in elite competition, players must not only watch their opponents' strokes very carefully but also note which side of the bat was used to hit the ball in order to work out the likely amount of spin! While the issue of different bat surfaces is not something that beginners need to worry about, if players want to go to the next level, they need to be prepared for it.

In a sense, target table tennis is the ideal Gallwey (1976) game, in which true competition does indeed become true co-operation. For when players strive to win a point, they make it easier for their opponents to improve and succeed. While a target the size of a video cassette is suitable for beginners, even novices may soon find this too easy, so smaller targets can be used. They can take many forms but the more interesting they are the better. Students can make their own targets even more exciting by pasting photographs of sports stars or popular entertainers on them. Encouraging children to bring their own 'grandparent-made' targets has been very effective in South Australian schools. However, no matter what targets are used, it is easy to differentiate learning by arranging a handicapping system, in which superior players must aim at a smaller target than their opponent, or by allowing players to choose the size of their targets.

Forehand Topspin Drive

The forehand topspin drive should be taught next. Players stand with their feet almost parallel with the table but with their shoulders turned. Because of the speed of the game, players cannot continually adjust the position of their feet and so must swivel from the hips to set up the correct shoulder and arm position. The natural swing of the arm and shoulders makes it easy to hit the ball crosscourt into the longest part of the target area.

However, hitting crosscourt all the time can lock players into a dead-end tactical method. Instructors therefore should encourage youngsters to play down the line of the table instead of always hitting crosscourt. This will force them to swivel at the hips and turn their shoulders more as they prepare for and execute the stroke. This will also mean that when both players are hitting forehands to each other, one will have to be positioned outside the line of the table. Of course, this also allows 4 players to use the same table.

The forehand topspin drive is played at about three-quarter's arm length. It begins at or just below table height and continues in an upward swinging motion to bring the bat level with the left side of the forehead, as shown in figure 10.5.

Beginners should feel that they are brushing the bat up the back of the ball, as the arm swings up to make the ball spin forwards and then drop as shown earlier.

While the sequence of practices outlined previously can be used effectively, a simple modification can slow play down further, giving beginners even more time to prepare for and execute the lifting, brushing motion necessary to produce topspin. All that is needed is a higher net. This forces players to lift the ball over the net and discourages them from hitting the fast, flat, risky shots that they would love to try out! This simple modification not only helps shape the correct technique but also ensures that both players have plenty of time to deal with the slow-looping ball. While it takes a little time and thought to set up, it is well worth it, even if only on one table, in terms of ensuring pertinent, purposeful practice.

At this point, youngsters should be encouraged to use their forehand topspin to deal with any ball they can reach. To that end, it is worth playing with the targets positioned deep in the backhand corner. Now they must be prepared to position themselves outside the line of the table to execute the stroke, a valuable preparation for the tactics of the real game.

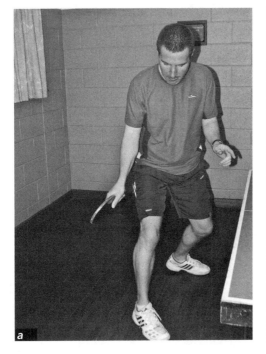 

FIGURE 10.5 The forehand topspin drive begins at or just below table height and continues in an upward swinging motion to bring the bat level with the left side of the forehead.

Backhand Block

The backhand block should be introduced next. This is a simple modification of the push stroke. It is valuable because it enables players to deal with topspin hits coming to their back hand. All they need to do is to position the bat on the line of the incoming ball, but with the top of the bat slightly angled forward to counter the topspin (figure 10.6). While players can take the ball at any point after it has bounced, they should gradually try to take it earlier, until it is almost a half volley. Now, of course, it is possible to play a target game in which one player hits topspin forehands while the partner counters with a backhand block. Whenever they complete a 3-point game, they exchange roles.

FIGURE 10.7 Forehand topspin serve.

FIGURE 10.6 Backhand block: Position the bat on the line of the incoming ball, with the top slightly angled forward to counter the topspin.

Forehand Topspin Serve

Next, the service action can be introduced. To keep things simple, introduce the forehand topspin service first (figure 10.7). The topspin service is a modification of the topspin drive, with the bat angle altered so as to drive the ball first onto the table, and then over the net to land deep in the other court. The backhand chop service, which can be introduced later, is a simple modification of the push stroke already mastered. The bat starts a little higher,

then brushes down under the bottom quarter of the ball to direct it onto the table close to the net. The backspin imparted will slow the ball down and, ideally, cause it to bounce low when hitting the table, thus making it difficult to attack.

Once players have grasped the basic pattern of both service actions and practised them in a target game, teachers and coaches should emphasise the legal service rule. This specifies that the ball must be thrown vertically upwards from a flat hand before it can be hit, must be played from inside the line of the table, and cannot be executed over the table. Armed only with these two variations, beginners can start to play competitive table tennis.

So far, we have introduced a limited range of working techniques and a working tactical model where beginners try to take as many shots with the forehand as they can, while using the backhand push or block to deal with balls they cannot hit with the forehand. Perhaps it is worth restating that this working tactical model can be used successfully up to the Olympic level.

More Advanced Strokes

Committed youngsters will find that they can easily master other strokes. For example, the backhand chop stroke (figure 10.8) is simply an extension of the push stroke.

Backhand Chop Stroke

Right-handed players should move their weight diagonally backwards onto the left foot to give themselves more time to prepare for and execute the stroke as the ball slows down. The bat starts from a slightly higher position to slice under the lower back quarter of the ball in a fast chopping motion that can produce considerable backspin. This causes the ball to slow down and, ideally, drop almost vertically, deep in the opponent's court, making it difficult for them to maintain a fast attack. To deal with faster attacking strokes, it will be necessary to take the ball even later. So, against a powerful attack, it will mean moving farther away from the table to allow more time to prepare for and execute the stroke.

The backhand drive also evolves from the backhand push. Players start holding the bat slightly lower, but now lift it up with a strong forearm movement to brush upwards through the ball, producing top spin. Initially, youngsters have to take the ball late, well after it has bounced, but gradually, they will learn to hit it earlier.

The forehand chop stroke (figure 10.9) will evolve as naturally as the backhand stroke did. Again, to give themselves more time to execute the stroke, players move back onto a flexed right leg to take the ball later. By now players will be able to track the ball and move into position with confidence, so it will be relatively easy for them to take the bat under the back quarter of the ball, as they have learned to do on the backhand. In other words, a transfer of concepts will occur that will make the new stroke easier to learn.

Shaping and Focusing Games

All strokes can be refined through the use of targets and by the process of shaping a play practice. For example, a game played only in the backhand court, in which players must hit only forehand strokes, forces them to really focus on footwork and positioning. Since a large number of kills in table tennis are made with the forehand, often with players standing outside the line of the backhand court, this practice is likely to transfer tactical understanding as well as good footwork. Running round the forehand, as this

FIGURE 10.8 Backhand chop stroke.

FIGURE 10.9 Forehand chop stroke.

tactic is called in tennis, is also an important element of tactical play in table tennis because it opens up a wide range of angles and allows the player to exploit the tremendous power that can be generated by the full swing of the arm.

Another example of shaping is to use a doubles game in which the players are only allowed to use forehand strokes. This will improve both their movement and footwork. Finally, it is possible to use a target game in which players must play alternate forehand and backhand strokes from their backhand court. This helps them develop the footwork needed to fully exploit the potential of the forehand smash. How far youngsters can go, as always, depends on how committed they are and how much they are willing to practise.

Tactics in Table Tennis

With young players, table tennis is largely a game of unforced errors, so the notion of tactical play is almost irrelevant. However, they can begin to work out whether they are better suited to building an attacking game, a defensive approach, or a balance in which they try to use their strengths against the relative weaknesses of any specific opponent. As players improve, the role of the service in tactics becomes increasingly important, as does what is termed the 'third ball attack' (similar to the serve and volley tactic in tennis). Here the player chooses a serve, often with large amounts of topspin or backspin combined with

sidespin, that will force the receiver to return a ball that can easily be put away for a winner or, failing that, allows the server to make best use of their technical strengths.

Badminton

Badminton presents unique problems for beginners because of the long handle of the racquet and the unusual flight path of the shuttle, which decelerates rapidly and drops suddenly in a way that beginners find very difficult to predict. In addition, the shuttle must be volleyed, which further adds to the complexity of the challenge for beginners. Here, perhaps even more than in the other racquet sports, players' ability to employ games sense and to apply tactics in the game depends on their technical ability.

The first step is to create learning situations in which beginners can initially focus on developing technical ability. This can be done by using challenges and games that are shaped to do the following:

- Eliminate the tactical demands in individual challenges, co-operative partner challenges, and target games.

- Reduce the perceptual demands by using shorter racquets and a slower shuttle, by increasing the predictability of the feed using a hand feed or a controlled racquet feed in challenges, or by playing target games using horizontal or vertical targets.

- Increase the time available to beginners by adjusting the start position of the racquet to simplify the timing of the racquet movement, and then emphasising racquet-up positioning.
- Minimise the agility demands by reducing the court space and by using target games that are personalised to individual needs.

Working Models of Technique

Working models of technique will foster early success for beginners. While elite players generate a powerful striking technique from precise timing and sequencing of body movements, culminating with a powerful wrist pronation on contact with the shuttle, beginners must focus closely on tracking the flight of the shuttle and co-ordinating their racquet movement to simply make contact with it—a difficult challenge indeed!

The challenge for teachers is they need to foster success whilst minimising potential dead-end techniques. This can be achieved through the use of challenges and target games. During these activities, learners build their confidence in striking the shuttle and begin to focus on using the racquet as a paintbrush when they strike the shuttle, rather than as a hammer (a firm-wrist hammering action). This is a simple way to visualise and develop the wrist action needed to accelerate the racquet head and strike the shuttle with some force. Other simple cues, such as 'throwing the racquet head at the shuttle', assist with the acceleration of the racquet head. The idea of reaching up for the shuttle as if it were a $100 bill floating down encourages players to reach upwards when striking the shuttle overhead.

Individual Challenges

With beginners many of the initial activities can include simple challenges to promote success in making contact with the shuttle, playing it over the net, and then maintaining a rally with a partner. Players can use shorter racquets as they undertake these challenges, for example building up the number of times they can continuously

volley the shuttle in the air. This enables them to improve their co-ordination and tracking of the shuttle onto the racquet. A simple extension to this task, such as asking players to try to increase the height they can hit the shuttle, enables them to focus on swinging the racquet head more strongly at the shuttle, using the wrist action to increase the racquet speed on contact. At any stage, players can decide to use the longer racquet and attempt to master the increased challenge in timing and co-ordination that this longer lever presents.

For some groups, the starting point might be balloon badminton, where the slow flight of the balloon and its increased size can create a fun and successful individual or partner challenge. Helium balloons can also be used as novel stationary targets to build confidence and give players a feel for the movement needed to throw the racquet head up to strike the target. Learners can hold the helium balloon in position, which gives them all the time they need to set their racquet up in back-scratch position and then hit through the target.

Partner Challenges

Partner build-up challenges can be introduced where players move onto a half-court badminton space and score a point for each continuous hit over the net. The net height can be extended to allow more time to play the shot. Players may choose to commence the rally with a backhand serving technique, which is easier to implement because the shuttle and racquet head are positioned close together. Beginners have also experienced success by placing the shuttle on the racquet, lifting it up and striking it in an overhead action. As youngsters improve, they can be encouraged to project the shuttle farther simply by including markers on the side of the court that indicate the distance back from the net. Now each pair attempts to increase the distance they can hit the shuttle.

The partner high-net target game can then be introduced. In this game, points are scored for striking the shuttle over a high stretch-cord net (2.5 to 3.5 metres, or 8.2 to 11.5 feet) tied to vertical uprights that are attached to the badminton uprights (figure 10.10). Initially, points can be awarded for any hit over the net, and partners

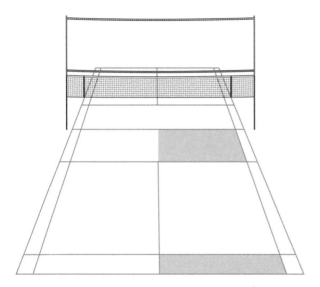

FIGURE 10.10 The horizontal and vertical target areas on the badminton court.

combine their hits into one total—perhaps in competition with other pairs. The game can then be modified so that individual players only score if the shuttle is hit over the high net, allowing each player to tally their own score in the rally.

4-by-4 Overhead Clear Challenge

The 4-by-4 task is a co-operative self-testing challenge where partners work together to improve the distance they can hit the shuttle using a 'clear' technique, which sends the shuttle high and deep to the back of the court. This technique not only forces the opponent to the back of the court, opening up tactical options for dropping the shuttle close to the net, but the height in trajectory also provides the player with time to recover their position on court. As players improve this challenge can be revisited, with a focus on generating power to increase the depth of the clear. The court area is set up with the four zones on each side of the court marked 1, 2, 3, and 4 (figure 10.11). Partners co-operate in this game by initially rallying using overhead clears. When the player who is scoring first calls out 'let it drop', the partner simply lets the shuttle drop to the floor and calculates the score. Points (1, 2, 3, or 4) are allocated according to the depth of the shot and then multiplied by the points (1, 2, 3, or 4) scored for the location of the player when the shuttle was cleared.

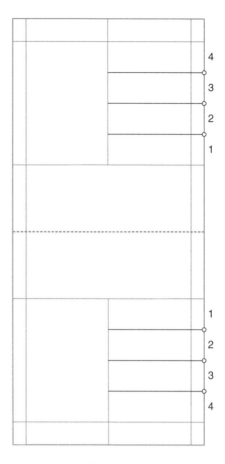

FIGURE 10.11 Set-up for 4-by-4 overhead clear challenge.

Find the Space

Players can be introduced to the 'find the space' game as a progression following the partner challenges using the higher net. After changing partners, they begin to play the 'find the space' game on the half-court area. The game is shaped to challenge players to land the shuttle on the floor space around their opponent. Points are only scored if the shuttle lands on the floor in front of or behind their partner. A co-operative backhand serve that clears the net and travels beyond the front serve line can be used to start this game, and no points may be scored on the serve. When short play-time intervals are used and players rotate frequently to different partners, this experience provides the opportunity for introducing the tactics for singles game play.

Singles Play

Singles in badminton is primarily based on developing the short–long game tactic, where players attempt to move their opponent to the front or back of the court to create space and opportunity for winning a point. While these tactical principles are relatively straightforward, developing the technical ability required to implement them is a major challenge. The player must be able to play the shuttle overhead to project it deep to the back of the court using an overhead clear and then combine this with the ability to drop the shuttle short near the net. Used in combination these shots create many opportunities for poor returns that can be attacked with a sharply downward angled smash.

The following target games can be used to maximise the opportunity for novices to focus on improving these techniques and applying them in game play.

Short–Long Target Game

The short–long target game is ideal for bringing together the techniques and tactics of singles game play. This game is an extension from the 'find the space' game. The play space is half the badminton court. The depth of the back boundary can be reduced to minimise the need for forward–backward agility. The challenge is to hit the shuttle and score a point by landing the shuttle in either of the target zones. Points cannot be lost even if the shuttle is hit out of bounds or into the net. Players can only win a game, of perhaps 3 or 5 points, by hitting the target more frequently than their partner. As both players strive to score points by hitting their short or long target zones, they begin to develop the agility needed to cover the court spaces to recover and respond in this game. It is possible to provide for a diversity of learners in this game simply by allowing players to set the back-court boundary and to select the size of their target areas (figure 10.12).

With the game shaped in this way, the context becomes authentic for introducing and refining the techniques required for singles game play, as well as challenging players to improve their agility, especially the forward lunging and recovery that are so important in badminton. Increasing the width of the playing space to the regulation singles court will further extend players' multidimensional agility.

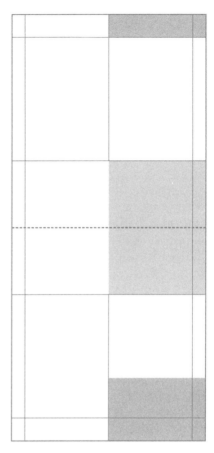

FIGURE 10.12 Short–long target game with personalised target zones.

Net-Roll (Drop Shot) Target Game

After playing the short–long target game, it is possible to identify the specific techniques that are needed to expand tactical options. The drop shot played from the front of the court can be practised in a net-roll target game, which is shaped by using a cord or tape extended 30 to 40 centimetres (12 to 16 inches) above the net to create a target zone. In this game, players only score points if the shuttle is played over the net through this zone. This game can be extended to focus on the lunge and recovery by adding a condition that players must return both feet behind the serve line after each shot they play (figure 10.13).

If needed, players can co-operate prior to starting the net-roll game by helping one another to improve their net-roll technique. One player adopts the coaching role and feeds the shuttle using a 'dart-feed' action close to the net cord so their partner can return it with a net roll. As the shot is played, the coach can observe footwork or contact point with the shuttle and comment on 'taking the shuttle as early as possible', or 'lunging with the racquet foot forward' to extend the reach to the shuttle. This can easily become a self-testing challenge for forehand and backhand net rolls. To further promote the use of the net roll in singles game play, any point won through the net-zone space can score double points.

Serving Target Challenge

The low-target zone located above the net is ideal for improving the backhand serve or for short forehand serves that are disguised. The initial challenge is to serve the shuttle over the net through the target zone, diagonally across to the serve area. This ensures that the shuttle trajectory remains flatter and closer to the net. By adding floor targets such as hoops or markers, the focus can also be directed to serve placement. The floor targets can be relocated to define back-court scoring zones when practising the deep serve (figure 10.13). The underarm deep serve is a more difficult technique to master due to the increased timing and co-ordination required to swing the racquet and contact the dropped shuttle using a powerful wrist flick. Players who may struggle with this technique initially can be helped by reducing the swing distance of the racquet and by shortening up on the racquet grip. In addition an understanding of how the shuttle must be allowed to drop down to meet with the head of the swinging racquet may assist them to be successful with this technique.

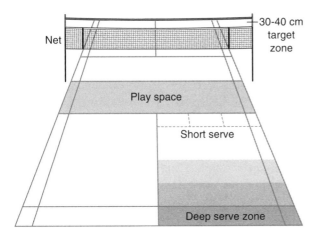

FIGURE 10.13 Net-roll target game and serving zones.

Continuing With Short–Long Game or Singles Game Play

The short–long target game and singles game play can continue to feature as key learning experiences, where rules can be clarified and scoring introduced in the context of the game. Where possible, youngsters should be matched to ensure even games, and opponents can be rotated after short periods, either in tournament play or when using action fantasy games. During these games, players can be encouraged to build their tactical game options by expanding their technical range. This will include learning to play a sharply angled shot to put away poorly directed serves or mis-hits that occur in the game, leaving the shuttle sitting up ready to be smashed downwards. Improving the smash technique played close to the net as the 'net kill' shot or in other areas of the court enables tactical options to expand. This is particularly relevant for doubles game play, where the strategy of hitting the shuttle downwards as much as possible is used frequently in attack formation.

Forecourt Net Kill and Smash Challenge

The forecourt net kill is a technique played close to the net, often in response to a poor serve that is lifted too high above the net cord or any return that has been lifted in a similar way. The player responds quickly by stepping forward onto the racquet foot and uses a rapid wrist snap with the racquet to strike the shuttle sharply downwards. Partners can work co-operatively in a self-testing challenge to improve this technique. With beginners it is preferable for one player to start with the racquet foot forward and the racquet raised, ready to play the shot. This reduces the timing demands and allows the player to focus on 'swatting' the shuttle down, by angling the racquet head downward to direct the shuttle to a target zone on the court. The co-operative partner assists by feeding the shuttle, using a lifted backhand serve from the side of the court and aiming at the lifted racquet head as a target. Points are scored depending on where the shuttle lands and aiming at horizontal scoring zones. If a player experiences difficulty in angling the shot downwards, a hoop can be held out flat at net height as an additional target to direct the shuttle through. A helium balloon can be used in a similar way, as a novel target floating at about half the net height (figure 10.14). The net

Receiver

Feeder

Helium
balloon

FIGURE 10.14 Feeding position and targets for improving the net kill.

kill technique also can be practiced in a serving context where the server varies each serve and the receiver must select the appropriate serve to step forward and swat downwards for a winner.

The mid-court smash challenge can be introduced simply by adjusting the depth of the feed so that the receiver has to reposition themselves to play the overhead smash (figure 10.14). As players gain experience, this can be extended into a smash-recovery game, where one player attacks using the net kill or smash whilst the other player works on reading the play and recovering the shot by lifting it back up into play. This game can be played in short time intervals, allowing regular change in roles. To further emphasise the use of the net-kill and smash techniques, singles games can be played with double points allocated for successful use of those shots.

The other important tactic used in badminton is 'disguise', particularly when playing the overhead shots. To do this, the player prepares to play one shot, for example the overhead clear, and then at the last second, when the racquet is about to make contact with the shuttle, they reduce racquet speed to lightly touch the shuttle to play a drop shot. This causes the shuttle to drop unexpectedly, with a trajectory angled down towards the net. The disguise of this shot makes it difficult for the opponent to quickly read and anticipate the return. This may catch them off guard in their recovery or force them to delay their response for an instant, resulting in a lifted return that is easily smashed away. The following activities illustrate how co-operative partner activities can be used to facilitate learning the techniques used to disguise play.

Overhead Drop Challenge

A partner co-operative practice can be used to improve the overhead drop shot in combination with the underarm lift technique. The underarm lift is a shot played from the front court using a powerful underarm swing to project the shuttle up high and deep to the rear of the court. It is an option for a return of any drop shot received in the singles game, particularly if the opponent has been brought to the front of the court. The cooperative task can be set up so one player works to keep the shuttle up high for their partner using the underarm lift whilst the other focuses on playing the overhead drop shot. Players should be encouraged to practise disguising the drop shot by making the shot look like the overhead clear and then, at the last moment, slowing the racquet head to softly touch the shuttle on contact to change its trajectory. Players can focus on tipping the racquet head forward when making contact with the shuttle to ensure that the shuttle's path angles downward towards the net. The low-cord target area located above the net is of value here, because players aim to drop the shuttle through this target zone. When players start to learn this shot, they may find it difficult to achieve the angled shuttle drop trajectory. To help with this, they can work on reaching high with the racquet to contact the shuttle and then aim to drop the shuttle into the net as a target. Once players gain confidence in playing this shot, they can return to normal game play, emphasising the use of the drop shot by allocating a double score for points won using this technique.

7-Zone Game: Half- or Full-Court Singles

This game can be played on a half-court or full-court singles space. It is a novel game that improves all aspects of skilled play. When playing in half-court, six spaces in the playing area are numbered 1 through 6. These areas can be determined by the players. Zone 7 is the body of the opponent. The aim of the game is to land the shuttle in a zone to claim it. The first player to claim all 7 zones wins.

Doubles Play

Students really enjoy the challenge of doubles, and games can be structured with a variety of partner combinations. Game play is developed around the tactics of using the additional width of the court space, directing the shuttle downward to maintain an attack position, and forcing the opposition to lift the shuttle. The challenge is for partners to co-operate to cover the court defensively and to transform this into attack. The rules of doubles can be introduced in the context of the game, and specific techniques can be developed by designing target games and play for co-operative pairs, similar to those outlined in the singles section.

Tennis

When played by experts, tennis looks like an easy game. However, beginners face all the usual problems posed by racquet sports. They have to track a fast-moving object, predict its flight path, and move into position to strike it so precisely that it will be returned to the other side of the net. All this must be done while trying to control an unfamiliar implement that may or may not be suitable for them. However, for many youngsters, the biggest challenge in tennis is simply to move to where the ball is going to be! Therefore, multi-dimensional agility is a critical element of skilled play in this racquet sport.

For these reasons, tennis is not an easy game to introduce to beginners in a class situation, many of whom will find it difficult to get to the ball to return it over the net on one occasion, much less maintain a rally involving several strokes. The complexity of this task increases when a class includes a diversity of participants, some of whom may be playing tennis for a club and others who may be rank beginners. Action-fantasy game cards provide a viable solution for differentiating learning and catering for this diversity in experience.

The challenge is to introduce this difficult game in a way that motivates youngsters to

The serve action can be difficult for young players to execute.

continue playing. The key to early success is using play practices that resemble the game closely enough for youngsters to feel that they are playing the real game but which are simplified and shaped to ensure success. Teachers and coaches must do the following:

- Provide a safe learning environment.
- Ensure that youngsters have fun.
- Ensure that they feel they are being successful.

Chris Deptula, who works with very young beginners in his tennis coaching school, suggests it is important to involve children in fun activities that build perceptual tracking and hand–eye co-ordination, as well as body awareness, balance, and agility, while they still believe they are playing real tennis activities. To continue the fiction, they can do these activities as part of a warm-up routine, just like real tennis players do! Naturally, these tasks must be challenging, exciting, and varied. Young children can be involved in having a rally when they are merely tipping the ball out of their hands, letting it bounce, then catching it with the same hand (palm up), with the other hand securing the catch on top of the ball. Chris uses his own version of 'table tennis' with very young players to develop tracking and hand–eye capabilities. Here, partners roll the tennis ball across a table, using their hands to stroke the ball back and forth in a rolling rally. Players are encouraged to use the flat side of their hands as a bat, brushing against the table top and stroking the ball with either the palm (forehand) or the back of the hand (backhand). This activity is extended to ground tennis, played on the ground on a marked-out court. Here, the ball also rolls between strokes. The hitting implement can be either the hand or a small bat. The level of engagement of the children in these challenges depends on many factors, not the least of which are the knowledge, experience, and enthusiasm of the teacher or coach.

Shaping Games in Tennis

In tennis, the following variables can be manipulated to create specific learning environments:

- How points are scored, including scoring that uses targets.
- The size and shape of the playing area.
- The ball type: its size, compression level, and colour.
- How the ball is struck. Limitations can be set on the type of techniques to be played in some of the shaped games.
- What implement is used to strike the ball. This of course can range from the hand or a wombat hand pad as a striking surface to a variety of padder bats and racquets of varying lengths and sizes.

Chris describes how many of these variables, particularly the court size and ball type, have formed the basis of recent changes in junior tennis development. The focus is on learning tennis on smaller courts and using slower bounce (low compression) tennis balls to make the game proportionally the same for the young beginner as it would be for an adult. This means that the average number of steps taken to reach a

shot is the same, the average time taken between hits in a rally is the same, and the proportional distance the player can cover when at the net is the same. This simplified learning environment enables game play to be integrated with individual challenges and target games to develop technical ability and other aspects of skilled play in tennis.

Individual Challenges

Individual striking challenges, using either the hand, a hand-pad bat, beach bat, or short racquet and a ball (using either a larger play ball or a slow-bounce or regular tennis ball) can be introduced to build confidence and technical ability. These challenges focus on tracking the ball and getting the racquet to hit the ball; they can begin with the challenge of building up the number of continuous hits of the ball with the bat's hitting surface. Variations include using first one side or the other of the bat, or alternating sides on every stroke. A target area, which can be a hoop or a chalked area on the ground, can be introduced to make this into an individual target game where points are only scored if the ball is struck into the air and then lands in the target area. The following conditions apply in this game: The ball can only be played after it bounces and it must be hit up into the air above head height to attempt a score. Each player starts their game by bouncing the ball and then striking it upward with the object being for it to land in the target zone. Once the ball is struck the player begins to track the ball and move to adjust their position, ready to play the ball again after it bounces. The fixed target minimises the agility demands and ensures a degree of consistency in the ball's direction. This allows beginners to focus on taking their bat back early, giving them more time to swing at the ball and contacting it 'in front of the body' as they swing through.

Partner Target Tennis

The individual target tennis game described previously can be played with a partner. Conditions of play remain the same, and points are scored in the same manner but now each player alternates hitting the ball. A court boundary such as a half-court badminton space can be defined with the target area located centrally in this space. This game provides players with many opportunities to improve their technical ability, and because they are required to strike the ball above head height in order to score, each player has time between shots to begin reading the play, adjusting their position, and implementing their technique accordingly.

Target Tennis Over a Net

The partner target tennis game outlined above can be easily transferred onto a court area where players are located on each side of the net. The net can simply be a mat or a marked space on the floor to divide the court or it can be any other elevated net. If a mat or marked floor space is used, then it is important to maintain the condition that the ball must be lifted above head height when it is played in the rally. If an elevated net is used then it should be raised to badminton height to ensure the ball is lifted to clear the net. Both of these conditions provide the learner with more 'time to be skilful'. Low-compression slow-bounce tennis balls and beach bats are other strategies to simplify the learning environment and foster success. Obviously the choice in equipment can be expanded if a larger tennis court space is available, but this will also depend on the range of ability and experience of players in the class.

Challenges and games can be started in a cooperative way by bouncing the ball and then striking it over the net as used previously; however, slight adjustments to this action will need to be made to direct the ball over the net to the target area. The target zone area can be the tram lines, the serving box if working on a tennis court, or the badminton singles serving area if working indoors or any other area marked on the court space. During these games, players can be encouraged to hold the racquet comfortably to ensure that the racquet face is contacting the ball in such a way that it will be propeled to its desired target area.

Beginners can also be reminded to start with their racquet back before they bounce the ball and to strike the ball out in front as they have practiced in the previous games. The over-the-net challenge will allow players to learn to adjust their position in order to play the

ball into the new target area. Before partners attempt to maintain a rally with the ball, they begin with a build-up challenge, similar to what was described in the table tennis section. This begins with a self-feed bounce and hit, where the player aims to clear the net and land the ball into the defined target space on the other side of the court. Their partner receives the ball and catches it after the bounce and then returns it in the same manner. A point can be scored for each shot that clears the net and lands in the target zone. Once each player has scored 3 points, the game is changed to build up consecutive hits in a rally. This build-up game starts with a bounce and hit over the net, and then the partner attempts to return the shot back to their partner. Once the rally breaks down the build up starts over. Players can change partners after scoring a set number of points or after a short time interval. If the regular tennis balls are used, it is possible to allow beginners to hit the ball after either one or two bounces so they have more time to prepare for and execute the stroke.

Partners can also be involved in reciprocal teaching during this progression to help each other improve their technical ability. One partner becomes a feeder who stands close to the net to throw the ball into a target zone for their partner to return. The feeder can provide some of the key points that will help their partner develop a working model of technique. This activity can be enhanced by adding in scoring zones and keeping a check on personal improvement. Roles can be rotated after six feeds, and each pair is able to extend their challenge by requesting variations in the placement or speed of the feed.

As players improve their technique, the shape of the game can be adjusted so the target size is personalised to suit the ability of each individual. Target tennis (similar to target table tennis) can be played. In this game points are only scored when the ball lands in the nominated target zone, for example in the tram lines, so this will quickly improve the line of shots and reduce the need for lateral movement to the ball, an element which many novices find difficult.

Target tennis can be progressively developed by adjusting the playing area and using a range of horizontal targets. When players change partners they can personalise the target size and the court space based on individual abilities of each player. For example, the width of the target zone might be increased on one side of the court in order to extend players' agility as they are forced to cover more space, whilst their partner uses a smaller target zone, enabling them to cover the space more easily.

Several of the target games outlined in this section have been also recommended by Tim Hopper (2009) to facilitate learning in tennis for beginning players. He views 'the game as teacher' and highlights how important it is to manipulate the game constraints to enable the learner to engage with them as they develop and transform their capabilities.

Backhand

Most of the progressions outlined previously can be used to improve the backhand technique. It is important to help players understand why a change of grip is needed in the backhand to ensure the racquet face's contact with the ball in the stroke is appropriate to direct the ball to the target. Discussion on the use of the two-handed backhand can also be included here. When introducing the backhand technique, partners can work co-operatively using the 'feeder coach' role described previously. The feeder positions themselves 1 to 2 metres back from the net, and they lob the ball in a direct line to their partner, who is also positioned 1 to 2 metres back from the net waiting to receive the ball. The receiver is facing the net, holding their racquet (with backhand grip) in front of their body. The racquet face is on edge ready to play through the ball and direct it back over the net. The feed is bounced in a direct line to the racquet, making it easier for the striker to simply swing the racquet forward and up (in a J movement) through the ball as it arrives. This activity can be progressed, with the receiver moving a little farther back from the net to play a backhand to a ball that is now fed between two marker cones. To do this the receiver must make a small adjustment in body position to move side on, turning the torso while taking the racquet back in preparation for the shot (figure 10.15). The feed target helps to ensure consistency in the line of the ball, and this enables the player to swing the racquet forward and through the ball to direct it over the net to a target zone. The games described earlier can be used to build the backhand stroke, and in

FIGURE 10.15 Racquet back with torso turned, ready to play backhand.

all of these outlined tasks players are gradually learning to adjust their positioning in relation to the placement of the ball.

Serving

Serving can be introduced using a working model of technique and practiced in a variety of individual challenges. Chris suggests an overarm throwing-and-catching game as a starting activity for beginners. The aim of this game is for one player to throw the tennis ball from behind the baseline over the net into the serving area to their partner, who tries to catch the ball after it bounces. This can be made into a game that can be used to introduce some of the rules for serving and scoring. The throwing action begins to replicate the movement pattern needed to build force in the serve, and the receiver learns to read the flight and direction of the ball as they move to position to take the catch.

A working model of the serve can be introduced with beginners to simplify the complexity of the full-swing advanced technique. To do this, a half swing is used where the racquet is held up with the arm and hand above the shoulder. This makes it easier to simply 'throw the racquet head' up at the ball as it is tossed up into the air. This technique can be practised by hitting balls into the fence initially and then brought onto the court, returning to the throw–catch game outlined previously.

The serving box provides a natural target, one that can be further divided into different scoring zones. Partners can design a variety of target games based on alternating serves back and forth to each other. Who can get 10 in first? Who can get 10 in first in the back third of the service box? Chris has found that a buddy system works well when beginners are learning to serve. One player practises the serve and the other player tries to catch the serve after one or more bounces, either by hand or in a bucket. This helps develop the receivers' ability to track the ball and respond by using their agility and co-ordination to catch the ball. As long as the server and non-server alternate roles relatively quickly, all participants typically stay on task. This can be extended into a serve and return game, where the ball is returned either anywhere into the court space or to a specific target zone.

Shaped Games and Bonus Points

Other variations on target tennis can be made by restricting the playing area in which points can be scored. An excellent example of this is a singles game where points can be won only if the ball lands in the service area. This very quickly leads players into making tightly angled shots with increasing use of topspin.

As other techniques are introduced, teachers and coaches can allocate bonus points for using them. One example is a singles game that encourages volleys. This is played in three-fourths of the doubles court area. In this game, the ball does not have to bounce. Any point scored with a volley receives 2 points instead of 1.

The serve and volley game can be further developed by conditioning the play. Now the server must volley the ball after both the first and second serves to win the point, whilst the receiver can win points only by returning the ball to marked areas on the court. In another game, after a co-operative feed, one player must hit every stroke crosscourt to win a point,

whilst the opponent can only win down the line. Clearly these are advanced play practices.

Players can also rally crosscourt for as long as they wish before one of them chooses to hit down the line to start the real game. Here, points can be won only with a shot down the line or with a crosscourt winner. This game focuses on improving games sense, particularly with an emphasis on tactics, strategy, and self-understanding.

Two target areas can be allocated at each end of the court, so that the agility and recovery of players can be stretched. For example, the left tramline and the right serve area might attract bonus points in the game. This focuses players on improving down-the-line and crosscourt shots, as well as court coverage, reading the play, responding, and repositioning.

The ideas presented for shaping the play and allocating bonus points can be extended and applied to foster improvement in all of the more advanced techniques and the tactical options they generate.

Volleyball

The key to teaching this game is to appreciate the distinction between 'volleyball' and 'power volleyball'. When William Morgan created minonette, the immediate forerunner of volleyball, he was trying to develop a simple game that could be played by ordinary people, a true recreational game.

Inevitably, the game he created evolved in a different direction to become power volleyball, a tactically complex game in which power and athleticism are as highly valued as in basketball. Volleyball is still suitable for the target audience Morgan was aiming at, and when taught correctly, it can lead towards the 'power' version of the game. However, even with the recreational version, good teaching is important because it is very easy to allow the process to become virtually a catch-and-throw game rather than one in which the volley is the defining feature. If this is not done, a dead-end game is created that is not particularly satisfying for players, and it will not help them to begin to master the techniques or tactics required to play competitively.

So teachers must decide which version of the game is suitable for their group, given the context in which they are working. Clearly they should not introduce the power game if the children are not ready for it or if there is insufficient time. This is because, unlike any other team game, the techniques of volleyball are sequentially dependent. For example, the 'spike' is only possible if the ball has been passed—'set' to the right spot at the right height. In turn, the set usually depends on the quality of the forearm pass (also termed 'bump' or 'dig'), which is a common technique used to receive the opponent's service. Finally, the bump is only possible if the server can actually get the ball over the net! And this is not an easy task for many youngsters. In other words three relatively difficult techniques must be mastered before a spike can be used to smash the ball down into the opponent's court!

Teachers should therefore initially focus on teaching players how to control and redirect the ball rather than worrying about introducing the spike and block. In a sense, they teach the equivalent of a ground stroke game in tennis, which relies on consistency to win points rather than trying for winners at the net. This provides a focus for technical practice and for improving games sense through simplified and shaped small-sided games as the key context for learning.

As mentioned previously, the sequential nature of the techniques in volleyball make it particularly difficult for beginners as errors are compounded. A poorly controlled or badly directed dig will make it very difficult for the setter to pass the ball accurately for a spike. As a result, games played by beginners are usually full of unforced errors. Because of this it is essential to reduce both the movement and perceptual demands for beginners so they can experience success in mastering the techniques needed to play the game. The over-riding aim of both teams should be to keep the ball in play for as long as possible so each team is able to practice using their three touches of the ball when it is in their court. This can be achieved by shaping the play to minimise the impact of the serve, adjusting the court space, reducing playing numbers, and conditioning the play to allow players to control the ball between shots. The way in which the ball is permitted to be controlled is important, and players should be encouraged to play the ball as it comes over the net using either the set or dig. This enables beginners to couple their perception and movement patterns as they learn

to read the flight of the ball and implement the technique. Once the ball has been played, it may then be caught (if needed) in order to control the ball before using a 'self-feed set' to move the ball to a team-mate to play over the net.

Shaping Volleyball

Dave Eldridge suggests that teaching volleyball effectively involves improving technical ability through a variety of shaped play practices that enable players to develop techniques in a game context. This maximises player enjoyment and success and facilitates the transfer of learning all aspects of skilled play from modified games to the full game.

He suggests that teaching a unit of volleyball involves finding a balance between giving students lots of contact with the ball, and then shaping play by employing scoring systems and rules that encourage the development of tactics and the advanced techniques of the game. The problem is that in beginning volleyball, the game is dominated by the serve or by players who merely play the ball straight back over the net (free ball) on the first contact (in whatever way possible). The aim is to help players to improve their technical ability so they are able to control the 'free ball' and then play a winning dig-set combination, sometimes with an added spike.

To promote this, he suggests that a team working hard to achieve the dig-set-spike sequence gets 10 points for winning with a spike, or 5 points for a point using only the dig-set combination—and perhaps no points from a free ball, even if it is successful. By rewarding them through the scoring system, players may then be encouraged to take the greater risk of attempting the dig, set, and spike sequence, which could involve an error on any contact. Once a class gets to the spiking stage, players will demand that their team does play with a dig (figure 10.16a) and a set (figure 10.16b), so that they can spike the ball down onto the opponent's court (figure 10.16c), which is truly one of the joys of the sport. Indeed, as soon as a class recognises the futility in giving the ball freely to their opposition, the scoring advantage given to a spiked ball can be scaled back.

Dave also suggests the game can be enhanced for some classes by adjusting the scoring system to focus on great floor defence. Here youngsters

FIGURE 10.16   *(a)* Dig; *(b)* set; *(c)* spike.

must be encouraged to move to the ball quickly and even get onto the court to keep the ball off their floor. *Tough play points* can be allocated to anyone in the class who does this well. An immediate 5 bonus points can be given or 10 points if the team go on to win the rally after this player's effort. If the teacher allocates tough play points on a scale of 1 to 10, players will quickly get the message that fast movement and getting down on the floor to keep the ball up will help their team score points. This soon creates longer rallies, which leads to more ball contacts for all players, which leads to better techniques, which leads to longer rallies, and so on.

Another way to shape the game is to adjust both the court size and the number of players. This is important because the large spaces between the 6 players on a full court can lead to short rallies simply because young players lack the agility to get to the ball. One effective solution to this problem is to play on smaller courts with smaller team sizes. Teams of 3 are better than teams of 6, since players will get more contacts and more chances to make errors and to learn; they will also have fewer people to criticise any mistakes! These smaller spaces can be set up by using badminton courts or by

moving the volleyball net antennas into the middle of the net, creating smaller courts. The sideline to the antenna then becomes court 1 and the antenna to the other sideline is court 2. The backline of the court can be brought in to further reduce the court space for beginners.

Short-Court Volleyball Rules

This game is played with 3 or 4 players on a team. To get the game started the ball is thrown underarm over the net by anybody in either team; however, points cannot be won on the serve. This means that the underarm throws should be easy to play. Spiking is not permitted, although overhead passes can be played. These games are restricted to 5 minutes each. At the end of this time, the winning teams move up a court and the losing teams move down. If the match is a draw at the end of the allocated time, the team who got to the tied score first wins. New matches can start immediately.

These games are fast and furious, since no time is wasted rolling the ball back to the serving team. The person nearest to the ball simply throws the ball underarm over the net to keep the action going. Since points cannot be won from the serve, players concentrate on the rally rather than being tricky with the serve. The rotation system ensures that opponents are changed regularly and quickly with minimal downtime, thus maintaining even competition and once again promoting longer rallies.

As players improve, the court size can be increased but the notion of small-sided teams should be maintained. Most importantly, games should always be structured so as to keep the rallies long and the number of ball contacts high.

The following practices may help improve play in this game.

Set Dump Practice

Players pair up and work across the net starting within 1 or 2 metres (3 to 8 feet) of the net. The challenge starts with one player throwing the ball gently over the net aiming to land it on the top of their partner's head. Their partner has their hands up ready to receive the ball, and they set the ball about 1 metre into the air before catching it and returning it back to their partner to set. When players feel confident they can receive the ball, they set it into the air and then gently dump the ball over the net, aiming to land it close to their partner's head for them to return. Both players work co-operatively to keep the practice going because they need to spend some time working on this in order to develop the technique required to control and redirect the ball. Players can change partners regularly to maintain the commitment of the group. The more experienced players can adjust the shape of this activity to create a partner target game by defining a small play area, and points are scored if the ball lands on the target floor space of your partner's court.

Dig, Set, and Spike Volleyball

Dave suggests that there are a variety of ways to facilitate the learning of 'three touch' volleyball using the dig, set, and spike techniques, and players must practice them at length in order to master the difficult sequence. The great thing about shaping games is that students can do the same sequence in 20 different ways and still have fun. In addition to small-sided games, players of all levels can benefit from participating in the passer-hitter practices described below (figure 10.17). This can be used both by players learning

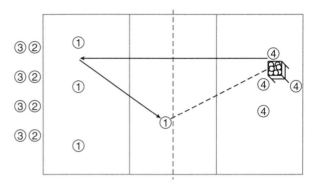

FIGURE 10.17 Passer-hitter practice with four teams (1-4).

the techniques and by athletes preparing for the Olympics.

The class is divided into teams of 3 or 4 players, and it is possible to work 2 to 5 teams per court; however, the lower the number of teams, the more opportunity each individual has to improve. One group (team 1) is on the court ready to receive the ball with one of the team members positioned on the net as a setter. Another group (team 4) is positioned to serve a series of easy underarm balls over the net. The ball cart can be located at this end, so there are at least 5 balls ready to use for the serve. Teams 2 and 3 are off court behind team 1 waiting for the rotation. After receiving a set number of serves, the passing team (team 1) move to become the serving team, while the serving team (team 4) move to the baseline behind team 3. Team 2 move onto the court to receive the serve.

Whilst it is quicker to have just one player in each team serving in any one rotation, there are benefits for sharing this role between at least two players. The team receiving the serve calls for the ball ('mine') and then directs the ball with either a dig or set to the setter, who is located in the front row central position about 1 metre back from the net. The setter watches the ball as the serve comes over the net and then gets ready to play the ball as it is passed towards them by the team-mate who received the serve.

There are a series of play options that can be applied in this practice to cater for the range of players from the basic level through to Olympic level. These are described below.

- The team receiving the serve aims to accurately pass as many balls as they can to the setter. The setter has to catch the ball to score a point. The team gets a score out of 5 or 10, depending on the number of serves delivered. The nominated server(s) initially give 5 easy serves to the receiving team. If the game is being played with 10 serves then the remaining 5 serves are slightly harder.

- The game can be varied slightly so that the setter now has to catch the ball above their head to score a point. If they can get on the ground to catch a low ball, bonus points can be allocated for spectacular efforts.

- The practice can be made more difficult by requiring the setter to set the ball 1 metre (3 feet) in the air before catching it. The passing team now remains on the court for as long as they can get the ball to the setter. Once they make a mistake, teams rotate. In order to include a diverse range of abilities, it is possible to allocate some teams with 'lives' that allow them one or two errors before they have to rotate off the court. No team can stay on the court for more than 10 serves.

This activity can be enhanced by keeping a tally of the number of successful passes a team makes before an error. Each team keeps their score and adds to it whenever they move to the position to receive the serve. The team that gets to 21 points first wins, and bonus points can be allocated for tough or spectacular plays.

This game can be extended further by adjusting its shape to include any of the playing conditions outlined here:

- After the ball is passed to the setter, one of the passers must spike the ball.

- After the ball is passed, the non-passer has to hit the ball.

- After the ball is passed, either player may hit the ball from the back court.

- Advanced: After the ball is passed, the non-hitter has to hit a quick set, which challenges both the placement of the quick set technique as well as the positioning and timing on the hit made by the spiker (non-hitter).

The previous team practice can also be set up as a more advanced passer-hitter individual practice with one setter who plays this position

for a period of time. One player (a) receives the serve, passes the ball to the setter (b), who sets it back up for them (a) to spike. After the player (a) has spiked the ball, she retrieves the ball and then joins the serving line. The server (c) takes her turn to serve and then joins the line to receive the serve. This practice can cater for up to 10 players. It works best with 2 or 3 players ready to serve and 2 or 3 players ready to pass and spike.

As the players' techniques improve, the server can serve the ball overhanded (figure 10.18), making the receivers work harder, since they will be challenged to read the ball earlier and move farther in order to pass the ball.

Once the passer-hitters are coping with this practice, the spikers can focus on concentrating their attack between the ball cart and the sideline. To force players to develop all three techniques of spiking, one strategy is to get the person next in line behind the passer-hitter to nominate the

FIGURE 10.18 Overhand serve.

technique the spiker must perform—for example, they can call out 'line,' 'crosscourt,' or 'dump and tip'. As the passer-hitters develop their range of attack options, they can discuss their strengths and weaknesses with their peers and the teacher while spikers can discuss their weakest shot and then practise it for a period of time. As the spiking techniques become more solid, a blocker can be introduced. However, because this is a demanding challenge, blockers should not attempt more than five blocks in succession. As soon as they finish their five blocks, they rotate out of that position and another player takes their place.

Two blockers can be introduced, and then this can be increased to three. Points can be allocated for each spike contest where the blockers score 5 points for a blocked spike; however, the setter and the next spiker in line can win back 10 points if the blocked ball is prevented from touching the ground. This encourages players to work on block cover. When the techniques of blocking start to match the efficiency of the spikers, there is an opportunity to teach the class about using the block as a tool for the spiking team and not as a threat. This can be achieved by helping players to understand how deliberately hitting the ball off the block can be a tactic for winning a point by redirecting the ball into a position that is difficult to return.

Adding another passer to the practice creates two passer-hitter options on the court. The passer can now hit backcourt or the spiker can hit frontcourt, depending on the quality of the pass. The shape of these games can be continuously varied to focus on specific aspects of game play. They are limited only by one's imagination!

Wash Practices

Players need to be immersed in the game context with maximum opportunity to contact the ball. Dave uses what he calls *wash* practices in his approach to create almost any scenario on a volleyball court and to focus on individual player techniques or team tactics and strategy.

Lucky-7 Wash Practices

This play practice can cater for between 8 and 24 students per court, although 12 students are ideal. Players set up in rotation on both sides of the net ready to play (figure 10.19).

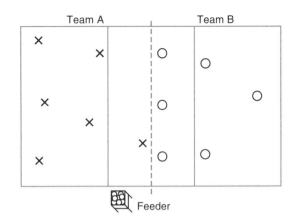

FIGURE 10.19 Lucky-7 wash practices.

At the basic level the ball is served softly underarm by the teacher or a student feeder at the side of the court as a 'free ball' into team A's court. This allows team A the opportunity to practice calling for the ball and using their techniques of digging, setting, and spiking with the end result of playing the ball over the net to team B. All rallies are played out to their conclusion. Team A receives seven balls in quick succession in this practice, with minimal downtime between balls. As soon as team A have had their seven balls, the feeder moves to the other side of the net to give team B their seven balls. While this is happening, team A rotate around one position. Team B do not rotate yet, and so are ready to receive the first of their seven free balls.

It is highly unlikely that classes will have perfect numbers for these wash practices, but it is possible to resolve this using a variety of team number combinations or by rotating players onto the court. Where possible aim to maximise participation.

At a beginning- or intermediate-level lucky-7 wash practice, teachers and coaches can focus on how the team is preparing to receive the ball and then observe passing technique. The observation of this aspect of skilled play is made easier because the team has an opportunity to receive a succession of free balls in a row, and these can be directed to any player in the group. Teachers and coaches can also observe the movement of the setter to the ball and their ability to set the ball up high enough for a spiker, and then track the spiker's movement as they prepare for the spike.

At a more advanced level, teachers and coaches can introduce back-row setting or review the team's ability to spike and defend against a block from the opposition. Now the focus is more on the team receiving the spike and their ability to block and implement blocking and team defensive tactics. At higher levels, coaches can also shape the play by only allowing the attacking team to play quick or back-row attacks, forcing them to expand their tactical options and improve their techniques to enable this tactic to be implemented.

Players can also have input into how the activity will be shaped by allowing each team to decide how they will play out the next 7, 14, or 21 balls. Will they concentrate on hitting the ball down the line, running quick attacks, or using tactical dumping of the ball? This option creates an extended challenge for the opposition, because once they realise what their opponents are trying to do, they have to adapt their play in order to counter these tactics.

A simple modification can be made to the method of feeding in order to include serving. A player (in the team opposite to the coach) serves one ball, which is played out and then immediately followed by a free ball to their team fed from the coach. The server gets to make three serves, and after the third serve the opposition team rotates positions before the new person starts their series of serves.

Player Free Balls

To make this game even more specific, another variation can be added. Instead of giving the free balls to the opposition, the teacher or coach high-bounces the ball to the team closest to their court. The players now have to give the free ball away to start the rally. Although these balls are bounced so the players can give the free ball relatively easily, the bounces can gradually be made harder, lower, and wider, placing greater movement demands on the players as the teams get better.

Factor Wash Practices

A factor wash practice is an ideal method of catering for teams of different abilities. The practice starts as a normal lucky-7 wash practice, but now the rallies are scored. The team that wins 7 points first gets handicapped by a *factor*. Although their opponents still win points just by winning

the rally, the better team can only win points by completing the factor—that is, serving, winning the point, and then winning a free ball point from the coach. If the same team again gets to 7 points first, they move to a *factor of 2*. This means they now have to win the serve along with two free balls to win points. If they fail to win the serve and the one free-ball factor, they go back to the even lucky-7 free-ball and start again. Teams have successfully worked with a factor of four free balls. If they win the serve but win only three of the free balls when they needed to win all four, it is called a *wash out*, hence the name of wash drills.

Managing Matches

It is clear that a combination of game play together with shaped and enhanced practices is the most efficient way to develop skilful volleyball players. Modified matches, court-size matches, scoring matches, and specific technique-reward matches can be used to make game time more efficient, fun, and varied. The following are examples.

Up-Down Matches

These matches are often timed or scored and are primarily played in short time periods. When the match is finished, the winning teams move in one direction on the courts while losing teams move in the other direction. If a match is tied, the team that got to the tied score first wins.

Rotational Tournaments

If there are six teams on three courts, the teacher or coach names one of the end teams as the anchor team. They do not move from that court and at the end of the match, the other teams rotate around the anchor team, finding a new team to play. Team names like China, Japan, and Cuba are used to enhance a tournament, which can be set up as a culminating event.

Pot-Luck Tournament

This strategy works well when setting up a tournament in a volleyball unit. In fact it has proved to be so successful that we recommend that it is used when teaching other games.

Teachers have a container with small discs numbered from 1 through 25 and each player is given a number. The discs are then spread out on the floor, number-side down, and then teams are randomly selected as the discs are turned number-side up. The tournament can be organised using a Sport Education approach co-ordinated by students in the management role. They allocate teams to courts for a series of timed matches. Players keep track of the score during the game, and when the time period ends players get the same number of points as their team. For example, if the score is 15 (A) to 13 (B) points, each player in team A gets 15 points whilst each player in team B gets 13 points. A sheet of paper, white board with a grid, or electronic pad can show the number of points a player scored in each round and the cumulative total of points a player has scored for the tournament. Students enjoy this structure, since the more experienced players are split up into different teams. Players then have to help their new team score as many points as they can so that they can get a good final score in the tournament.

eleven

Teaching Striking and Fielding Games

Cricket, Tee Ball, Softball, and Baseball

> ## Cricket is essentially a sport of individual contributions masquerading as a team game.
>
> Christian Ryan

Striking and fielding games take many forms, from rounders, the probable ancestor of both softball and baseball, to Finnish baseball and the peculiarly English game of cricket, a game which is now played in many countries, but especially in those of the British Commonwealth. Although it is hardly known in large areas of the world, including the United States, cricket is one of the most widely played and watched games on the planet, mainly because it is the major sport of India, a country of more than one billion people. However, it is interesting to ponder the possibility that the Civil War prevented cricket from becoming the dominant summer game in the United States, because in the 1820s, large crowds attended cricket games in New York, and it is even rumoured that George Washington played the game.

Striking and fielding games are based on the simple notion of a batter striking the ball into opposition territory to elude the fielders and to then to use the time gained to score runs. The advantage of both baseball and softball is that, at the lowest level, they require only a single bat and a ball and they can be played on any reasonably flat piece of ground. This simple fact may have been decisive in establishing the pre-eminence of baseball in the United States in the 19th century.

Interestingly, while all are thought of as team games, the critical phase in each occurs when one player, the batter, faces up to the pitcher (or in cricket, the bowler). As suggested previously, this one-on-one confrontation means that technical ability is initially the critical component of skilled performance. Indeed at the highest level, the batter in baseball needs highly developed technical ability, along with exceptional reflexes, to strike a ball delivered at high speed, especially when its path to the plate may be changing because of spin imparted by the pitcher. In cricket, the challenge for the batter is compounded because the ball may change direction in the air because of spin or swing and then again when it hits the pitch, either because of spin imparted by the bowler, the impact of the seam of the ball as it hits the turf, or simply because of irregularities in the surface the ball landed on!

So the first task for the sport educator is to find ways to help youngsters master the techniques needed for success in these games. While this is relatively straightforward in softball and baseball, where the essential techniques are based on very natural movement patterns, cricket can present special problems. The ball must be delivered in an artificial manner—that is, bowled with a straight arm rather than thrown naturally—while batters must master a wide range of specific techniques if they are to be successful.

The second task can also be difficult to resolve because in striking and fielding games, most players spend considerable time doing nothing! In Test match cricket, for example, players on the batting team have been known to sit and watch the action for more than two days while team-mates pile on the runs. Meanwhile, the members of the fielding team must stay completely focused for long periods of time, even though some may only occasionally touch the ball. While this situation is never so extreme in the case of baseball and softball, players may still endure long periods, at least as youngsters perceive them, where they sit or stand around waiting their turn to be involved in the action.

Because of these two factors, some teachers are reluctant to include cricket in the physical education curriculum. This is unfortunate, because the Loughborough group provided a potential solution to both of these problems with their use of sector games. However, it should be noted that while they intended these games to be used to develop tactical understanding, in Play Practice they are used primarily to improve technical ability. Examples of these games are covered in the cricket section. However, the general process is outlined in the sections relating to tee ball, softball, and baseball.

Organising these games is a relatively easy process, especially with tee ball, softball, and baseball, which are already played in a sector. However, by reducing the angle of the sector—for example, adjusting the angle between bases, as shown in figure 11.1a—it is possible to play up to five or even six 3-a-side sector games on a large field (see figure 11.1b). At the very least, this gives large numbers of youngsters the chance to hit the ball, either off a tee or from a co-operative feed, to beat fielders positioned in the sector. This also gives them the opportunity to improve their fielding and catching ability and to build their understanding of rules and other aspects of games sense.

Sector Games With a Scoring Zone

With tee ball, baseball, and softball, the sectors are extended out to home-run range. Marker cones indicate the distances the ball has to be hit to score one, two, three, or four runs. The experience level of the players and the type of equipment used will influence the distance the ball must be hit to score. Each batter steps up for three consecutive hits (which means that

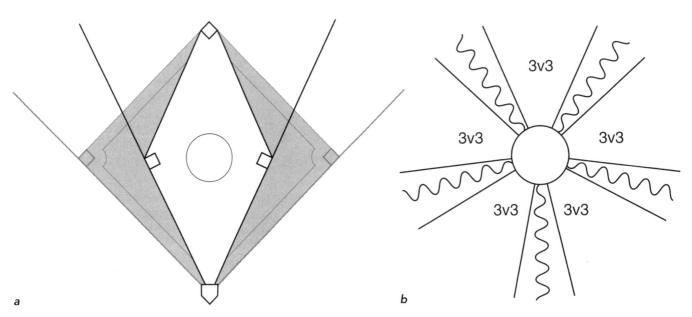

FIGURE 11.1 Reducing the sector (a) by using the angle between first and second base or second and third, or (b) by having five or six 3-a-side sector games on a large field.

each group must have several balls available) and tries to hit the ball past or over the fielders. Any ball that is caught costs the batter two runs, unless it goes over the four-run line. If so, it is treated as a sacrifice fly, and a single run is scored. On the changeover, the team that was fielding comes in to bat and tries to score more runs than their opponents. In these games, while one batter is up hitting the first of their three attempts, a team-mate is getting the next ball ready on the tee, while the third can be acting as a combination feedback giver and commentator. When games are completed, teams can rotate to face new opponents.

Sector Games With Base Running Added

It is easy to extend the initial sector game simply by adding a rule that for any scoring hit to be valid, the batter must run and beat the ball to first base, which is positioned at a distance that will allow some chance of success. This adds another level of complexity to the sector game, increasing its alignment to the real game while still retaining a high level of participation. The fielders are challenged to consider tactical positioning to cover the space available and to develop the technique needed to field the

Using a large ball simplifies the challenge of hitting off the tee.

ball and throw it quickly to first base. Batters continue to practice their technical ability as they strike the ball, and they begin to develop games sense as they consider their own ability, the space available in the field, and the fielders' capabilities in this challenge.

Sector Games With All Bases

From here it is easy to add in the remaining bases so that the game is now more closely aligned to the real game. It is important to ensure the bases are distanced appropriately to establish a diamond and field space that balances fairly with the playing numbers. The game continues to be the central learning experience, and players can be introduced to increasing levels of complexity in the game as rules associated with base running, infield and outfield fly balls, and tagging are clarified. Tactical positioning and situational decision making also feature. However, as particular issues emerge from this context they can become the focus for more specific practice. For example, when the concept of tagging is introduced, it can be practised in a small tagging game that is shaped to help players solve the problem set up when a baserunner is caught between bases. This can also be applied with a variety of other game situations, such as fly balls or double plays.

As we suggested earlier it is possible to include tournaments and culminating events, such as 'world championships'. This promotes fun and a feeling of festivity and provides youngsters with opportunities to take on other roles.

Bowling and Pitching

Bowling a cricket ball and pitching a baseball or softball accurately are very difficult tasks unless youngsters have grown up in a culture that values either of them. What is clear is that it takes considerable practice to deliver a ball close to the target in both cricket and baseball. So, unless there is a great amount of time available for practice, it is unlikely that many beginners will master either of these techniques well enough to apply them in a game.

Despite this, youngsters love to aim at targets, which attract a lot of interest. These can be set up in any free space. They may also be the stimulus for a lifelong interest in the sport.

- In cricket, the target shown in figure 11.2 has proven to be immensely popular, both because it is easier to hit than the regulation cricket stumps and because of the noise created when it is hit. This larger vertical target can be complemented by the use of horizontal ground targets for line and length.

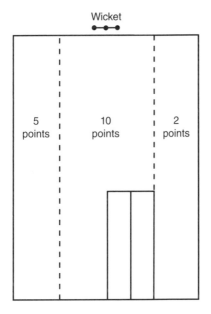

FIGURE 11.2 A cricket bowling target made of steel or solid wood is used. It is based on the real target zone; the regulation wicket is unrealistic and too small. Individuals or small teams compete in games of six balls to each player.

- A novel target for pitching in both baseball and softball can have either a cutout area below the bat, through which the ball must be pitched, or a tin plate hanging down from the bat (figure 11.3). The latter is especially popular because a good pitch is obvious to everyone within hearing distance! Other targets can be set up by attaching hoops to a fenced court area at the appropriate height and in line with a base.
- Partners can also work together in a co-operative way as pitcher and catcher or bowler and keeper to improve these techniques.

FIGURE 11.3 An example of an easily made wooden figure of a batter with a metal plate hanging on to the bat to represent the strike zone.

Teachers need to decide when to introduce pitching and bowling into the games. With beginners, eliminate the pitch by using a batting tee and then progress to striking a moving ball fed cooperatively from team-mates. Sector games can also be set up so that the pitcher or bowler is initially provided by the batting team. In other instances where pitching is allowed it may be necessary to introduce a rule restricting the pace of the pitch such as in slow-pitch softball.

To bridge the gap between the basic technical practice and the real game, both sports use net practice. Here, the batter stands in an area surrounded on three sides and the top by mesh netting. No matter how hard the ball is struck, it is contained, except from where the bowler or pitcher is operating, so everyone in that area needs to be careful. Now batters can face one ball after another and can begin to learn to track and hit the ball. Most importantly, in baseball and softball they must learn to make the critical decision of whether to try to play the ball at all or to let it go by. In cricket, they have to make similar decisions, but if they do decide to play the ball, they must decide which stroke to employ. Clearly, decision making becomes an important aspect of net practice.

The final dilemma to be resolved is that the only place to develop games sense is in a game, but in all three games, a full game takes too long to be completed in a physical education lesson, and of course there is always the problem that players may not always be actively involved. So to help youngsters become competent players, a small-sided version of these games (5v5 softball and batting pairs cricket) can be used in lessons, coupled with the opportunity to play limited over or limited time games, such as 20–20 games. However, even shortened games of this kind must be played out of regular school hours. Of course, the ideal situation is a link with a local club so participants can extend their playing experience.

Cricket

This section is intended to present some innovative ideas on teaching cricket for sport educators who already understand some of the complexities of this great game. And it certainly is a complex game! So while many young players can master working models of some of the techniques of cricket, it takes years of practice and playing experience to really understand all of its complexities. This is one of the reasons it is regarded by many as one of the great games of the world, but it is also the major reason why many schools have given up including it in their physical education programs. In fact, while it is possible to introduce young players to some aspects of the game through sector games, fielding games, and challenges, it will only be possible for most youngsters to play the full game if they are in a school or community where cricket is given a high priority.

As indicated earlier, while the primary focus of the Loughborough group was to use sector games to develop tactical awareness in cricket, they are in fact superb vehicles for developing technical ability in batting. Equally important, they get all students involved and give them a chance to improve their fielding. The basic pattern is the same as for softball or baseball sector games, but with modifications to meet the specific needs of this game. So, the sectors are now approximately 45-degree arcs positioned to represent productive scoring zones for a right-handed batter (figure 11.4). These scoring zones are based on our analysis that it is possible to succeed at the highest level in cricket with a

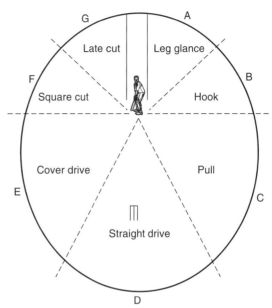

FIGURE 11.4 Sectors showing productive scoring zones for a right-handed batter.

relatively limited range of batting techniques. This is what we term a *working method.*

Each team of three players gets the chance to hit six consecutive strokes. Depending on the specific stroke to be practised and the level of the player, this can involve the use of a batting tee or even a dropped or lobbed ball. As with baseball, each batting team needs several balls available to keep the action flowing. While one batter is hitting the first of six attempts, one team-mate is getting a ball ready for the next stroke, while the third can be acting as a combination feedback giver and commentator. Because of the precise nature of the techniques of batting in cricket, the feedback role can be of considerable importance.

However, unlike baseball and softball, where the batter usually only executes one basic striking movement to hit the ball into a defined sector, the batter in cricket must be able to first select from and then execute any of a range of techniques to direct the ball through 360 degrees. At the highest level, this could mean hitting a ball bowled at close to 160 kilometres per hour (100 mph), a ball that may change direction in the air because of aerodynamic factors and then change direction once again when it hits the ground! If hitting a pitch in the major leagues is one of the most difficult challenges in sport, then batting at Test level in cricket presents a similar level of difficulty!

It will not be possible to introduce all of the techniques used by batters at the top level in the time available in many school programs, so the Play Practice approach is based on what can best be called a working method, where the technical requirements are stripped back to the bare bones. If batters can punish any overpitched ball into the area shown in figure 11.4, sector D, and can either hook or pull balls that are pitched short, shown in sectors B and C, they can be successful at the highest level. This assumes, of course, that they can also play with soft hands in defence and nudge, dab, push, and nurdle the ball to pick up singles, often a tickle into the area shown in sector A. They must all do this without being bowled out, caught out, run out, or given out leg before wicket, and no, that complex scenario is not going to be explained further to those who do not already understand it! Of course, young players can continue to develop their technical ability and thus the tactical options available to them by learning to drive overpitched balls landing wide of the off-stump through the covers (sector E), to square cut short balls pitched wide of the off-stump (sector F), and at the absolute elite level, to late cut the ball (sector G).

Batting Strokes

Experience suggests that it is best to begin with attacking strokes because this is more likely to motivate youngsters. However, it is as important for batters to understand the concepts of line and length as it is for the bowlers. Clearly, the bowler's object is to make it as difficult as possible for the batter to score runs. They do this by trying to deliver the ball on a length that prevents the batter from hitting it either before or just after it has bounced. The length may also make it difficult for batters to move back to hit it with a cross-bat shot. If bowlers do this, they are bowling on a good length (figure 11.5). Fortunately, they don't always manage this, and batters get the chance to play attacking shots to balls that are either overpitched or underpitched.

Finding the answer to the question of which stroke should be introduced first confirms the complexity of the process of teaching this game. If it is being introduced in an area where cricket is not already a major sport, it is best to begin with the most natural of the attacking strokes, the hook stroke, and its partner, the pull stroke. Both of these strokes are used to hit short-pitched balls to the leg side. While not identical, they are very similar. The key difference is the

FIGURE 11.5 Bowling a good length.

line of the ball as it approaches the batsman. If it is on or outside the line of the leg stump, it can be played into sector B. This is the hook stroke. If it is on the line of the stumps or just outside the line of the off-stump, it can be played into sector C. This is the pull stroke. For both strokes, the movement sequence is as follows:

1. Lift the bat into position.
2. Take the right foot slightly back and across.
3. Move the left leg back to open the body up to the ball.
4. Swing the bat across and down to hit the ball into the defined sector.

The sectors should have markers at set distances for scores of one to four runs, with six runs for a clean hit over the last line. If the ball is caught, the batting team can be penalised one or more runs.

However, to further simplify the task, beginners learning these strokes should position themselves with the bat lifted and their feet already in position. This means that they only have to concern themselves with hitting the ball with a very natural arm swing—almost the same swing as in baseball. After playing sector games using this technique, it is a relatively simple step to ask them to start in the stance shown in figure 11.6 and then go through the same sequence as before. Note that beginners should always take this stance with the bat picked up, as shown in figure 11.6. This approach is used by many top-class batters because it gives them more time to actually play the stroke, but it is especially valuable for beginners because much of the early practice will involve hitting balls lobbed or thrown from a short distance. As they improve, youngsters can hit a ball thrown and bounced into position by a team-mate.

Against top-class fast bowlers, where there is little time to select and execute this stroke, the batter merely swivels on the back foot to get into position to hit the ball. Players do not need to be taught to roll the wrists to keep the ball down (a common but unnecessary focus point) because this action occurs automatically as they follow through with the shot. In fact, in both strokes the

FIGURE 11.6 A left-handed batter demonstrates the stance with the bat lifted.

ball can only be kept down if the bat is moving from high to low as it strikes the ball.

In a school or a community where youngsters already have some understanding of the game, the straight drive might be the first stroke to be introduced. While it is less natural than either the pull or hook strokes, it emphasises the importance of playing with what is termed a *straight bat*—that is, where the bat is vertical when it strikes the ball. This stroke is played against balls that are overpitched and either on or just outside the line of the stumps. In simple terms, the player prepares with the bat picked up and then swings down through the ball to hit it with the meat of the bat. Because the ball can be hit very hard using this stroke, all practices should initially be carried out using tennis balls! It does not take much practice for young players to execute the basic elements of this technique—in a practice environment!

The key elements of the drive for a right-handed batter are as follows:

- Before the ball is delivered, lift the bat up into the ready position.

- As the ball approaches, move the head and shoulders towards the line of the ball (figure 11.7).

- Follow this by moving the left foot as close to the pitch of the ball as possible.

- And then, almost simultaneously, swing the bat down from its high position in a vertical arc to strike the ball in the sweet spot of the bat and send it away along the ground.

Because unlike the pull stroke this is not a natural hitting action, beginners may need to undertake some shadow practice—that is, practice without a ball—in which they learn the elements of the stroke as outlined previously. With large groups, this should be done in a very controlled manner with players following clear instructions. After taking guard, on the command 'one,' they all pick up the bat; on 'two,' they move their head and shoulders towards the line of the ball (a chalk mark on the ground will suffice); on 'three,' they swing the bat down to hit the ball. Ensure that every child has a bat for this practice, even if they are merely the affordable, lighter plastic bats now available or even simple wooden bat shapes. Following this practice, youngsters can first move to driving the ball from a low tee. Then they can proceed to working in pairs, with one dropping the ball onto a marked spot for their partner to drive on the second bounce, preferably into the netting of a tennis court. This practice can cater for large numbers. By the time youngsters move to the sector game, they have already begun to develop a working model of technique. While we appreciate that this direct teaching approach is not especially favoured in our profession at this time, we believe that it is the most efficient way of helping youngsters become competent players of this great game.

FIGURE 11.7 For the straight drive, the bat is lifted and the head and shoulders move towards the line of the ball.

It is possible to use the same technique to hit the ball using virtually the same technique when the ball is pitched wider. This is called the *cover drive*. It is a more difficult stroke than the straight drive because the batter is often hitting slightly across the line of the ball. Despite this, any youngster will find it easy to transfer the basic technique to deal with balls that are pitched in different areas.

Defensive Play

In cricket, defensive play is also important, and a simple play practice can be used to develop good technique in which the batsman plays with a vertical or *straight* bat and soft hands. The batting crease is surrounded by a marked area, as shown in figure 11.8. An opponent tries to lob spinning balls into a target area, thus forcing the batter to play correctly. The closer the batter can drop the ball to his bat, the more points he gets. While this game can be played 1v1, there are advantages to a 2v2 game. Two players can serve as bowlers, each taking their turn (6 balls each), while the second batter acts as an umpire until it is his turn to bat. This is because the opposing bowlers may be tempted to serve the batter unplayable balls by delivering them too fast or with great spin. Inevitably, this will lead to some debate, but once the notion that the

umpire's decision is final is accepted, some valuable learning and practice can result. The 2v2 game also provides an opportunity to introduce a close-in fielder who attempts to catch any ball that might be popped up by the batter.

Again, with beginners, the shadow-play approach is recommended to introduce the basic defensive strokes. Fortunately, the forward defensive stroke evolves quite naturally from the straight drive already introduced. The only difference is that if batters cannot reach the ball to drive it along the ground, they check their stroke and play the ball with soft hands. Here, the sequence is as follows:

- Pick the bat up into the ready position.
- Move the head and shoulders to the line of the ball and the left foot close to the pitch of the ball.
- Simultaneously bring the bat down in a vertical arc to play the ball with soft hands, ideally in the sweet spot.

Back Defensive Stroke

Clearly, if the ball pitches shorter, it may bounce up around the hands of someone playing forward. The back defensive stroke can then be used. As figure 11.9 shows, the batter learns to move the weight back onto the right foot and

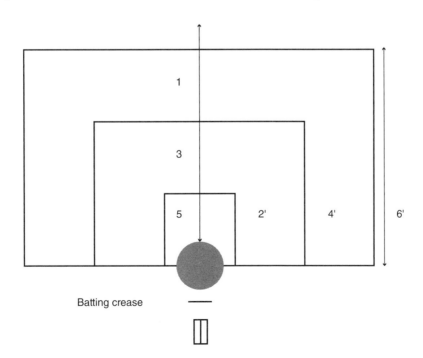

FIGURE 11.8   Batting crease surrounded by a marked area.

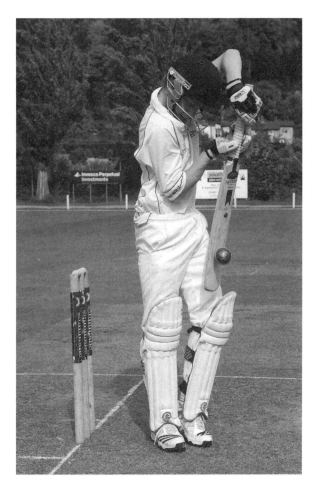

FIGURE 11.9 Back defensive stroke: The batter moves his weight onto the right foot and brings the bat down onto the line of the ball.

to bring the bat down onto the line of the ball. As players improve, it may be useful to use a lacrosse ball instead of a tennis ball because this will markedly increase the degree of difficulty for the defending player. Although both of these strokes are primarily defensive strokes, if the ball is pitched on the leg stump, it is possible to score runs simply by slightly angling the bat to glance the ball down the leg side into that scoring area.

Again with large groups, use a direct approach to carry out shadow practice of all the strokes. When working to develop the back defensive stroke, the sequence will be as follows:

1. Pick up the bat.
2. Take the right foot back and across to the line of the ball.
3. Bring the bat down onto the line of the ball.

It is possible to repeat this pattern 10 or 20 times in a very short time period.

Once youngsters have a working model of this stroke, they can play the soft-hands game outlined previously. This approach may appear to be the worst kind of isolated technique practice, for initially, there is not even a ball. However, we make no apologies for this because it is the most effective way of helping novices master the complex techniques of this game. Remember that once the basic techniques are mastered, even at a working level, it is possible for any committed person to play cricket into their 70s, so this is a worthwhile investment.

Again, the degree of emphasis on good technique depends on the place and importance of cricket in any school or community. The challenge for the teacher is finding the right balance between practice and games of the kind described previously for any specific group of children in the context in which they are working.

While the catching and ball-stopping aspects of fielding can be improved in the sector games, throwing for accuracy cannot. It is possible to use the bowling target described previously for accuracy practice, but the challenge for sport educators in these games is to develop realistic and challenging play practices that emphasise this aspect of good play. The previously mentioned baseball game in which the hitter has to beat the ball to first is one example of this kind of practice. Many more are waiting to be developed!

However, teachers, especially those working with younger players, may find the game of bombardment an enjoyable and useful practice for improving some elements of throwing and fielding. Here, two teams set up facing each other, preferably behind lines 12 or 15 metres (40 or 50 feet) apart (depending on the level of the learners); every player has a tennis ball, and their aim is to drive a basketball positioned equidistant between the teams over their opponent's goal line by hitting it with the tennis balls thrown as hard as possible. The action can become fast and furious and will last a considerable time simply because the closer the basketball gets to a goal line, the easier it is for the defenders to drive it back the other way.

Cut Strokes

Aficionados of this great game will have noted that so far, we have omitted cut strokes from the batting sequence. This is because these strokes are difficult to teach in a group situation. They may be best left until youngsters make a commitment to the game and can practice in the nets. The fundamental problem is that the ball must come onto the bat quickly if these strokes are to be executed well, playing the ball into the offside area towards the point area or backward of the point area shown in figure 11.4, sector G. This creates a dilemma: If the ball is delivered too fast, novices will not be able to hit it, but if it is too slow, they will hit it early into the covers area shown in figure 11.4, sector F. The solution (again, this is only recommended for those who are seriously committed to teaching cricket) is to introduce the late cut first! This may seem strange because the late cut is a difficult stroke to execute, it does not bring many runs, and it is dangerous to play in the real game. However, it is in fact an excellent progression towards the square cut that has been used with great effect by all successful batters.

The critical point is that in mastering the late cut, youngsters must learn to move their weight onto the back foot and to wait for the ball to come past the body into a position where they can chop down on it with the bat. After shadow practice, where the emphasis is on hitting the ball after it has passed their body, youngsters can practise the stroke with a lacrosse ball bounced in at the right speed and height. This ball is ideal because it bounces and maintains its speed even when it is not thrown very fast.

Square Cut

Once youngsters start to master the late cut and learn the risks involved in using it in a game, they can be introduced to the square cut, one of the most productive scoring strokes in cricket (figure 11.10). Now the notion of playing the ball as it passes the right shoulder, along with the technical elements of transferring the weight onto the right foot and executing an early high preparation of the bat and a downward slashing movement, transfer easily from the practice of the late cut.

The ball can be hit from a high batting tee. However, because there is no ball speed, this tee should be placed much farther back than where the ball would normally be contacted in a game so that the student can punch the ball into the indicated sector with a strong swing of

FIGURE 11.10　Square cut.

the bat face. The next practice should be with a well-thrown lacrosse ball or, ideally, a bowling machine! The preparation is the same as for the late cut, but now the ball is taken a fraction earlier and is hit into the point area shown in figure 11.4, sector F. The lengthy explanation of how to teach this stroke confirms the need for teachers to fully understand the critical issues when teaching games. However, we must restate that the previously outlined approach is only possible in a school or community where cricket is really valued. In the majority of situations, the teacher is forced to settle for the basic pulling, hooking, and driving strokes using sector games, along with the soft-hands defending game, to give young players a feeling for cricket. Unless youngsters have made a great commitment to cricket and have already mastered the strokes detailed previously, there is no point in introducing the sweep stroke.

Bowling

While everyone usually gets to bat in cricket, not every player has the opportunity to bowl in the real game. Despite this, every youngster in a cricket culture should be helped to master the basic bowling action. This is a very specialised form of throwing in which the arm must be kept athletically straight throughout the delivery. However, most youngsters can easily master this apparently complex skill if they are introduced to a working technical model of the bowling technique.

While elite players can hold the ball in many different ways, depending on what they want to achieve, with beginners the simplest method is to hold it with the thumb and first two fingers (figure 11.11). Although the ball shown here is a regulation ball made of leather, it is possible for young players to use composition balls for both practice and games.

In the working technical model, youngsters stand sideways, looking at the target over their left shoulder, with the left arm held high. They then rock forward to deliver the ball with a high straight arm (figure 11.12). In this way, with the front shoulder pointing at the target until the last instant, and a high swing of the arm to the vertical, players should be able to deliver the ball close to the line of the target wicket at the other end of the pitch.

Once this action has been mastered, it can be developed by starting with the ball in front of the chin. Now the hand and arm execute a long

circle to deliver the ball with an easy follow-through over the left leg. Even young players can quickly master the movement patterns of this technique. But, and this is a big but, they will only be able to deliver the ball consistently and accurately on the line of the target after considerable practice.

Players then move on to the basic bowling action. Here, they take five to seven running steps to arrive in the original basic bowling position to deliver the ball. Young bowlers can begin their run-up facing their target but can then jump into a sideways delivery position in the last two steps to ensure that the left shoulder is pointing at the target as the delivery action begins. However, as with all sport techniques, considerable practice will be required to ensure the level of accuracy necessary to bowl in an actual game. That thousands of youngsters set out to master the bowling action every year is a testament to the pulling power of challenges of this kind.

Remember that most youngsters love to aim at targets. They will attract a lot of interest and may even be the starting point for a lifelong interest in sport. These can be set up in any free space. Because of the size and weight of the target, it is better left in position in the practice area.

These targets give youngsters a good idea of the direction or line they should deliver the ball. Because, unlike baseball, the ball should strike the ground before it reaches the batsman, it may be useful to put out a second target to give the bowler an aiming point. This can be used to introduce the concept of length in bowling, one of the most misunderstood aspects of the game. With beginners, the length target can be fixed to give an approximate aiming point for all bowlers.

Line and Length in Bowling

Like all games, cricket has developed a long list of specific terms to describe elements of the game. Two of these are *line* and *length,* both of which have implications for the batter and the bowler.

With beginners, *line* is the most important aspect of bowling. In cricket terms, the line of a ball simply means the path it travels down the pitch. Beginners should be encouraged to bowl along that line. This aspect of accuracy is closely linked to the effectiveness of the working model of bowling technique, because if the youngster

FIGURE 11.11 Beginners should hold the ball with the thumb and first two fingers.

FIGURE 11.12 Working technical model for bowling: *(a)* Stand sideways, looking at the target over the left shoulder with the left arm held high; *(b)* rock forward to deliver the ball with a high straight arm.

starts sideways on and then rotates to bring the bowling arm over high and straight, there is a very good chance that the ball will travel on the correct line.

Amazingly, the concept of length does not appear to be understood by many who have played the game for years, even expert commentators. The problem is that the term *a good length* is used as though it was a specific area of the pitch. In fact, good length is always relative. It will vary according to the type of the bowler, especially their speed, the nature of the pitch, and the strengths and weaknesses of the specific batter they are facing.

In basic terms, a good length is one that forces a specific batter to defend rather than hit the ball. This is shown in the preceding figure 11.5. This figure also shows overpitched balls that the batter can drive and short-pitched balls that can be hit, pulled, or hooked away to the leg side. Finally, it shows approximately where young bowlers should attempt to pitch the ball.

As a rule of thumb, young players will be more successful if they overpitch the ball than if they pitch it short! The reason is simple. Even when pitched on the line of the stumps, short-pitched balls rise up into the natural hitting zone of a beginning batter, who can pull or hit it with full power. On the other hand, full-pitched balls exploit the tendency of beginning batters to swing around the ball instead of straight through it. Gradually, bowlers must learn how to modify both the line and length of where they pitch the ball.

While line is determined by the basic bowling action, and so is reasonably easy to master, length depends on the kinaesthetic awareness that can only come from repetitive practice.

Spinning and Swinging the Ball

While it is possible for young players to learn how to use both spin and swing to make the ball deviate in the air and off the pitch, this is best left until they have fully mastered the bowling action and can control line and length in their bowling. It is worth remembering that the bowling action is especially important because to a large degree, it can contribute to both of these methods of confounding batters. However, even at the highest level, bowlers will do well to pitch the ball up because it allows batters more time to swing and will encourage attacking strokes against spinning balls.

Fielding

While it is possible for youngsters to improve their stopping and catching with sector games, many simple games can be used to improve the throwing skills that can produce run-outs. A target game, where partners aim at a single stump (or any suitable target), provides an excellent challenge that can be differentiated for various experience levels. The game includes fielding, since players must back up and retrieve their partners' throw before having their shot at the target. By varying the distance from the target or including time challenges, the focus can be directed to longer throws or short, quick deliveries to the target. Partners can also play another challenge game where each player is trying to protect a score line defined by markers (the length of the score line varies from 2 to 5 metres, or 8 to 15 feet). One partner tries to roll the ball past their partner and over the line. The partner who is protecting the line tries to field the ball and stop it from going over. Partners change roles after each roll of the ball, and they score a point for each ball saved from going over the line.

Net Practice

Although it is possible for youngsters to move from sector games and target bowling straight into a real game, net practice can be an important bridging activity. It gives both batters and bowlers a chance to get a great deal of experience without the pressure of the game. It is especially important for batters because it gives them the opportunity to begin to read the line and length of balls and to select the appropriate stroke to deal with them. Indeed, well-organised net practice becomes one of the most critical elements in developing good players in a cricket culture. Note that it is possible to use concrete pitches and mesh fencing to construct practice nets.

Full Game

While it is impossible to justify the inclusion of the full game in a physical education program, it is clear that youngsters do need an opportunity to play in the game if they are to develop those elements of games sense involved in fielding and running between the wickets that are critical to skilled play in cricket. In many schools, it is impossible to provide a grass wicket good enough for safe game play, so artificial pitches with a concrete base will have to be used. There can be no prescription for this. It is up to teachers to consider what they might be able to do to give their students some experience of the game, always bearing in mind that they may be opening up avenues of enjoyment that can last a lifetime!

That said, none of the above applies to the private schools of England and many other former Commonwealth countries because there is not only time to play games during the school day but also money available to ensure good grass pitches. That is one reason why such schools provide a high proportion of their country's leading players.

Softball and Baseball

Fortunately, the games of softball and baseball can be introduced through the lead-up game of tee ball, which simplifies the batting technique by allowing players to hit a stationary ball from a tee. The reduced perceptual and timing demands allow beginners to focus on developing a natural swing pattern as they strike the stationary ball. Other small-sided (3- to 5-a-side) games can be played as introductory activities using the diamond sector with a batting and fielding team structure. The equipment and scoring system can be varied in these games. For example, grip-ball pads and a Velcro ball can be used with beginners. The batter must throw the ball out and run the bases, scoring a point per base covered. While the batter runs, fielders gather the ball and throw it to each of the bases, calling stop when the ball reaches home base. Batters keep a tally of the total points they score in an inning before changing roles. Different balls and striking implements can also be used in these introductory games. The key factors in promoting learning in these introductory games are the following:

- Maximising the opportunity for learning through the use of small-sided sector games
- Shaping the appropriate play space to establish a fair contest between batters and fielders
- Selecting appropriate equipment for individuals in the class or group
- Allowing participants a degree of choice in the selection of equipment or play conditions

Teaching Progression

The following series of small-sided sector games can be used as a progression for introducing softball or baseball. The equipment can be chosen to suit the developmental needs of the group, and the dimensions of the game can be adjusted accordingly.

Sector Game With Scoring Zone

This game is described in the introduction, and it can be played initially with a group of 3 students per sector. The batter tries to hit the ball from the tee, past or over the fielders, and they tally the runs scored from 3 hits. Each player then rotates roles from batter to front fielder to back fielder, with each batter keeping their score. During these games, players focus on their batting technique, first ensuring they are set up an appropriate distance away from the batting tee with their bat back ready; second initiating a small leading step, turning the belly button forward to initiate the swing; and finally focusing closely on the ball as the arms extend and the bat drives through the ball. This game can easily be converted into a 3v3 game simply by combining groups from two sectors. When this occurs the batting team can have one player undertake the role of feedback giver who helps to coach using some of the key focus points introduced earlier.

Running the bases can be introduced in small-sided sector games after players have experienced success with batting.

Sector Games With Baserunning

As indicated in the introduction, the initial sector game can be extended simply by adding a rule that for any scoring hit to be valid, the batter must run and beat the ball to first base, which is positioned at a distance that will allow some chance of success. This adds another level of complexity to the sector game, increasing its alignment to the real game while still retaining a high level of participation.

It is possible to vary the playing area in sector games. For example, a smaller section of the diamond can be used for a 2v2 sector game. In this game, the boundary for fair and foul territory can be defined by a line extending from home through first base into the outfield and a line extending from home through second base into the outfield. An outfield boundary can be included by running a line of markers across from the extended lines. The distance between first and second base must be shortened, and a 'fair hit line' 3 meters (10 feet) out from home base can be included to ensure the playing space can be covered by 2 fielders. The batter must strike the ball, land it within the boundaries, and then run to first base, scoring one point for making it safely. The fielders must gather the ball and get it to first base before the runner. If the runner makes it safely to the base, she is faced with a 'forced run' to second base, when her team-mate has the bat. This means the player at first must run to second base as soon as the ball is struck and reach the base before the fielders gather the ball and throw it to second base. In this situation the fielders are faced with a decision of throwing the ball to either first or second base in order to get a batter out. They can of course try for a double play by quickly moving the ball to one base and then the other before either runner makes it safely. Once the baserunner reaches second base, she returns to home to continue batting in the next innings. The batting pair complete three innings, then tally their score (1 point for each safe base gained) before changing roles. The focus for this game can be directed to batting technique, baserunning, fielding, accurate throwing to bases, or specific components of games sense.

3v3, 4v4, or 5v5 Sector Games Using All Bases (Diamond)

As indicated in the introduction, the natural progression is to include all bases in the diamond and to play either 3v3, 4v4, or 5v5 sector games. The number of players can be extended further depending on the class and the nature of the unit plan; however, small-sided game play has the benefit of involving more players in the action. When smaller numbers are included, it is important to adjust the bases in the diamond to create a fair contest for batters and fielders. It is possible to include a back boundary and a fair hit line forward of home base to ensure a fair contest. Home base for baserunners may also be moved about 10 metres (35 feet) to the side of its normal position, particularly when a batting tee is being used, to improve safety by avoiding congestion at this area. A batting team area can also be defined to ensure player safety. As outlined in the introduction, these games can be used to improve games sense, particularly in relation to applying an understanding of the rules and tactics.

The progression for sector games outlined above provides a platform for development for all aspects of skilled play. With beginners it is possible to initially play with a softer ball so that fielders do not need gloves, and batters can easily strike this ball from the batting tee. Gloves and the specific softball or baseball can be introduced at any time, through individual and partner challenges initially and then by returning to the variety of sector games using the mitt and either a softball or baseball.

Individual and Partner Challenges for Fielding Technique

Grip-ball pads are an ideal way to introduce players to the concept of catching the ball with a glove before they actually start using the mitt and a harder ball. This novel and engaging equipment promotes success, since the bright catching surface provides a good target for partners to throw to. The sound of the ball hitting the pad provides immediate feedback when a catch is made, and it is possible to extend the throwing range using the smaller ball. Learning to use the mitt for catching and fielding progresses on from using the grip-ball pad as a new challenge for individuals to master. The challenges and target games outlined in the lacrosse section can be applied. Some examples are outlined below.

- Players work with a glove and ball in their own space on individual challenges including catching the ball with the glove up high overhead and catching the ball as it drops lower with the glove held out in front. Throwing technique can be developed concurrently by including distance and accuracy challenges or by playing the bombardment game described in the cricket section.

- Partners can work co-operatively on throwing and catching, roll-and-field, and high-catch challenges. Combining techniques, variation, and time challenges all help to enhance motivation. These games can be developed into partner target games when the challenge is to try to roll the ball across your partner's endline as they try to field the ball and prevent it from getting past. Distances between partners and the length of the end zone can vary according to the individuals in the group. Similar games can be designed to improve high catching technique.

Striking the Moving Ball

Players can progress from striking the stationary ball on the tee to striking a moving ball fed cooperatively by a team-mate. The feeder positions themselves 3 to 4 metres away from the batter in line with home plate and at a right angle to it. The ball is fed to the batter using an underarm slow pitch with a level trajectory aimed at the front hip of the batter. This can initially be practiced in pairs with one player feeding the ball to their partner, who strikes the ball into a fence or net area. Once they become confident in feeding and in hitting the moving ball, they can revisit any of the earlier games, using this method to replace hitting from the tee. As mentioned in the introduction, once pitching has been introduced, it is possible to play sector games where the batting team provides the pitcher or where there is a restriction on the nature of the pitch. In these instances it is possible to play with a 'backstop' who is positioned several metres back from home base, rather than including the role of 'catcher' using full protective equipment. These pitching conditions allow a transition in game development to occur without letting the pitch completely dominate the game. Teachers will then need to decide whether it is appropriate to include full pitching and catching into the game using all of the appropriate safety equipment.

twelve

Teaching Target Games

Archery, Golf, Tenpin Bowling, and Lawn Bowls

One of the advantages of bowling over golf is that you seldom lose a bowling ball.

Don Carter, U.S. tenpin bowler

Success in archery, golf, tenpin bowling, and lawn bowls depends on sound technique, mental toughness, and resilience, along with the ability to focus tightly at the crucial instant. The interesting thing about this group of sports is that, despite the fact that they all present similar challenges, they differ greatly from each other in terms of their origins, equipment, and technical demands. Their major advantage is that they can be played across a wider age range than is seen in any other game. It is not uncommon to find 90-year-olds still enjoying the challenges they present, and archery is a major sport in the Paralympics, providing athletes with a range of disabilities an opportunity to compete at the highest level.

However, we must understand that youngsters perceive missing a target as clear evidence of failure. And since, as we have already suggested, they do not like to fail, especially in front of classmates, teachers must create a variety of practice situations where beginners can experience initial success and are thus encouraged to persist long enough to develop at least a working model of technique.

Archery

Student safety is obviously critical, so teachers must make sure that the whole area is completely safe. Two major issues exist. First, the area must be carefully selected and should accommodate at least 50 percent more distance than the maximum range of the equipment being used, unless there are protective banks behind the shooting area. Second, the teacher needs high-level management skills, especially the ability to establish and strictly enforce very tight rules controlling the firing line. No one, absolutely no one, is allowed to go over the firing line without a very specific signal from the teacher! Even the slightest infringement must be dealt with by the simple consequence of taking the culprit's bow away for a period.

It is also important to provide safety equipment, such as finger tabs and wrist guards, and to teach youngsters how to use both. Finger tabs allow youngsters to draw the bow without cutting their fingers, while the wrist guards protect their arms when the string flashes forward to release the arrow. These are especially important with beginners, who often hyperextend their arms as they deal with the pressure of drawing the string back. Beginners can use bows with a simple fibreglass construction, although a mixed group may require bows in a range of poundages. Note that the more complex composite bows used in competition are not necessary.

The teaching sequence should show students how to do the following:

- Use the safety equipment.

- String the bow. In the first session it may be worthwhile ensuring that all bows are already strung so that actual shooting can start quickly. However, students do need to learn to string their own bows, so this issue can be addressed at the end of the session, not at the beginning.

- Nock an arrow with the fletching in the correct place.

- Position the tabbed fingers to draw the bow back.

- Maintain a strong but slightly flexed arm while holding the bow.

- Draw the right hand to the chin, keeping the right elbow in a high, strong position (figure 12.1).

Shooting for Distance

The Play Practice approach begins with students shooting for maximum distance rather than at targets. While many might question this approach, it has several advantages, and it works! In the first place, beginners will more readily appreciate the potential danger of a missile that can travel 200 metres (660 feet) or more. Second, as they try to shoot greater distances, their technique will improve. They will begin to draw to the chin with a correct finger position on the bowstring while maintaining a strong front arm, instead of the short draw, poor finger position, and weak front arm that tend to occur when aiming at nearby targets.

An added bonus is that the landing angle of the arrows will be such that none will be lost snaking under the grass, as often happens when arrows are fired at a normal target. This saves arrows and the time spent looking for them, and so contributes to plenty of perfect practice!

FIGURE 12.1 Bow drawn: right hand to chin, right elbow in a high, strong position.

Firing High

The second practice involves firing high to drop the arrows into a horizontal target, such as the centre circle of a soccer field. This is done from gradually decreasing distances. Volley firing on a signal is always a popular variation with children in both of these initial practices.

All these practices shape the correct draw and help youngsters understand the relationship among a good draw, the release angle, and the flight characteristics of the arrow. If the group is split into two, while one archer is shooting, the partner can provide feedback on one or two carefully defined aspects of technique, such as drawing to the chin or keeping the bow arm strong.

When a good draw has been achieved, regulation targets can be introduced, again with a Play Practice twist. Large coloured balloons can be secured to each target, and a special award can be given for every one that is hit. Naturally, other targets can be used. However, for children, little beats the dramatic bursting of a balloon. One final variation is shooting at moving targets. A cardboard box can be drawn slowly across the shooting area. Teachers can decide for themselves how the box is decorated.

Clearly, regulation shooting and scoring can be introduced at any point, but a culminating competition for the prized golden arrow will create considerable interest.

Golf

As one of the great games of the world, golf is the ultimate target sport. Hitting a small ball long distances is challenge enough, but getting it close to a specific target (i.e., a small hole) when faced with the terrors of bunkers, trees, lakes, or rivers appears almost magical. Fortunately, millions of people of all ages take up the challenge. So, where possible it should be included in every program of sport education.

Teachers and coaches must understand that golf is made up of two separate and distinctly different games. On the one hand, the player has to be able to strike the ball with a full swinging action, rather like swinging a flail or executing an upright baseball swing. One of the major

Golf is made up of two separate and distinct games: full swinging and putting.

challenges here is to develop a repeatable and accurate swing in order to hit the ball medium to long distances using irons or woods. Fortunately, once the swing is mastered, it can be generalised and modified to hit the ball different distances through the air simply by changing the club used. The second game of golf is putting. This involves hitting the ball along the green into the hole. Clearly, the techniques involved are completely different, so much so that a player may be masterful at one and poor in the other. While both are important, it is not for nothing that golfers repeat the old saying 'Swing for show, but putt for dough.'

Complete mastery of golf depends on not only the mastery of these techniques but also the ability to decide when to use a particular club and to play a particular stroke. This can only be gained from playing on a real course. Because of limitations of time or facilities, it is only possible to introduce some elements of the game in a physical education unit, so tight priorities must be established. Much depends on the proximity of the school to a course, even a par three, but this would only be needed for a culminating activity where youngsters can be introduced to both the joys and the mores of the game. The vast bulk of instruction can be carried out on school grounds, even if a real course is accessible. The initial focus should be on the great satisfaction that comes from hitting the ball cleanly, no matter how far it travels.

The Play Practice approach is simple. From the very beginning, students, using 7- or 9-irons, hit towards or even onto a series of replica greens. These greens, which can be marked out with ropes, or better still, cut out on a playing field with a mower, should be the exact size and shape of famous par-three holes from around the world. Of course, the distance between the tee and green can be reduced to whatever length best suits a group. The actual hole can be any size the instructor wishes, but with beginners this hole should be significantly larger than the real one. Whatever the size of the hole, there must be special prizes for a hole in one!

This can easily lead into a series of tests that enable youngsters to get a feel for golf, even if they never have the chance to play on a real course while at school. These tests could include the following:

- Hitting for distance using tape measures. This can be as far as the ball travels, no matter the direction. It could also be a test conducted alongside a tape measure or distance markers, with the distance from the line of the tape subtracted from the overall distance of the hit, thus rewarding straight hits. However, students should use 7- or 9-irons instead of drivers.

- Putting from set spots perhaps 9 metres (30 feet) away to get as close to the pin as possible.

- A bunker shot could be played from a long jump pit or even a relatively small hole filled with sand. Again, the aim is to gain points by hitting the ball into a range of circular targets on the green.

- A short iron shot played with a 9-iron or wedge from 18 metres (60 feet).

Instructors can also use modified target areas to help players develop a range of shots. For chipping practices, try placing hoops, cones, or drawn targets on the green or other cut-out areas. Chipping over a football crossbar to a target can be an enjoyable challenge. The target areas can

either offer a larger hole or a defined area where a player should land a chip from off the green to run up near the hole.

Bunker shots, which appear complicated, nonetheless lend themselves well to the use of Play Practice. In bunker play, the club should not actually strike the ball. Instead, it should enter the sand behind the ball and lift both the ball and the sand on which it rests. How far behind the ball the club head should enter depends on the type of sand and whether it is wet or dry. These variables tend to make getting out of sand difficult because the decision-making element is greater than for most shots. Applying a Play Practice approach, however, simplifies many of the demands. For example, teachers can use the bunker sand to draw markings that show where the club should strike the sand to get the ball out. Markings may vary from simple lines or semicircles to shapes or even faces drawn in the sand.

Softer modified golf balls allow increased opportunity in driving challenges, since the distances hit are shortened. They also allow a variety of safe partner chip-and-catch challenges.

This approach can lead easily into the series of tests used in some special, unofficial tournaments for U.S. professional players. These tournaments are virtually a Play Practice approach to golf. They include the following tests:

- Driving for distance
- Putting from set spots to get as close to the pin as possible
- A bunker shot from set spots to get as close to the pin as possible
- A short iron from set spots to get as close to the pin as possible

In the tests that require getting closest to the pin, distance is marked with a tape measure, although distance rings can also be drawn. These tests could all be fitted into a relatively small area. Youngsters can work their way around each activity in pairs or small groups. Naturally, all performances should be recorded with a view to improvement. In addition, 'the Open' can be held at the end of a unit of work. Ideally, this should be on a real golf course, although a par-three course would be suitable. If this is not possible, the test series outlined above would be appropriate, with suitable adjustments made to the length of each hole.

The innovative approach of JOLF (Junior gOLF) developed by Jonathon Shipstone and Neil Plimmer (2012) for introducing junior participants into the sport is worthy of attention. The comprehensive program reflects Play Practice principles and features JOLF challenges and game experiences as the central learning experiences, suitably shaped for the developmental level of the children.

Tenpin Bowling

Although tenpin bowling has a professional circuit in the United States, for most people, it is a recreational sport. The attraction of this game is that it can be great fun, even when it is played badly. It can provide a focus for social activity for friends, work groups, and clubs of all kinds, so it is well worth including in a sport education program. The biggest problem is the cost, which can make it difficult for all but the most committed bowlers to become highly skilled.

The automation of the scoring system has made playing much simpler, and the addition of on-screen bells and whistles that accompany a strike or a spare brings a Play Practice feel to the experience. Side bars that can be raised or lowered to accommodate beginners also reflect a Play Practice approach, since they simplify the challenge for beginners. Above all, they eliminate the humiliation that accompanies bowling a ball into the gutter.

The first task is to introduce beginners to the process of going to the desk to book a game and to order a pair of shoes. The next is learning how to select a ball. This involves going to the racked balls and selecting one that is the right weight for the player's strength and that has finger holes with the correct spacing. Here, the thumb goes into the single hole, while the second and third fingers go into the side-by-side holes.

Instructors may be tempted to allow players to do their own thing, wandering in and simply throwing the ball down the lane. Do not allow this. Instead, teach a formal four-step approach. Although some may find this a challenging task, it is worth persevering, since it provides the foundation for a move towards successful bowling at any level. This means that a part of every session should be devoted to developing this technique. Try asking the operators to allow free

practice of this movement on adjoining unused lanes. If this is not possible, have students use the spaces between the lanes for practice.

Teach a working model of the approach and delivery. Here, the right-handed bowler stands in a stable position with the left foot slightly in front of the right. The ball, held correctly, rests comfortably on the left hand, which is kept fairly close to the body in this initial stance.

The movement begins as the bowler steps smoothly onto the right foot while simultaneously extending the right arm forward. Then the bowler allows the ball to swing down in a long arc as she continues to move forward. This arc brings the ball up behind the bowler just as she prepares to take the final delivery stride. The action is completed as the ball is swept forward and delivered onto the lane in the area shown in figure 12.2, with a final upward lift of the fingers.

Once this working model is mastered, the notion of an aiming point can be introduced. The natural tendency is to simply aim at the pins, but this will not lay the groundwork for

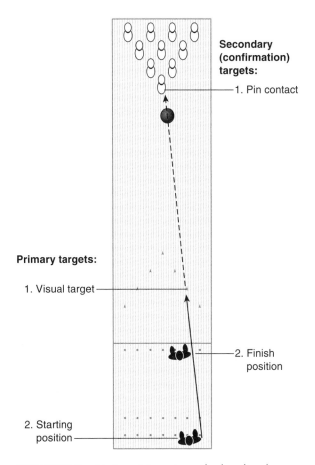

FIGURE 12.2 Aiming at targets on the bowling lane.

future improvement. Improvement will only come from learning to use the much closer aiming points (the arrows) on the lane, as shown in figure 12.2. It is important to get players to develop consistency not only in their delivery but also in their starting positions and aiming points. Here, the marks on the approach and the arrows on the lane will help enormously once they get comfortable with using them.

It is pointless to even consider introducing the advanced methods of experienced bowlers who impart great spin on the ball as they deliver it. This spin causes the ball to hook into the critical pocket between the one and the three pins, but it also transfers energy to the remaining pins, causing them to rocket into each other. This increases the likelihood of a strike. However, this advanced technique requires considerable strength in the bowling arm and fingers, and it often involves the use of specialised equipment. Above all, it requires immense amounts of practice for mastery. This is where a working technical model comes into its own because it can be mastered quite quickly and it allows the player to be relatively successful.

What do we mean by success? No gutter balls, some pins knocked down with every ball, and occasionally a strike! Players get the feeling that they know what they are doing, so they develop the desire to continue playing. This is the Play Practice way. Using modified foam bowling balls and a series of targets, it is possible to introduce some aspects of the working technique at school prior to visiting the bowling centre.

Lawn Bowls

Lawn bowls is a highly popular game in the Commonwealth countries. Although it is usually seen as a game for older players, it can be played from the ages of 8 to 80 and beyond, and in fact it is increasingly being taken up by younger players.

Although categorised as a target game, lawn bowls is unusual in that the actual target, the jack, is never actually aimed at, except when employing the drive shot (i.e., a direct shot at the jack to knock it off the green). This is because of the nature of the actual bowling ball, simply called 'the bowl' because it is not a true sphere.

The bowl has a bias, so its path to the jack is a curve. The nature of this curve differs according to many variables, ranging from the type of bowl (there are many in the modern game), the weather, the type of surface, and, of course, the speed of the shot.

Having said all that, the basic and most essential skill of the game is the draw shot. This involves getting the bowl to stop as close to the jack as possible. It can be argued that all other shots, with the exception of the drive, are merely modifications of the draw shot. With beginners, the draw is the essence of the game, the shot that must be mastered. Without this, there is no basis on which to become a successful player.

The main elements of lawn bowls shots are 'green' and 'weight'. Mastery of green, or the line that the bowl takes, depends purely on technique. Weight is more dependent on the kinaesthetic awareness of the bowler, who must rely on his experience and muscle memory as he releases the bowl. Fortunately, the game has built-in feedback on both of these two elements: that is, where the bowl comes to rest after it has been bowled. This supplies the feedback the bowler needs to store in his muscle memory and the information needed by the teacher if she is to provide praise or feedback to the bowler.

To be able to bowl consistently, lots of repetitive perfect practice is required. There is no other path to consolidation and success in this game or indeed any of the other sports in this category. However, practices must be varied if young players are to maintain their motivation. Plenty of different practices using novel targets, drills, and modified games not only provide a fun element but also can be used to gauge progress.

Early activity should be a feature of all sessions. Set induction is a principle often ignored in what is still a very conservative game, although instructors should always stress respect for the nature and importance of the playing surface. There is certainly little need for theory, since the essence of the game is simple. The finer points and nuances of the game can be learned later as the need emerges.

After an initial demonstration in order to set a clear goal, the first session can quite rapidly move through correct bowl selection (these can range in size from 00 to approximately 4) for each student, to grip, stance, delivery, and

the tracing paper, with the year's results on it, could be kept. In this way, a whole year's group of 110 boys could record their performances during the winter.

An additional advantage of this system was that the same boards could be re-covered with tracing paper and used to record performances in track and field during the summer! Nowadays with the prevalence of computers, recording of data can be more easily undertaken, referred to, and applied.

While the results of this approach were manifest at Wymondham, at Dr. Challoner's its effectiveness was almost amazing, because again without any coaching or organised training, the school cross country team would have finished third while competing against 36 county teams in the English Schools Championships of 1965.

Track and Field Athletics

Because each event makes different demands on the physical and mental qualities of the participant, students with widely different abilities can find enjoyment and experience success in track and field. Indeed in recent years, there has been a huge expansion in the range of people taking part in this great sport. Now, people of all ages as well as those with a wide range of disabilities participate in every level, up to the Olympic Games.

Although this should give it an immense advantage as an educational and developmental activity, track and field rarely takes the place it deserves in the physical education curriculum. In fact, along with gymnastics and swimming, track and field should be central to any worthwhile program of sport education. Unfortunately, it is all too often reserved for the physically gifted child, and in Australia, as in many other countries, it enjoys status only as an inter-school and inter-club sport.

The Play Practice approach to track and field developed in the early 1960s as the author attempted to introduce the sport to large classes of children in physical education lessons. What evolved was the notion that track and field was merely a series of specific challenges in which students strove to improve their personal best by finding out how fast they could run, how high they could jump, and how far they could throw

or jump. To achieve even this objective in the limited time available meant that the challenges had to be reduced to the simplest possible level. The criteria arrived at was that while each test should be simplified, it should still conform to the fundamental rules of the event and should not be a dead-end technique. In other words, it would not prevent further development if youngsters wanted to continue with it in their own time. Thus the concepts of working technical models and indirect competition were born.

Five-Star Approach

After a period of reflective tinkering, the five-star award approach to track and field evolved at the school. The principles and methods developed at that time not only led to a complete revision of the teaching of track and field in many countries but also helped to lay the foundations of what was to become Play Practice. The relationship between the two becomes clear when studying the basic principles of the five-star approach, which were first spelled out in the 1960s. This approach is based on the following tenets:

1. Children like to be challenged, but most of all, they like to succeed and to have their successes noted. They do not like to fail or to be beaten, and they certainly do not want to be last at anything. Thus, one of the most important factors in the learning process is early and continued success for each child. Even in the tough competitive sport of track and field, all children can succeed if the process is based on indirect competition, where children strive to beat their own previous best performance rather than direct competition in which each competitor struggles to beat opponents.

2. Children like to see how fast they can run, how far they can jump or throw, and how high they can jump or vault. They are much less concerned with how correctly they perform these activities. Good technique, while important to ultimate performances, is only a means to an end, not an end in itself.

3. The apparently complex events of track and field evolved from the natural play activities of running, jumping, and throwing. At the senior level, the sport is made up of stylised events and formalised versions of these natural activities with a strong emphasis on direct (that is, head

to head) competition. Clearly, with children, it is important to emphasise the play element and to eliminate this head-to-head direct competition because it tends to turn youngsters—the losers—away from the sport.

Using this approach, track and field becomes a series of varied and enjoyable challenges that allow all youngsters to improve their performance and thus succeed. With the increased skill and fitness that comes with participation, children can experience success and gain the satisfaction of mastery and improvement throughout this vital early learning period. Then if the track and field events are viewed as challenges rather than as a series of complex movement patterns for children to master, the task of the teacher or coach is far easier. It takes very little knowledge to introduce the various tests of running or even those of hurdling, long jumping, and high jumping using a working technique that enables children to do the following:

- Perform the event within the accepted rules. Even here, some modifications can be made that can simplify the test without changing its essential nature.

- Master the basic elements of the challenge as quickly as possible.

- Begin testing themselves almost immediately.

- Develop a technique that is simple but sound and, most importantly, has the potential for continued development.

Working Technical Models

The notion of introducing a working technique is critical to the success of this approach, and it parallels the way in which Play Practice modifies games to reduce their complexity. Nowhere is this better illustrated than in the pole vault. Here, by introducing a working model of technique, ordinary children can vault above their own height after 30 minutes of practice in a sand pit.

The technical skill and knowledge needed to introduce athletics in this way is surprisingly small. Any committed sport educator can quickly build an enthusiastic and committed group of young athletes. Youngsters will not

only enjoy the challenges of this sport but also begin to improve their agility, which is clearly essential to success in many other sports.

However, track and field is a great sport in its own right. While working models of technique can be used to introduce children to the varied and interesting disciplines of athletics, teachers should be prepared to help children progress from the working model towards more advanced models. Clearly, it will be easier to make this transition in some events than in others. However, ample evidence suggests that many youngsters have the talent and desire to become competent performers, even in events as complex as the hammer throw and the pole vault. While this may seem like a daunting task at first, any committed teacher can learn more about track and field, even if only by studying one discipline at a time.

Since the primary emphasis in this approach is placed on personal performance and improvement, it is important to record all students' performances. This can be done by the children themselves.

The following basic plan can be used to introduce track and field to youngsters between the ages of 10 and 14.

Time Trials

While the group is warming up, remind them of the importance of personal improvement and doing their best. Organise a time trial over a standard distance. The distance chosen can be determined by the nature of the class. The whole class can start at the same time in the 800 and 1,500 metres. The teacher simply calls out the students' times as they pass the finish line. In the 400 metres, it is best to set them off in groups of three or four at 10-second intervals. The groups start as the instructor calls 'Go, 10, 20, 30, 40, 50,' and so on. They subtract this figure from that called out to them as they finish. While students are recovering from their effort, talk with them, praise their general performance, and recognise all personal improvements if they have run the distance before.

Once children have been introduced to the use of stopwatches, it is possible to time groups over 100 and 200 metres. However, do not waste time attempting to teach the crouch sprint start because (1) children in a class do not wear running spikes, (2) the sprint start is complex and cannot be mastered in the time available, and (3) starting blocks are rarely available.

Introduce a new test. Start with the simpler events first. The following sequence is suggested.

Long Jump

This is the most natural of the field events and hardly needs teaching at all. It can be further simplified by the use of a take-off zone that is 1 metre (3 feet) wide instead of the usual 20-centimetre (8 inch) take-off board, which even experienced athletes have great difficulty hitting accurately! With very young children, simply measure their jump from their take-off point.

Encourage children to use short-approach runs of around 15 metres (50 feet). This will give them sufficient speed while allowing control at take-off. At this stage, about all that can be said is to run fast and jump high. Certainly no time should be wasted on techniques such as the hang or hitch kick. From the very beginning, try to give the youngsters an idea of approximately how far each jump is by stretching tape measures from the take-off zone through the pit.

Track and field athletics comprises a series of individual challenges. The long jump is shown here.

High Jump

Bearing in mind that the event is structured by only one rule, that the jumper must take off from one foot—two-footed leaps are not permitted—this event is again easy to introduce.

While any style of jumping off from one foot is allowed, the old-fashioned scissors style has many advantages. Despite the poor layout position over the bar, it is both simple and safe, and it provides good lift at take-off. In fact, it is used as a primary training exercise by elite high jumpers. Children who have special ability or interest can switch to the flop technique later on if suitable landing pads are available and they are already jumping high enough to be able to exploit this more advanced technique.

Hurdles

One successful approach is to start with hurdles, preferably those with elastic tops at the accepted height for the particular age group. The distance between hurdles should be varied to accommodate different stride lengths. Once again, depending on the nature of the group it may be necessary to adjust the height of the hurdles.

Shot Put

When children are asked to nominate the most boring event, they will invariably choose the shot put. The following section illustrates how Play Practice can turn this supposedly boring activity into an enjoyable challenge in which youngsters are highly motivated to do their very best. It also illustrates the importance of good preparation and the simple, subtle, but highly effective elements that make up really good instruction.

The teacher or coach begins the process by ensuring that at least one shot of approximately the right weight is available for every two children. The second task is to select and mark out a suitable piece of ground for the activity. It must be dead ground (i.e., not usually used for other activities), and it should be set out as shown in figure 13.1. The limits of the area must be clearly defined by a border of some kind. Limiting the distance to 20 metres (66 feet) or less will put the group's efforts into perspective. If the activity were turned around, and the children were to face a limitless field in front of them as they tried to throw or put, their efforts would seem puny.

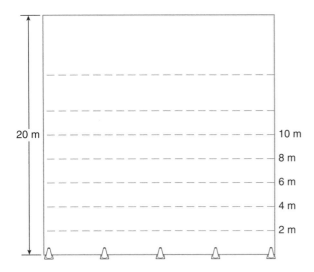

FIGURE 13.1 Sample setup for the shot put.

The area is also marked in a way that will convey a sense of achievement to everyone. The first line is only 2 metres (8 feet) from the throwing line, a distance all can attain. If, on the other hand, the first line is set at 10 metres (35 feet), many children will automatically be condemned to 'failure', no matter how hard they try. Simple, subtle, but effective!

The third element of preparation can involve the students. They are asked to find or make their own personal marker that can be used throughout a track and field unit for measuring run-ups, as well as distances achieved. It can be something as simple as an old tennis ball or a screwdriver painted brightly, or it can be something specially made by Grandad for the unit. Naturally, the school can provide these markers, but it can be valuable to involve family or friends in the experience.

After the teacher or coach explains and emphasises the safety rules, students can begin to practice by executing a backwards overhead throw with two hands. This commonly used training and warm-up activity is simple enough for beginners as they are introduced to the important progression when throwing a heavy implement: legs first, then trunk, shoulders, arms, wrist, and fingers.

Initially, instructors should introduce only the basic putting action, which is the safest throw to teach. Here, the shot is pushed away from the neck with a powerful punch of the shoulders and a driving extension of the arm. Depending on the time available and the interest and knowledge of the teacher or coach, this can be an excellent opportunity to examine the issues of strength, power, force, release speeds, and delivery angle.

The group has three warm-up throws each, during which time the safety rules are re-emphasised, and then three more attempts, after which the best distance thrown is marked. The distance of the best attempt can be measured either by estimation or by using tape measures that are placed strategically in the throwing area. Now the Olympic challenge is introduced! The children are told that if they can beat their best throw to date, they gain a bronze medal in the Olympic shot put event. If they succeed in that, they try for a silver medal with the second throw. If not, they try again for the bronze! Finally, on the third throw, those who have managed to improve twice already can go for the gold medal.

This approach generates considerable interest and not a little fun. It is then carried over to at least one of the progressions for teaching the actual technique of putting the shot. Experience suggests that it can completely change the attitude of young people towards the challenge of throwing heavy weights.

Triple Jump

The triple jump is also easy to teach as a test. It provides the immense satisfaction of jumping a long way and offers great prospects of rapid improvement. Teachers can introduce it initially as a standing 'hop, step, and jump', with the stress on the 'dah-dah-dah' rhythm, once the children have mastered the correct foot pattern. With all of these early attempts, instructors should give the youngsters an approximate idea of how far they are jumping. If they then allow the group to add a 15-metre (50 foot) run-up, they will have a class of triple jumpers.

Javelin

If taught properly and with stringent safety rules enforced, this is not a dangerous event, and most youngsters can quickly master the basic elements. As always all throwing should be done from behind a scratch line, with the landing area marked so that the children can immediately see how far they are throwing and can note their improvements.

Pole Vault

The pole vault is surprisingly easy to teach. All that is required is a large sand pit and some stout wooden staves or bamboo poles 2.5 to 3 metres (8.2 to 10 feet) long. The students can be introduced to holding the pole with the top hand 30 to 60 centimetres (1 to 2 feet) above their stand-and-reach height, with the bottom hand 45 centimetres (18 inches) lower. The palm of the top hand should face them, while the bottom hand should be turned away. Now, students should run about 9 metres (30 feet), plant the pole into the sand pit, and hang on, riding past it on the same side as their top hand to go as far down the pit as possible. As they gain confidence and skill, youngsters can hold the pole progressively higher so that they can vault farther down the pit. Planting the pole in the sand eliminates the need for an accurate approach run.

The next step is to put high-jump standards on each side of the pit. Instructors can set a soft crossbar at 60 centimetres (2 feet) and ask the class to vault over it. Initially, there is little difference between this requirement and the skill needed to vault for distance. However, as teachers raise the bar by 15-centimetre (6 inch) increments, they can emphasise the need for students to swing the legs and hips up over the bar. Finally, students can turn and face back towards the run-up as they pass over the bar.

Discus

The discus is probably the most difficult and dangerous of the events to teach because it is difficult to control the implement. In fact, this event should be omitted from the program unless teachers have complete confidence in their ability to maintain a safe learning environment.

First, instructors should show the group how to hold the discus on the top joints of the spread fingers. Next, students can practise rolling it along the ground as far and as straight as possible to learn how to correctly release it off the index finger. Finally, instructors can teach the standing throw, flinging the discus out with a loose and sweeping horizontal arm pull. This is initiated by punching the right side of the body around the left.

Hammer Throw

It is highly unlikely that hammer throwing will become an accepted part of many programs, but it has been introduced on a class-by-class basis to 14-year-old boys in some British schools. With all of the events, instructors must remember that children only need to perform the test within the rules and with prospects of improvement.

Remember that it is important to teach the basic rules of each event so that the children know how to judge and measure correctly, and it is particularly vital to teach and continually re-emphasise the safety rules. If it is easy to do so, youngsters can be organised into groups to test themselves in the events already introduced. As more tests are mastered, smaller groups can be used. Because of the problems with raising and lowering the high-jump bar, it may be convenient to base groups roughly on ability if only one high-jump area is available.

During this period of group work, teachers can teach an event for which limited equipment is available—for example, the hammer or pole vault. Each group can be rotated in turn to the teaching station, while the rest of the class are testing themselves in known events. During this time, it is also possible to give groups a chance to test themselves in the 100- and 200-metre runs and in the hurdles when a shortage of stopwatches permits only a few children to be timed at once.

Relays

If time is available, instructors can conduct an occasional continuous relay, either with or without batons. With teams of 7 to 12 spread around a 400-metre track, these relays provide fun and hard running. They can be based on running for a set time or a specified number of laps.

Teaching Progression

Track and field can be introduced to beginners in the following manner:

- Introduce each event as a challenge.
- Test or allow the children to test themselves and time or measure.
- Record the performance in the challenge.
- Re-test frequently, recording and praising all improvements.

This approach to introducing athletics has the following advantages:

- It gives all children a chance to grow fully as they experience the success and satisfaction that come from improvement.
- It both recognises the performance of individual youngsters and encourages them to accept individual differences.

- It creates a highly favourable climate of opinion among the peer group; this encourages gifted youngsters to make full use of their talent. It exposes all children to these great disciplines and gives them a chance to discover an interest or talent that could be the basis of a lifetime of commitment and enjoyment.

- While it requires enthusiasm and good organisation, since no teaching method can be effective without these, it requires little technical knowledge on the part of the teacher.

Swimming

Millions of children around the world learn to swim by playing with their friends in rivers, ponds, lakes, reservoirs, and the sea. In the process, they simply imitate those who appear to look good. Unfortunately the number of children worldwide who drown during this experience has never been determined!

That, of course, is the point. Every child, especially in countries like Australia, should be able to swim by the age of 11. Ideally, they should be able to help anyone else get out of trouble by the time they are 16. However, equally important is that swimming can provide us a vast range of 'I can do this' experiences that can lead to personal growth. Even the simple thought, 'I can swim', can have a huge effect on a child's self-image.

Although it is possible to introduce beginners to a range of swimming strokes, anyone who has ever taught children, especially adolescent boys, knows that the only stroke most are interested in learning is what is termed the *freestyle, overarm,* or even the *Australian crawl.* This is the cool stroke used by real swimmers. Most youngsters dream of being able to dive in and power down the pool with feet churning and arms cycling in front of a host of admirers. However, this dream will only be fulfilled with the usual hard work necessary to develop at least a working model of technique. Here, it is worth understanding some simple principles.

The resistance of the water increases four times with speed of a body moving through it. This means that everything possible must be done to reduce that resistance by minimising the surface area of the body exposed to the water. In turn, this means that the swimmer must be flat and high in the water. This position not only reduces drag but also enables the swimmer to fully exploit the pulling power of the arms and the drive of the leg kick. However, it also means that the head must be down and the nose and mouth close to the water or even under it at times.

However, this is neither normal nor natural for most youngsters, who have to lift their heads up and out of the water to breathe. This impulse inevitably destroys the good body position they should be aiming for: As the head goes up, the trunk and legs drop. Now the swimmer is in a very inefficient position in respect to the resistance of the water and so cannot effectively use her arm pull or leg kick. Therefore, she has to expend a great deal of energy and rapidly tires. We commonly see swimmers swallowing water as they try to get their heads up. This situation is neither pleasant nor encouraging!

Breath Control

The fundamental issue for beginners is to learn to control their breathing when their faces are close to the water. Only then will they feel comfortable in this new environment. In order to breathe properly in water, they must master a specific technique that allows swimmers not only to breathe without lifting their heads out of the water but also to keep more air in their lungs. This helps them maintain a higher body position, thus reducing water resistance.

Some methods of helping youngsters master breath control in water are formal, but the following playful activities can also help:

- Blowing table-tennis balls across the surface of the pool in a race

- Duck diving to pick up items from the pool floor

- Holding the side of the pool in the horizontal position with the head down, but turning it to the side to breathe

Challenge Approach

Even before children have mastered the basic stroke, instructors can help them build their confidence in water through a challenge approach. Students begin by attempting to cross the

1-metre diagonal at the end of the pool. With a good push-off from the side, this is easy. Next, they move a bit farther back and try the same thing. Gradually, they get to a point where they can see that swimming a pool's width is possible! By that point, they are usually hooked.

As they improve, it is possible to encourage them to build a breathing pattern based on one breath for every two strokes. With growing confidence in this process, they can begin to breathe out explosively before their nose and mouth are clear of the water so that they can then use all the time available to suck air back in before their head goes down again.

By combining these simple challenges with games to improve their breath control, they will gradually move towards an effective and safe swimming technique.

Skiing

Play Practice principles can be applied to skiing to create more dynamic, effective, and enjoyable learning situations. Here, traditional methods have been bogged down by an over-emphasis on technique to the point where the joy and exhilaration of moving on skis is lost.

In fact, one of the major reasons behind the explosion of interest in snowboarding among young people may be that adolescents much prefer to go off and try the real thing, even risking bumps and bruises, than to be pinned down waiting for their turn to attempt the repetitive and boring technical practice typical of many ski lessons.

Given the constraints the average skier usually faces, such as cost and limited time to practise, sport educators must determine just how much a learner really needs to know in order to ski safely and enjoyably. As always, the Play Practice approach revolves around three simple questions:

- Where are the learners now, and what do they want from the sport of skiing?

- What is the fundamental nature of the sport?

- How can we get beginners involved in the real activity as quickly as possible?

Traditional methods are based on a misconception about what most beginning recreational skiers expect from the sport. This misunderstanding is a product of the socio-cultural aspects of ski instruction, which is dominated by young men and women whose lives have revolved around competitive skiing. Since many ski instructors are expert skiers first and teachers second, they tend to over-emphasise technique. Recreational skiers, however, do not spend much time racing down marked courses. They prefer a touring approach, where they select a route and its challenges to match their own technique and that of their friends. For them, technique is a means to an end—that is, travelling safely and enjoyably on snow-covered slopes.

Therefore, teaching should not be based purely on isolated technique practice but should encourage learners to begin the process of learning to read both the slopes and the snow conditions. One of the most important aspects of performance in any sport is that participants must understand their own capabilities and limitations. Nowhere is this truer than in recreational downhill skiing, with its ever-present threat to limbs and even to life itself.

From the very beginning, skiers must learn to ski safely on terrain they can cope with. Out-of-control skiers risk not only their own safety but also that of others on the slopes. This important aspect of wise skiing is highlighted in a section titled 'Saying No With Grace' in the excellent book *Skiing Out of Your Mind* (Loudis, Lobitz, & Singer, 1988). The authors remind us that it

Skiing is a challenging sport that people of all abilities can enjoy.

is not always easy to resist pressure from well-meaning friends.

Although most resorts employ a colour-coding system to mark the difficulty of ski runs, no international standard exists. Many skiers, partway down a slope, realise to their dismay that they do not have the technical proficiency required to ski it. Learning skiing must therefore move beyond the repetition of practising technique in isolation and encourage learners to begin the process of reading both the ski slope and snow conditions. At the simplest level, the latter may involve simply learning to stay away from icy patches or deep powder. Elite skiers must also learn to avoid hidden obstacles when skiing off-piste and, above all, to stay away from slopes where avalanches are likely.

Ski instructors, especially those working with beginners, should therefore take learners on a mini-trek around carefully selected terrain with many wide, gentle slopes. Here, they can introduce and develop techniques and key concepts when necessary to deal with the terrain encountered. Again, this is Play Practice in action.

Clearly, technical ability is important in skiing, so this trek should not merely be a wander across the snow. The route must be carefully planned to take advantage of terrain best suited to introduce and improve basic skiing techniques in a logical sequence. It should also incorporate an almost unnoticeable progression to increasingly challenging slopes. The selection of the learning environment is therefore a critical aspect of good ski instruction. A simple example is the importance of the area selected for one of the most basic practices, a downhill run or schuss with skis kept parallel. Obviously, the slope needs to be just steep enough to allow some acceleration, but, and this is most important, it needs a flat run-out where the novice can slow and stop without having to do anything special and certainly without having to dodge other skiers, pedestrians, dogs, or snowmobiles. Similarly, using a gentle gully or couloir to practise turns can make learning this technique easier because the slide up the gully wall bleeds off speed and removes one of the major problems learners confront as they prepare to turn.

A trek approach has many advantages. Learners readily see the need for a particular technique to deal with a problem posed by a slope and will commit themselves more purposefully to mastering it. The varied challenges the terrain presents naturally varies the stimulus, keeping learners alert and motivated and giving them the fantastic sense of achievement that comes from moving around a mountain environment on skis. It naturally encourages learners to read the terrain and pick a route that they can ski safely and enjoyably.

Instructors can make their students aware of the reasons for choosing or avoiding particular terrain. Most slopes have a number of route options. By using different-coloured flags or slalom gates, instructors can mark out several routes of varying difficulty, and learners can select their own routes. Instructors might point out the options at the top and ask students to evaluate the choices and describe where and how they will ski them. If students encounter difficulty, the instructor should provide both technical feedback and guidance related to their choice of terrain: Was it too difficult or did they try to apply the right technique in the wrong place?

Ski resorts should go a step further and create safe and effective learning environments. If they can take the time and trouble to build special areas for hotdogging, boarding, and aerials, then surely it is not too much to expect them to put as much effort into building suitable teaching stations.

Such stations might include a series of low bumps on a gentle slope, positioned so that students could bleed off the speed they gained going down the first slope by going up the next, so that they are always able to feel in control. Another possibility could be a gully created with the turning points built up by carefully sited and sculpted banks of snow. This would pay off by making it easier for beginners to master important techniques, and it would also demonstrate the commitment of the instructors involved to excellence.

Ultimately, the Play Practice approach to teaching skiing takes the activity back to its roots—that is, travelling across snow that was impossible to walk through.

fourteen

Sport for All

All great successes, all great lives have involved the coincidence of aptitude and talent, but also the luck of meeting people who have believed in you. At some point in your life you need to meet someone who will tap you on the shoulder and say, 'I believe in you.'

Arsene Wenger, coach,
Arsenal Football Club

Play Practice attempts to engage youngsters through the enjoyment, exhilaration, and even the tiny frisson of fear that comes with taking part in new challenges and so induce them to participate in a sport. However, no matter how successful we may be, this process is only a means to an end. We must now take the connection children have made to a specific sport and encourage them to do the following:

- Continue their involvement
- Progress as far as they wish to go in that sport
- Develop a more general love of sport and physical activity
- Begin to take pride in a healthy, efficient body
- Make a life-long commitment to maintaining that healthy and efficient body through sport and physical activity

Understand that success in sport has as much to do with the opportunities to play, practise, and fail as it has to do with what is commonly thought of as talent. While this notion may challenge both received wisdom and practice in our field, it underpins the entire philosophy of Play Practice.

Talent Versus Opportunity

Fortunately, recent books such as *Outliers* by Malcolm Gladwell (2008), *Bounce* by Matthew Syed (2010), and *The Talent Code: Greatness Isn't Born, It's Grown* by Daniel Coyle (2009) are confirming that talent is everywhere. All three have built on the work of Anders Eriksson, whose study of violinists led him to the conclusion that the only factor distinguishing those who became concert soloists from those who became music teachers was the hours of purposeful practice that each had undertaken: 10,000 hours in the case of the former, 4,000 in the case of the latter. Gladwell extrapolates this evidence to suggest that talent in every field is more about where the person comes from than any inborn qualities. He suggests that those who excel in any field have benefited from a range of factors that lead them almost unknowingly to success. Professor Benjamin Bloom at the University of Chicago arrived at the same conclusion after his 1985 study of 120 elite athletes, musicians, artists, and mathematicians. He wryly observed, 'We were looking for exceptional kids and what we found were exceptional conditions.'

Syed provides many examples to support his argument, but none is more persuasive than his own journey to become an international table tennis player, a journey that began simply because he grew up close to a club with a highly committed coach available almost 24 hours a day. On its own, this could hardly be conclusive. However, when he goes on to show how, at one point, half the British team came from Silverdale Street in the town of Reading in England, it becomes much more credible!

Indeed, between them, these authors provide ample evidence ranging across music, literature, education, and sports of all kinds to support the notion that skilled performance in many activities really comes down to the opportunity first to participate, and then to practise persistently and purposefully. However, their greatest contribution may be their suggestion that rethinking the roots of excellence can have a major effect on all that we do as teachers and coaches. For as long as we believe that talent is fundamentally genetic, we are likely to devote considerable time searching for students who seem to possess it, and then to spend even more time, effort, and money trying to develop it once we have found it! While this in itself is not bad or even wrong, the danger is that it can distort our whole approach to working with young people. In the

first place, coaches will miss many youngsters, those children who have had limited or even no exposure to an activity or who are disadvantaged by their physical characteristics—for example, a very rapid growth spurt that may limit their performance at that point in time.

These late developers, of whom Michael Jordan is perhaps the best known example, may simply be ignored, so that both they and the coach miss out.

However, the most serious problem occurs when the belief that success in sport depends on talent is communicated to children, as it almost invariably will be. If they believe that the key to success in sport is something called 'talent', they may give up because they feel they obviously have no talent for that activity. However, if youngsters can be helped to understand that they hold their future in their own hands, that talent is really only another word for commitment and pertinent practice, they can set out to achieve their goals with confidence.

Of course, many sports do require specific physical qualities. Coyle recognises this when he says, 'In the interest of clarity, we'll define talent

Paul Mildren is an elite South Australian athlete who has pitched in several World Baseball Classics and who benefited from ample opportunities to participate and practise.

in its strictest sense: the possession of repeatable skills that don't depend on physical size' (2009). This is an important proviso because regardless of the available opportunities and the willingness to practise, the nature of some sports precludes players from reaching the absolute elite level. The sheer size required to be an Olympic discus thrower or shot putter, or a world-class rower or basketball centre, means that it is difficult for people outside a certain range of height or weight to make it to the Olympic medal podium.

A study carried out by Jean Côté and colleagues (2006) at the University of Queensland in Australia also raise questions about talent, albeit from a slightly different perspective. What is especially interesting is their finding that children born early in the qualification period used by a sport have a significant advantage over their peers born only months later. They suggest that this head start leads to early success, to the recognition from important others, including peers, that comes from this success, and the development of an 'I am good at this' attitude. This leads in turn to a greater commitment to practise. This then becomes a self-fulfilling prophesy, simply because more practice leads to improved performance, which leads to greater success. Thus the drive towards excellence begins. One suspects that the reverse is also true, that children who do not experience early success and who are left behind do not go on to make a commitment to sport.

Coaches should therefore be aware of a huge pool of children who may have been overshadowed by more precocious youngsters in the early part of their sports career but who might flourish if given the opportunity.

The second major finding of this research was that growing up in small communities appeared to make it easier for youngsters to become stars. A youngster who might be lost amid the plethora of talented individuals in a large city would have a chance to shine in the smaller talent pool of their local area. Small communities also give youngsters the chance to compete in a range of sports and to compete against more experienced opponents in situations where the result is not as psychologically critical. Here, they are less likely to specialise in a sport too soon and avoid the pressure of head-to-head competition in specific age groups. This is a near-perfect learning environment, where the opponent almost

acts as a coach to draw out the best from the younger player.

Indeed, the major contribution of this work may lie in the suggestion that sport administrators in schools and communities should look for ways to create the equivalent of small-town environments and small sport communities. In fact, this solution was discovered virtually by accident in the English public schools of the 19th century. In order to accommodate hundreds of boarders (boys who lived at the school during term time) and to provide pastoral care in smaller administrative groups, the concept of 'houses' was developed. A boy belonged to his house, which might in fact be an old house, for the duration of his stay at the school. It became a central part of his life; in many cases, the right to enrol in a specific house was passed down through generations of one family.

These houses became the focus for the comprehensive intra-school sport programs, often organised and administered by senior students, that came to underpin the notion of muscular Christianity so often associated with the English public school system of the 19th century. Inevitably, versions of this house system were built into British state schools as they gradually evolved, even though the students were not boarders. In many schools in the Commonwealth countries, it continues to be used as a basis for organising intra-school sport.

Identifying Talent

While all of this is interesting, it is also worth considering the other side of the argument: that the best way to develop elite sport performers is to identify those with potential early on and to provide them with the coaching and support necessary to maximise their talent.

Although this view remains very common, several studies have shown that early specialisation is unnecessary at best and counterproductive at worst. Among the most damning of these studies was one reported by the late Jess Jarver (2001), an Australian authority on talent identification in track and field, who detailed a project conducted in Finland where a 10-year plan was initiated to find and develop potential Olympians in track and field. The children who appeared to have the greatest potential were selected, provided with excellent coaching, and subjected to intense training to prepare for national championships at the under-12 and under-14 levels. While the majority of the youngsters selected were still competing 10 years later, and some had reached the national championship finals, not one of the top 100 children in the selected 12-year-old group had made the Finnish national team!

In 1984, a study by the Swedish Tennis Association also suggested that early specialisation is unnecessary for players to achieve high performance levels (Barrett, 1984). Among other things, this study found that the players who were part of the Swedish tennis miracle of the 1980s, including the great Björn Borg, were keenly active in a range of sports until the age of 14. They did not begin to specialise in tennis until about the age of 16. They also noted that many of these youngsters came from small rural communities, where they had the opportunity to compete with older players in a range of sports.

Perhaps of even greater significance is this study's suggestion that there was a disadvantage in learning to play in the larger clubs typical of cities and bigger towns. The cut-throat nature of early competition in these situations was seen to outweigh the benefits of better coaching. Many players who had been superior to the eventual elite while competing in the 12-to-14-year age group had been burned out by the sport before they ever fulfilled their potential.

A study by Côté, Baker, and Abernethy (2007) of a group of outstanding international players in a range of team games also confirmed that early selection and specialisation may be unnecessary for youngsters who have the potential to become elite players. Their findings parallel those of the Swedish study. They emphasise the importance of abundant free and deliberate play, as well as involvement in multiple sports until the beginning of specialisation from age 12 to 14 and a commitment to excellence around the age of 16. Once again, small rural communities gave talented youngsters a good start, not least because they provided children with an opportunity to play with adults. This study also found that although excellence was achieved only through a large volume of deliberate practice, the commitment was significantly lower (a mean of 3,939 hours) than suggested by earlier studies.

Perhaps the biggest problem with the early selection of potential stars is that it often means early rejection for many youngsters, who then choose not to take part in that, or any other, sport. This is especially insidious when, as we have already seen, it may simply be because of an unfavourable birth date! Even if a talent identification process guaranteed success for the chosen few, it would still be impossible to justify on educational grounds. However, the evidence suggests that, despite obvious exceptions like Tiger Woods, it does not always ensure success at the adult level!

To summarise, as long as the belief remains that one requires special talent to become a good performer, there will be a temptation to search for talented youngsters and to provide special development programs for them. This has several unfortunate consequences. The first is that early specialisation often leads to early burnout, with youngsters dropping out of a sport prematurely, even after they have demonstrated considerable potential. The second is that the initial talent selection process, however inadvertently, tends to write off children who appear to have little or no potential. Consequently, these youngsters may never begin to discover that they are in fact talented.

Developing Elite Athletes

Inevitably, all of this leads to an awareness that if children are to become involved in sport and perhaps move towards the elite level, the key factors are as follows:

- An opportunity to participate in a positive environment
- A feeling that they are being successful
- Recognition by significant others
- An event or person that ignites their passion for an activity

All these, in turn, lead to increased commitment, more practice, more success, and greater recognition. Therefore, the drive towards excellence may begin. However, for this to occur it may be necessary to do the following:

- Rationalise the physical education curriculum.
- Ensure that school sport programs benefit all the students.
- Create many opportunities for informal participation in sport in both schools and communities.

- Bridge the gap between school and community sport programs.
- Give youngsters the opportunity and the skills they need to organise their own competitions.
- Ensure that the play of young children is not replaced with adult sport forms.

Rationalising Physical Education Curricula

Little doubt exists that a major weakness in the physical education curricula of many schools in Australia and elsewhere has been the increasing prevalence of the 'mile wide, inch thick' philosophy, commonly known as the multi-activity curriculum in the United States. Here, teachers argue that by sampling a variety of activities, students can get a sense of what they like. Unfortunately, this 'taste it and leave it' approach leaves many youngsters stranded without the knowledge, skill, or desire to continue participation in an activity that they have barely been exposed to. Sadly, this approach has dominated the physical education curricula of many countries for nearly a century.

Opportunity, interest, and acknowledgement are the keys for promoting physical activity.

The Play Practice position is that after completing a physical education experience, youngsters should believe that they are competent enough to continue to the next level. They should know that they will enjoy that participation and should be confident enough to pursue available opportunities. At the very least, they must emerge from exposure to even the most complex of sports with their optimism and hope undimmed.

So while the curriculum must be broad enough to provide the range of experiences necessary to cater for different interests, it must also be deep enough in specific activities to ensure that students have sufficient time to develop the essential feelings of competence and confidence. A starting point would be to ensure that the time allocated to an activity reflects its complexity and the difficulties it may present to learners. All too often, the curriculum is chopped up into arbitrary blocks of six, four, or even a derisory two weeks. This is based more on administrative convenience or even the limited domain-specific knowledge of the teacher than on the needs of the students or the demands of the activity.

Unfortunately, the reality is that the nature of the curriculum in many schools does sometimes reflect the limited content knowledge of the modern physical education teacher. This problem has been steadily escalating in the English-speaking world as the preparation of physical education teachers moves from an approach based on a thorough background in physical activity and sport, with relevant practice-referenced theory, to ever-increasing volumes of theory separated from the realities of the context. David Kirk (2010) addresses this issue in his excellent book *Physical Education Futures*. However, it will not be resolved until more universities reorientate their direction and centralise sports and physical activity as the core of their formation programs for physical education teachers.

Ensuring That School Sport Programs Benefit the Majority of Students

It may not be easy to resolve this particular issue because, in many cases, it will involve challenging long established, even entrenched, positions and practices. The problem is especially acute in the United States, where school sports are often hijacked to become a component of the entertainment schedule for the local community. Unfortunately, when community pride and individual egos are involved, winning becomes increasingly important, and the potential of sport to positively influence the lives of young people may be eroded.

The only way this situation can be resolved is for the school and its community to face the situation head-on and to ensure that every student who wants to play has the opportunity to do so. Of course, this takes planning, organisation, and money, but probably no more than is invested in a single football team in many American high schools. Examples of schools very close to making this happen include Epsom College in Surrey, England, and Trinity College in South Australia. On any given Saturday in October, Epsom College, a fee-paying school of 750 boys and girls, may be fielding 17 rugby teams for boys and 14 field-hockey teams for girls. This program is supplemented during the week by a range of other sports played against schools. Although tuition at Epsom is very expensive, it is not at Trinity College. The annual program of both schools can be accessed through their respective websites.

It is therefore critically important to ensure that sports are for the benefit of the players, not the adults organising or supporting the program. In the United States, 70 percent of children who play a sport end up quitting by the age of 13, a statistic probably replicated in most developed nations. Again, the reasons for this are detailed at length elsewhere, but the factors most usually mentioned are boring practice sessions, an overemphasis on winning, and control by adults.

Creating Opportunities for Informal Participation in School and Community Sport

Most authorities agree that simply by providing basic facilities and equipment, it is possible to allow youngsters to continue the development process. This can be done by putting up basketball backboards, making futsal pitches available, putting cricket nets with a set of stumps in place, opening up tennis courts to everyone who wants to play, and making tables and equipment for table tennis available in any space that can accommodate them.

All will have a positive effect on continued participation.

This idea was mooted in the original version of Play Practice, which suggested that enthusiastic parents with no prior background in a sport can grow into many roles. With the involvement of the young players in officiating, parents can certainly organise low-level leagues and tournaments with an atmosphere little removed from pick-up games. In fact, one attractive idea is to have all the youngsters who want to play turn up at a set time, pick teams, and take part in tournaments based on small-sided and limited-time games. In individual sports, each child would play every other in a round-robin system. In team games, sides could be randomly chosen, with youngsters taking turns officiating.

Indeed it is vital to retain the mores of pick-up games. Even when these are played with great intensity, results are not recorded, statistics are never kept, and mistakes are not perceived as crucial, nor are they long remembered. Most importantly, the open environment of pick-up games gives players the freedom to experiment, to try out new moves and tactics, and to take on different roles, all without the threat of criticism from authority figures if they fail. This is important because, as emphasised earlier, success is usually built on failure that is often repeated but usually remembered only for an instant by those who are playing. The message is simple: If adults are to be involved, they must focus on any success, no matter how small, and must let mistakes go by unnoticed.

Parents are often the key. They need to become activists who involve themselves in the sport education process to ensure that every child in a school or community can be involved, not just the select few. Once parents begin to see the advantages of this approach for their children, indeed for all children, they are far less likely to support distortions in either a school or community sport program.

Among many excellent examples of community-based sport programs is the Midnight Basketball League, a concept that is affecting communities in the United States and around the globe. Founded by the late G. Van Standifier in Glen Arden, Maryland, to provide an alternative to drugs and crime, the Midnight League gets young adults off the streets by offering late-night basketball and mandatory education, counseling,

The View of One of the World's Most Successful Coaches

'I was a coach for under 16s and under 14s in my home city. In the summer before the season, we had a period of trials where we had to choose 10 or 15 from 100 kids to make the squad for the next year. This was heartbreaking because football is for all, sport is for all. The road to competition, to excellence, is another thing. When kids do not have the talent for that road to excellence, I think that the school should provide protection, give them conditions to participate. If a kid is not good enough for a club competition, for sure he's good enough for school competition. I think the school system, the government, the country should provide protection against this kind of disappointment.'

With these perceptive words, José Mourinho, one of the most successful soccer coaches of the modern era, presents one of the major challenges facing junior sport and simultaneously touches on one of its greatest myths—the myth of talent!

mentoring, and personal-development workshops in a safe environment. The program develops discipline and direction and, as always with sport activities, provides youngsters with a source of pride and achievement.

Bridging the Gap Between School and Community Sport Programs

In an ideal situation, there should be a seamless progression from the physical education experience through a broad-based school sport program and into community-based sport activities. A first step would be simply to ensure that all school and community sporting facilities are made available every possible minute of the day throughout the year. It is often said that children bring a fast-food approach to recreation and sport. If this is the case, perhaps we should note that fast-food franchises are open 24 hours a day!

Because of the importance of maintaining continuity of experience, schools must make a real effort to bridge the gap to community sport. One possibility is to have at least one member of the physical education staff work during afternoons in the school and then early evenings as the coordinator of an after-school sport program, staffed by club coaches or students training to become coaches. Another alternative is to appoint a staff member to generate and maintain school and community sport links. One of the best examples of this is found at Trinity College, north of Adelaide in South Australia, mentioned earlier. Here, the transition between school and the community is almost seamless, involving a whole range of sports and physical activity. Another example is Heathfield High School in

South Australia, where the volleyball program ties the school and the community together.

Remember that cost is becoming an ever-important factor in sport participation. Schools should negotiate with clubs to eliminate or minimise costs for youngsters for at least the first year. But for the support from a teacher who paid his annual subscription to the local cricket club, this author might not be writing these words now.

Helping Youngsters Organise Their Own Training and Competitions

Here it may be worth considering the words of David Maraniss (2005):

> But the reality of my childhood, the dominant theme of my youth, in fact, is that my friends and I grew up with the coach who wasn't there. We were almost utterly free from adult influence, good or bad. Parents, in any case, were not part of our shadowy world of barely organized low level baseball. Once in the summer after sixth grade, a few of us went out to watch an official Little League game. They had full cloth uniforms, not our synthetic pullover jerseys, and bright white bases, and dugouts and outfield fences—wow! But they also had adult coaches ordering the boys around and a group of loud-mouthed parents in the stands, including one particularly obnoxious mother who was merciless with the umpires. We

saw an adult-run system out there that seemed important and alluring, yet also frightening and repellent. The ambivalence I took away from that experience was one that would stay with me for many years.

This example confirms that it is possible, and perhaps necessary, for children to organise play experiences more in line with their needs, not those of adults. Why not take this idea and allow young people to organise play experiences for themselves and for others? They know what is required and understand the potential problems. Why not build on this and offer a high school course in sport leadership that covers the basics of organising, administering, and officiating junior sport? Here, it is worth noting the 'Fit to lead' approach and other mentoring programs that have been successfully introduced in many South Australian schools.

Indeed, a much greater involvement on the part of youngsters in sport is long overdue. Because of this, schools are urged to adopt the Sport Education model proposed by Daryl Siedentop. A well-structured sport education program of the kind he recommends can introduce youngsters to the varied roles of player, official, recorder, coach, and trainer. For some youngsters, this will be a critical, life-changing experience. It should give participants a chance to feel competent and worthy and help them begin a life-long commitment to sport and a healthy lifestyle. At the very least, this may help them become more informed and sympathetic parents for the next generation.

Preserving Children's Natural Play Activities

There is little point in advocating an innovative approach to teaching and coaching sport in middle schools and high schools if children have already been turned off by earlier experiences in elementary schools or, as seems more likely, by negative experiences in community sport. While youngsters can be introduced to games of low organisation from a very early age, and may even begin to master many of the techniques of the major games, it is generally accepted that most young children do not even begin to develop the cognitive and social ability needed to play complex team games until at least the age of 8.

Indeed, this developmental process continues through to the age of 12 and beyond. This is why games played before this age are so often chaotic and error ridden. Of course, as suggested earlier, some youngsters can begin to master the techniques of many sports. Some 10-year-olds can become competent at tennis, table tennis, baseball, softball, soccer, and even cricket, especially when adults are available to help them make tactical decisions. They can also excel in gymnastics, skiing, and swimming. However, this again raises one of the most critical issues in sport for young people, that of early specialisation. As sport physician Dr. Joseph Torg noted, 'One of the most serious crimes of our day is robbing children of their childhood.'

Unfortunately, there will always be parents and coaches who are tempted, perhaps unthinkingly, to risk the long-term futures of children in the hope that they will reap some of the obscene financial rewards available to elite performers in sport. Inevitably, they will point to the exceptions, examples of the great players who began kicking, shooting, or hitting a ball before they could walk, who began competing in a specific sport as early as it was possible to do so, and who practised relentlessly to become successful.

They should be aware, however, that the July 2000 edition of *Pediatrics*, the journal of the American Academy of Pediatrics, carried a new and defining policy statement on the risks of early specialisation in a single sport (Committee on Sports Medicine and Fitness, 2000). This policy states that children should be discouraged from doing this before adolescence to avoid physical and psychological damage. They argue that the risks, which range from overuse injuries to delayed menstruation, eating disorders, emotional stress, and burn-out, outweigh the advantages of a possible professional career.

As sport scientist Peter Keen observed, 'Starting kids off too young carries high risk. The only circumstances in which early specialisation seems to work is where the children themselves are motivated to clock up the hours, rather than doing so because of parents or a coach. The key is to be sensitive to the way the child is thinking and feeling, encouraging training without exerting undue pressure'(Syed, 2010, p. 63).

On the same topic, Steven Anderson, chairman of the American Academy of Pediatrics' committee on sport medicine and fitness, said,

'Waiting to specialise until the age of 12 or 13, when children are more emotionally and physically mature, helps ensure that they are pursuing an activity that really interests them, rather than fulfilling a parent or coach's dream.'

Summary

The essential theme of this book has been the importance of bringing the joy of play back to the sport experience for participants at every level. A simple extension of this is the notion that we should never distort sport for young people. No matter how cleverly and fervently the arguments are made for pre-adolescent competitive sport, adults who encourage children to take on adult play forms before they are ready are stealing children's play and denying them some of the experiences essential for a well-adjusted life.

The final words here must go to Michael Novak, who stunningly captures the essence of sport and its place in our culture in *The Joy of Sports* (1988). He writes:

Sports are not merely entertainment, but are rooted in the necessities and the aspirations of the human spirit. They should be treated with all the care, intelligence, and love the human spirit can bring to bear. It is a corruption, not only of sports but of the human spirit, to treat them as escape, entertainment, business or a means of making money. Sports do provide entertainment, but of a special and profound sort. They do depend upon a financial base, and it is not wrong that they should repay investors and players decent returns. Yet sports are at their heart a spiritual activity, a natural religion, a tribute to grace, beauty and excellence. We ought to keep the streams of the spirit running clean and strong.

This must surely be the rallying cry for all those who choose to devote their lives to helping young people discover the joys of sport.

resources

Abernethy, B. 1986. Basic concepts of motor control: Psychological perspectives. In B. Abernethy, V. Kippers, L. Mackinnon, R. Neal, & S. Hanrahan (Eds.), *Biophysical foundations of human movement* (pp. 295-311). Melbourne, Australia: Macmillan.

Abernethy, B., Baker, J., & Côté, J. 2005. Transfer of pattern recall skills may contribute to the development of sports expertise. *Applied Cognitive Psychology, 19*, 705-718.

Abernethy, B., Farrow, D., & Berry, J. 2003. Constraints and issues in the development of a general theory of expert perceptual-motor performance: A critique of the deliberate practice framework. In J.L. Starkes & K.A. Ericsson (Eds.), *Expert performance in sport: Recent advances in research on sport expertise* (pp. 349-369). Champaign, IL: Human Kinetics.

Almond, L., Bunker, D., & Thorpe, R. 1983. Games teaching revisited. *Bulletin of Physical Education (UK), 19*(1), 32-35.

Arnold, P. 1968. *Education, physical education and personality development.* London: Heinemann.

Australian Sports Commission. 2010. Participation in sport motivation. Available: www.ausport.gov.au.

Baker, J., Côté, J., & Abernethy, B. 2003. Learning from the experts: Practice activities of expert decision makers in sport. *Research Quarterly for Exercise and Sport, 74*, 342-347.

Balsom, P. 1999. *Precision football.* Kempele, Finland: Polar Electro Oy.

Bandura, A. 1994. Self-efficacy. In V.S. Ramachaudran (Ed.), *Encyclopedia of human behavior, Vol. 4* (pp. 71-81). New York: Academic Press.

Barrett, J. 1984. The Swedish miracle. Available: http://wilandertribute.com/resources/The + Swedish + Miracle.pdf.

Berry, J., Abernethy, B., & Côté, J. 2008. The contribution of structured activity and deliberate play to the development of expert perceptual and decision making skill. *Journal of Sport & Exercise Psychology, 30*, 685-708.

Bigelow, B., Moroney, T., & Hall, L. 2001. *Just let the kids play: How to stop other adults from ruining your child's fun and success in youth sports.* Deerfield Beach, FL: Health Communications.

Blake, M. 2009. The masters of sports psychology. *The Melbourne Age,* November 23. Available: www.theage.com.au/news/sport/cricket/the-masters-of-sports-psychology/2009/11/23/1258824670291.html.

Blauner, A. (Ed.). 2005. *Coach: 25 writers reflect on people who made a difference.* New York: Time Warner Books.

Brooking, T. 2009. *Saturday Telegraph,* November 22.

Brown, S. 2009. *Play: How it shapes the brain, opens the imagination and invigorates the soul.* New York: Penguin Books.

Bugelski, B. 1956. *The psychology of learning.* London: Methuen.

Bunker, D., & Thorpe, R. 1982. A model for the teaching of games in secondary schools. *Bulletin of Physical Education, 18*(1), 1-4.

Burton, D., & Raedeke, T. 2008. *Sport psychology for coaches.* Champaign, IL: Human Kinetics.

Campbell, M. 1998. *Ultimate golf techniques.* London: Dorling Kindersley.

Chandler, T. 1996. Teaching Games for Understanding: Reflections and further questions. *Journal of Physical Education, Recreation & Dance, 67*(4), 49-51.

Charlesworth, R. 1994. Designer games. *Sports Coach,* Oct-Dec, 30.

Chow, J., Davids, K., Button, C., Shuttleworth, R., Renshaw, I., & Araujo, D. 2007. The role of nonlinear pedagogy in physical education. *Review of Educational Research, 77*(3), 251-278.

Clarke, J. 1995. On becoming skillful: Patterns and constraints. *Research Quarterly for Exercise and Sport, 66*(3), 173-183.

Cleary, M. 2010. Agustin Pichot: The greatest player of the decade? *London Telegraph,* December 29. Available: www.telegraph.co.uk/sport/rugbyunion/international/6900560/Agustin-Pichot-the-greatest-player-of-the-decade.html.

Committee on Sports Medicine and Fitness. 2000. Intensive training and sports specialization in young athletes. *Pediatrics, 106*(1), 154-157.

Côté, J., Baker, J., & Abernethy, B. 2007. Practice and play in the development of sport expertise. In G. Tenenbaum & R.C. Eklund (Eds.), *Handbook of sport psychology* (3rd ed., pp. 184-202). Hoboken, NJ: Wiley.

Côté, J., Macdonald, D., Baker, J., and Abernethy, B. 2006. When "where" is more important than "when": Birthplace and birthdate effects on the achievement of sporting expertise. *Journal of Sports Sciences, 24*(10), 1065-1073.

Cox, M., & Gould, D. 1990. *The Swedish way to tennis success.* London: Wiedenfeld & Nicholson.

Coyle, D. 2009. *The talent code: Greatness isn't born, it's grown.* London: Arrow Books.

Csikszentmihalyi, M. 1990. *Flow: The psychology of optimal experience.* New York: Harper & Row.

Davids, K., Button, K., & Bennett, S. 2007. *Acquiring movement skill: A constraint-led perspective.* Champaign, IL: Human Kinetics.

Deci, E., & Ryan, R. 1985. *Intrinsic motivation and self-determination in human behavior.* New York: Plenum.

Fogerty, R. 1997. *Brain-compatible classrooms.* Victoria, Australia: Hawker Brownlow.

Frederick, C., & Ryan, R. 1995. Self determination in sport: A review using cognitive evaluation theory. *International Journal of Sport Psychology, 26,* 5-23.

Gallwey, T. 1976. *Inner tennis: Playing the game.* New York: Random House.

Gladwell, M. 2008. *Outliers: The story of success.* New York: Brown.

Glasser, W. 1998. *Choice theory. A new psychology of personal freedom.* New York: Harper Collins.

Hannaford, C. 1995. *Smart moves: Why learning is not all in your head.* Arlington, VA: Great Ocean Publishers.

Hopper, T. 2009. *Game-as-teacher in TGfU and video games: Enabling constraints in learning through game play.* Extended paper on keynote address, ACHPER 2009, Brisbane, Australia.

Hopper, T., & Sanford, K. 2010. Occasioning moments in the game-as-teacher concept: Complexity thinking applied to TGfU and video gaming. In J. Butler & L. Griffin (Eds.), *More Teaching Games for Understanding* (pp. 121-138). Champaign, IL: Human Kinetics.

Hopper, T., Sanford, K., & Clarke, A. 2009. Game-as-teacher and game play: Complex learning in TGfU and video games. In T. Hopper, J. Butler, & B. Storey (Eds.), *TGfU Simply good pedagogy: Understanding a complex challenge* (pp. 201-212). Ottawa, ON: Physical Health Education.

Jarver, J. 2001. Talent identification. *Leistungssport, 31*(4), July.

Jensen, E. 1998. *Teaching with the brain in mind.* Alexandria, VA: Association for Supervision and Curriculum Development.

Jensen, E. 2005. *Brain-based learning: The new paradigm of teaching* (2nd ed.). Alexandria, VA: Association for Supervision and Curriculum Development.

Jones, K., & Welton, P. 1978. *Soccer skills and tactics.* New York: Crown Publishers.

Kidman, L. 2005. *Athlete-centred coaching: Developing inspired and inspiring people.* Christchurch, New Zealand: IPC.

Kirk, D. 2010. *Physical education futures.* London: Taylor and Francis.

Kretchmar, S. 2005. Teaching games for understanding and the delights of human activity. In L.L. Griffin & J.I. Butler (Eds.), *Teaching Games for Understanding: Theory, research, and practice* (pp. 199-212). Champaign, IL: Human Kinetics.

Lanker Family Foundation. 2010. Spectrum Institute for Teaching and Learning. Available: www.spectrumofteachingstyles.org.

Launder, A. 1973. Soccer for schools: A modern approach. *Journal of Physical Health Education & Recreation, Nov-Dec, 44*(9), 25-27.

Launder, A. 1989. The Ps of perfect pedagogy. *Sports Coach, April-June,* 21-23.

Launder, A. 1993a. Action fantasy games. *Aussie Sport Action, 4*(3), 26.

Launder, A. 1993b. Coach education for the twenty-first century. *Sports Coach, 16*(1), 2.

Launder, A. 1993c. Target games: To improve technique in racquet sports. *Sports Coach, 16*(3), 13-15.

Launder, A. 1994. A simple approach to teaching track and field. *Modern Athlete and Coach, 32*(4), 23-26.

Launder, A. 2001. *Play practice: A games approach to teaching and coaching sports.* Champaign, IL: Human Kinetics.

Launder, A. 2003. Revisit 'game sense.' *Sports Coach, 26*(1), 32-34.

Launder, D. 2008. *Implications of decision theory for emergency services and application within the South Australian metropolitan fire service.* Paper presented at the International Bushfire Research Conference, Adelaide, Australia.

Launder, A., & Piltz, W. 1992. An innovative approach to teaching touch. *Sports Coach, 15*(1), 12-17.

Launder, A., & Piltz, W. 2006. Beyond 'understanding' to skilful play in games, through play practice. *Journal of Physical Education New Zealand, 39*(1), 47-57.

Lehrer, J. 2009. *The decisive moment: How the brain makes up its mind.* Melbourne, Australia: Text.

Lopez, S. 2008. *Positive psychology: Exploring the best in people.* Westport, CT: Praeger.

Loudis, L., Lobitz, C., & Singer, K. 1988. *Skiing out of your mind: The psychology of peak performance.* Champaign, IL: Leisure Press.

Maraniss, D. 2005. The coach who wasn't there. In A. Blauner (Ed.), *Coach* (pp. 116-117). New York: Time Warner Books.

McNab, T. (Ed.). 1970. *Modern schools' athletics.* London: Hodder & Stoughton.

McPhee, J. 2005. VBK. In A. Blauner (Ed.), *Coach* (p. 69). New York: Time Warner Books.

Michel, R. 2001. *Team building: The road to success.* Spring City, PA: Reedswain.

Mosston, M. 1966. *Teaching physical education: From command to discovery.* Columbus, OH: Merrill.

Mosston, M., & Ashworth, S. 2002. *Teaching physical education* (5th ed.). San Francisco: Cummings.

Myrer, A. 1968. *Once an eagle.* New York: Berkley Medallion Books.

National Institute for Play. 2009. What is the National Institute for Play? Available: www.nifplay.org/about_us.html.

Novak, M. 1988. *The joy of sports.* Lanham, MD: Hamilton Press.

Pajares, F. 2010. Information on self efficacy: A community of scholars. Available: www.uky.edu/~eushe2/Pajares/self-efficacy.html.

Perkins, D. 1999. The many faces of constructivism. *Educational Leadership, 57*(3), 6-11.

Phillips, J., Klein, G., & Sieck, W. 2004. Expertise in judgement and decision making: A case for training intuitive decision skills. In D. Kohler & N. Harvey (Eds.), *Blackwell handbook of judgement and decision making* (pp. 297-315). Malden, MA: Blackwell.

Piltz, W. 2003. Teaching and coaching using a play practice approach. In J. Butler (Ed.), *Teaching Games for Understanding in physical education and sport* (pp. 189-200). Oxon Hill, MD: National Association for Sport and Physical Education.

Piltz, W. 2006, December. *Influencing professional practice in games education through working models and principle based experiential learning.* Paper presented at the Asia-Pacific Conference on Teaching Sport and Physical Education for Understanding, Sydney, Australia.

Piltz, W. 2008a, January. *The advantages of sector games for promoting quality teaching and learning in batting and fielding games.* Paper presented at the Association Internationale des Ecoles Superieures d'Education Physique (AIESEP) World Congress, Sapporo, Japan.

Piltz, W. 2008b, January. *The influence of play practice principles and processes on pre-service teachers' conceptions and capabilities in games teaching.* Paper presented at the Association Internationale des Ecoles Superieures d'Education Physique (AIESEP) World Congress, Sapporo, Japan.

Pink, D. 2009. *Drive: The surprising truth about what motivates us.* New York: Riverhead Books.

Read, B. 1989. Artisans, players and gods: A reflection on the teaching of games. *Physical Education Review, 12*(2), 134-137.

Ross, K., Klein, G., Thunholm, P., Schmitt, J., & Baxter, H. 2004. The recognition-primed decision model. *The U.S. Army professional writing collection.* Available: www.army.mil/professionalwriting/volumes/volume2/october_2004/10_04_2_pf.html.

Ross, K., Shaffer, J., & Klein, G. 2006. Professional judgments and 'naturalistic decision making.' In K.A. Ericsson, N. Charness, R.R. Hoffman, & P.J. Feltovich (Eds.), *The Cambridge handbook of expertise and expert performance* (pp. 403-419). New York: Cambridge University Press.

Rotella, B. 2008. *Your 15th club: The inner secret to great golf.* New York: Free Press.

Ryan, R., & Deci, E. 2000. Self-determination theory and the facilitation of intrinsic motivation, social development and well-being. *American Psychologist, 55,* 68.

Ryan, R., Williams, G., Patrick, H., & Deci, E. 2009. Self-determination theory and physical activity: The dynamics of motivation in development and wellness. *Hellenic Journal of Psychology, 6,* 107-124.

Schon, D. 1987. *Educating the reflective practitioner.* San Francisco: Jossey Bass.

Seligman, M., & Csikszentmihalyi, M. 2000. Positive psychology: An introduction. *American Psychologist, 55,* 5-14.

Seligman, M., Ernst, R., Gillhum, J., Reivich, K., & Linkins, M. 2009. Positive education: Positive psychology and classroom interventions. *Oxford Review of Education, 25*(5), 293-311.

Shipstone, J., & Plimmer, N. 2012. *JOLF: Junior golf coaches handbook.* England: JOLF Ltd.

Shulman, L.S. 1986. Those who understand: Knowledge growth in teaching. *Educational Researcher, 15*(2), 4-31.

Shulman, L.S. 1987. Knowledge and teaching: Foundations of the new reform. *Harvard Educational Review, 57*(1), 1-22.

Siedentop, D. 1991. *Developing teaching skills in physical education* (3rd ed.). Mountain View, CA: Mayfield.

Siedentop, D. 1994. *Sport education: Quality PE through positive sport experiences.* Champaign, IL: Human Kinetics.

Siedentop, D. 2009. National plan for physical activity: Education sector. *Journal of Physical Activity and Health, 6*(suppl. 2), 168-180.

Siedentop, D., Hastie, P.A., & van der Mars, H. 2011. *Complete guide to sport education* (2nd ed.). Champaign, IL: Human Kinetics.

Siedentop, D., & Tannehill, D. 2000. *Developing teaching skills in physical education.* Mountain View, CA: Mayfield.

Silberman, C. 1971. *Crisis in the classroom: The remaking of American education.* New York: Vintage.

Slade, D. 2003. *Stick2Hockey* [DVD]. Palmerston North, New Zealand: Stick2Hockey Ltd.

Slade, D. 2005. *Teaching attack and defence in team games: A TGfU approach.* Massey, New Zealand: Massey University Press.

Slade, D. 2010. *Transforming play: Teaching tactics and game sense.* Champaign, IL: Human Kinetics.

Smith, A. 2009. Frank Lampard vs Steven Gerrard: Who's the midfield maestro? *London Telegraph,* January 31. Available: www.telegraph.co.uk/sport/football/competitions/premier-league/4403519/Frank-Lampard-vs-Steven-Gerrard-Whos-the-midfield-maestro.html.

Stork, S. 2001. When playing is learning. *Teaching Elementary Physical Education, Jan,* 30-31.

Syed, M. 2010. *Bounce: Mozart, Federer, Picasso, Beckham and the science of success.* New York: Harper Collins.

University of Pennsylvania. 2007. Positive Psychology Centre. Available: www.positivepsychology.org/publications.htm.

Wade, A. 1997. *Teaching the principles of soccer.* Spring City, PA: Reedswain.

Walls, J., & Basham, G. 2008. *Basketball and philosophy: Thinking outside the paint.* Lexington, KY: University of Kentucky Press.

Whitehead, N., & Cook, M. 1984. *Games, drills, and fitness practices for soccer coaching.* London: Adam and Charles Black.

Wideman, J.E. 2005. Passing it on. In A. Blauner (Ed.), *Coach* (pp. 51-52). New York: Time Warner Books.

Williams, J. 2008. *SANFL vision and record: Modified football 'nines'.* Presentation to AFL Women's Development, Sydney, Australia.

Worthington, E. 1974. *Teaching soccer skill.* London: Lepus Books.

index

Note: Page numbers followed by an italicized *f* or *ff* indicate a figure or multiple figures will be found on those pages, respectively.

Alan Launder has been involved in sports for more than 50 years as a competitor, teacher, and coach. He has worked in Great Britain, the United States, and Australia.

He has taught at elementary, secondary, and tertiary levels with considerable success. His period as head of the physical education department at Dr. Challoners Grammar School in England in the 1960s was especially rewarding because in a relatively brief period the school became a sporting powerhouse.

For the last 20 years of his professional career he was a senior lecturer at the University of South Australia, where he helped to develop a four-year degree course in physical education teacher education that became a model for programs in other countries. He won the 1992 Rothmans Prize in recognition of his ability to develop and communicate innovative ideas in sport education.

Launder holds senior coaching qualifications from Great Britain and Australia in soccer, cricket, basketball, track and field, and table tennis. In 1984, he was a coach of the Australian track and field team at the Los Angeles Olympics. In 1986 and 1988 he was the head coach of the Australian team at the World Junior Championships. In 1991, 1993, and 1995, he was a coach of the track and field team at the World University Games. Most recently he has served as a consultant to the Australian Track and Field Coaches Association and to the Australian Lacrosse Association as they revised their coach education programs.

Since 1973 Launder was also involved in developing and teaching the curriculum for the Australian Track and Field Coaches Association and was a primary contributor to the internationally respected coaching magazine *Modern Athlete and Coach*. As the national event coach for pole vault, he has seen Australia move into world-class standing with many fine results, including a female world-record holder, the men's world champion in 2001 and 2009, and the men's Olympic champion in 2008.

Launder considers his major career achievement to be the development of the philosophical and pedagogical principles that underpin the Five Star Award, an innovative approach to teaching track and field that has been adopted by more than 20 countries. In 2000, Queen Elizabeth II made Launder a member of the Order of Australia for services to Australian sport.

In his spare time, Launder enjoys sporting art, travel, snow skiing, and fine wine. He lives with his wife, Jennifer, in Salisbury East, South Australia. He has two sons, David and Richard, and four grandsons.

Wendy Piltz has been involved in physical education and sports for many years as a player, teacher, and coach. Her involvement in a range of sports and various outdoor pursuits is a significant aspect of her lifestyle and expertise. An accomplished athlete, Piltz has competed at the district level in basketball and netball, the state level in touch, and at the national level in women's cricket and lacrosse.

Wendy is a committed and enthusiastic educator who has worked in elementary, secondary, and tertiary sectors. She completed her undergraduate degree in physical education from the University of South Australia (formerly ACAE) in 1978 and her master's degree in social psychology from the University of Oregon in 1980. Wendy taught in the public secondary school system in South Australia for 10 years as a specialist health and physical education teacher and a school coach of basketball, lacrosse, cricket, volleyball, touch, athletics, and netball. In addition, she worked with elementary-aged children and served as a volunteer for 5 years as the basketball coach of children in grades 3 to 7 at her daughter's primary school. Her coaching experience extends to a state level in women's cricket, and she is currently coaching lacrosse at the North Adelaide club in South Australia.

Wendy began working at the University of South Australia in 1990, where she joined Alan Launder as a colleague on staff in the health and physical education faculty working in teaching and curriculum, sport pedagogy, and group dynamics. Since 1998 she has redesigned the preservice programs in health and physical education to accommodate changing program structures and has embedded Play Practice models into these programs. A key area of Wendy's research focuses on teaching and learning oriented to practice-based study on the efficacy of this approach. Her expertise in teaching, innovation in course and program design, leadership, and mentoring have been acknowledged through numerous teaching awards at the university. In addition, Wendy has received two national Australian Sports Commission awards for outstanding services to sport and innovation in lacrosse coach education.

Wendy regularly presents at international and national conferences in sport pedagogy, focusing on teaching and learning using Play Practice, team development, and teacher and coach education. She also maintains a sustained service to local communities, conducting professional development workshops for teachers through the Australian Council for Health, Physical Education, and Recreation (ACHPER), sporting clubs, and state departments of sport and recreation. Wendy has served as a consultant for the American Sport Education Program (ASEP), Australian Sports Commission (ASC), Australian Football League, South Australian National Football League, Women's Lacrosse Australia, and Australian Touch Association.

In her free time, Wendy enjoys being with friends, swimming, cycling, and adventure travel. She loves the mountains and is passionate about snow skiing. Wendy resides in Adelaide, South Australia, and has one daughter, Kelsey.